D0938687

The Philosophical Frontiers of Christian Theology

The Philosophical Frontiers of Christian Theology

Essays presented to

D. M. MACKINNON

Edited by
BRIAN HEBBLETHWAITE
and
STEWART SUTHERLAND

CAMBRIDGE UNIVERSITY PRESS

CAMBRIDGE

LONDON NEW YORK NEW ROCHELLE

MELBOURNE SYDNEY

Published by the Press Syndicate of the University of Cambridge
The Pitt Building, Trumpington Street, Cambridge CB2 1RP
32 East 57th Street, New York, NY 10022, USA
296 Beaconsfield Parade, Middle Park, Melbourne 3206, Australia

First published 1982

Printed in Great Britain at the University Press, Cambridge

Library of Congress catalogue card number: 81–10132

British Library Cataloguing in Publication Data
The philosophical frontiers of Christian theology.
1. MacKinnon, D. M. 2. Philosophical theology
- Addresses, essays, lectures
I. Hebblethwaite, Brian II. Sutherland, Stewart
III. MacKinnon, D. M.
230 BT40
ISBN 0 521 24012 3

Contents

Preface

One of the 'borderlands' of theology is undoubtedly the area in which its concerns overlap with those of philosophy. The intention of this book is to chart some of the frontiers which are of most concern in contemporary discussion. Two convictions underlie the choice of topics: on the one hand it is clear that many of the central questions of theology can only be thoroughly articulated and explored if they are set within a philosophical context. On the other hand the object of theological study has encouraged theologians to paint on a broader canvas than contemporary philosophical discussion encourages. It is arguable that this should render theology less vulnerable to intellectual fashion. Thus each discipline in its respective way has much to contribute to the other. The essays written for this collection are intended to explore and evaluate specific examples of such contributions. The themes have both historical and contemporary dimensions, but the emphasis in each case is on contributing to a specific continuing debate, rather than on a survey of the main options.

Donald MacKenzie MacKinnon began his academic teaching career as Assistant in Moral Philosophy to Professor A. E. Taylor at Edinburgh in 1936. In the following year he returned to Oxford as Fellow and Tutor in Philosophy at Keble College. During the war he directed special courses in philosophy for naval and air force cadets in Oxford. From 1947 to 1960 he was Regius Professor of Moral Philosophy at Aberdeen, moving to Cambridge in 1960 to take up a Fellowship of Corpus Christi College and the Norris-Hulse Professorship of Divinity, which he held until his retirement in 1978.

He has been Wilde Lecturer in Natural and Comparative Religion at Oxford (1945–47), Scott Holland Lecturer (1952), Hobhouse Lecturer (1953), Stanton Lecturer in the Philosophy of Religion, Cambridge (1956–59), Gifford Lecturer, Edinburgh (1965–66), Prideaux Lecturer, Exeter (1966), Coffin Lecturer, London (1968), Riddell Lecturer, Newcastle-upon-Tyne (1970), D. Owens Evans Lecturer, Aberystwyth (1973), Drummond Lecturer, Stirling (1977), and Martin Wight Memorial Lecturer, London School of Economics (1979). In 1976–77 he was President of the Aristotelian Society, and in 1980 he was elected President of the Society for the Study of

Theology. In 1978 he was elected Fellow of the British Academy. A bibliography of his published writings appears at the end of this volume.

The essays that follow are presented to Donald MacKinnon by colleagues, pupils and friends with gratitude, affection and respect.

Abbreviations

CD Karl Barth, *Kirchliche Dogmatik*. Zurich, 1932–67. English translation: *Church Dogmatics*. Edinburgh, 1936–69.

CG F. Schleiermacher, *Der Christliche Glaube*, edited by M. Redeker, Berlin, 1960. English translation of second edition: *The Christian Faith*, edited by H. R. Mackintosh and J. S. Stewart, Edinburgh, 1928.

CQR *Church Quarterly Review*

ET English translation

fr. Fragment

GG *Friedrich Schleiermacher's Sämmtliche Werke* part III, volume I. Berlin, 1846.

JTS *Journal of Theological Studies*

KD F. Schleiermacher, *Kurze Darstellung des theologischen Studiums*, edited by H. Scholz. Darmstadt, 1969. English translation by T. N. Tice: *Brief Outline on the Study of Theology*. Richmond, Virginia, 1966.

PAS *Proceedings of the Aristotelian Society*

PG *Patrologia cursus completus, series graeca*, edited by J. P. Migne.

PR L. Wittgenstein, *Philosophical Remarks*, edited by R. Rhees, Oxford, 1964. English translation: Oxford, 1975.

SF *Kants Gesammelte Schriften*, volume VII. Berlin, 1917.

SJT *Scottish Journal of Theology*

ST Thomas Aquinas, *Summa Theologica* (*Summa Theologiae*), 1265–1273. English translation: New York, 1947 (Blackfriars edition, London, 1963–75).

SVF *Stoicorum Veterum Fragmenta*, 1903– , edited by H. von Arnim.

VC *Vigiliae christianae*

WiA Immanuel Kant, *Was ist Aufklärung*, edited by Norbert Hinske, Darmstadt, 1973.

ZKG *Zeitschrift für Kirchengeschichte*

PART ONE

Athens and Jerusalem

1

The Borderlands of Ontology in the New Testament

C. F. D. MOULE

The notes to this essay will be found on pages 10–11

The recipient of this volume has steadily refused to detach philosophical theology from biblical studies. It is only this that emboldens a student of the New Testament who, at best, is only an amateur in D. M. MacKinnon's field to hope that an attempt to assess the relation of the two will not be unacceptable to him. All that is attempted here is to point to some of the data that might be significant when considering the relation between the implications of the religious experiences reflected in the New Testament and the ontological statements of traditional Christian doctrine, and to draw some provisional conclusions.

There are two separate but interlocking questions here, namely, how far, if at all, the New Testament actually uses philosophical or quasi-philosophical language; and whether philosophical, and, in particular, ontological, language (even if not used in the New Testament) is necessary when it comes to defining the implications of what the New Testament seems to reflect.

It has been suggested that there may be something deliberately philosophical in the use of the neuter in the phrase on the lips of Jesus in John 10: 30: *egō kai ho patēr hen esmen*. Is it not a deliberately contrived surprise when the unity between Father and Son is expressed by this neuter numeral, *hen* – 'I and the Father are one thing' (or, if not 'one thing', then 'belonging to the same category' – so Barnabas Lindars)?[1] May it not be the purpose of the surprising gender to express something that, in Chalcedonian terms, might be called a unity of substance between Father and Son? By contrast, it might be observed, St Paul uses a masculine numeral in Gal. 3: 28. Referring to the unity in Christ of all believers alike, whether Jew or

Greek, slave or free, male or female, he says that they are all 'one person' – *heis* (masculine). That the Johannine neuter, by contrast, is used with deliberately philosophical intent is something that one would like to be able to affirm. In fact, however, such parallels to this neuter usage as are to be found in the New Testament do not favour this conclusion. In St John's Gospel itself, in the great 'High Priestly prayer', Jesus asks for the disciples *hina ōsin hen kathōs hēmeis* (17: 22). In that case, not only Father and Son, but also the disciples with them, are to make up 'one thing' (or to belong in 'one category'); and this, if taken as a statement of a unity of substance, would lead to the conclusion that human beings are regarded as of one substance with the divine – which would be incongruous not only with developed Christian doctrine but with many features of Johannine thought. Further, in 1 Cor. 3: 8, the one who plants and the one who waters are 'one' (neuter) – that is, they belong to the same category,[2] as servants together of God; and this is manifestly not intended as an ontological statement.

However, if New Testament usage does not allow a philosophical meaning to be claimed with any confidence for St John's expressions with the neuter numeral, that is not to say that there are no philosophical terms or ideas in the Fourth Gospel or elsewhere in the New Testament – still less that the implications of the New Testament can be defined without the use of such language or ideas. If one asks where the New Testament comes nearest to drawing explicitly upon philosophical concepts, one's first thought will probably be of logos-doctrines. In the prologue to the Fourth Gospel it is stated that the eternal, divine 'utterance' of God, the logos that was his agent in creation, became flesh – became a man in time and space. About the term 'logos', one must certainly not jump to conclusions, before trying to hear it as nearly as possible as it would have sounded in the writer's own days. If, as it is reasonable to believe, there is a tradition of Hellenistic Judaism behind it, what would this term have meant in such a world of discourse? It was not necessarily a philosophical term. The personification of the divine wisdom in Proverbs 8 or of the logos of God in the Wisdom of Solomon, chapter 18, is not philosophical. These are only pictorial ways of saying that God in his wisdom created the world and that it was by his irresistible fiat that Egypt was visited with the plagues. There is nothing in such language to compel the reader to think of a pre-existent, divine hypostasis. It is the same with Philo's frequent use of logos. But in John 1: 14 the logos *became flesh*, and this is a statement of a different order. It carries a philosophical meaning, and moreover, a novel one. In a familiar passage in the *Confessions*, Augustine recognizes both its philosophical character and its novelty. In the books of the neo-Platonists, he says, 'I read – not indeed in these words, but the very same thing...that the Word was in the beginning, and that the Word was with God and the Word was God...But that the Word was made flesh and dwelt among us, I found not there'.[3] Here is an ontological statement, and one that implies something on a different level from inspiration. That the word of God came to a prophet is a common idea. Indeed, according to the verses immediately preceding verse 14 in the Johannine prologue, even supernatural birth is something that belongs to all who receive him, and not to Christ alone. But that the word became a man – that is special, as patristic exegetes insisted.[4] For Christ alone is reserved this actual identification with God's utterance, his logos. It is difficult not to concede that this is tantamount to an ontological statement – a statement about the being of Christ as identical with the being of God.

Something similar may be intended, in more oblique language, in St Matthew's Gospel, if it is true, as is held by many,[5] that it identifies Christ with the divine Wisdom. The theory is that, whereas the gospel traditions that are commonly labelled 'Q' represented Jesus as the bearer or transmitter of God's Wisdom, this Evangelist took the further step of actually identifying Christ and Wisdom. (Contrast Matt. 23: 34 with Luke 11: 49: in Luke, Wisdom speaks, in Matthew, Christ speaks.) In effect, this would be to say that the Wisdom became flesh. It would be by implication an ontological statement.

Besides John 1: 14, the other most explicit identification in the New Testament of Jesus with the logos of God is in Rev. 19: 13. But here the circumstances and context are different. The victorious figure on a white horse, clearly intended to be Christ, is explicitly said to be named 'the logos of God'. But this is really a functional rather than an ontological description: Christ is God's fiat embodied: he victoriously carries out the divine decree. It is like the personified word of Wisdom 18, except that the Person is now known and identified.

Much closer to an ontological logos-Christology (although the word logos happens not to occur in it) is the exordium of the Epistle to the Hebrews:

> God...in these last days...has spoken to us by a Son, whom he appointed the heir of all things, through whom also he

> created the world. He reflects the glory of God and bears the very stamp of his nature [*charaktēr tēs hupostaseōs autou*], upholding the universe [*pherōn ta panta*] by his word of power. (Heb. 1: 1–3)

Here, Christ is God's final and definitive utterance, the effulgence of the divine glory, the impress of his very substance; and it is by Christ's powerful utterance, in turn, that the universe is sustained. This last thought is parallel to Philo, *De plant.* 8f, which says that nothing in creation is strong enough to bear the burden of the world (*ton kosmon achthophorein*), but that the eternal word of the God of the ages is the strongest and firmest support of the sum of things (*logos...ho aidios theou tou aiōniou to ochurotaton kai bebaiotaton ereisma tōn holōn estin*). The Christian reader is reminded by this of the hymn tentatively attributed to Ambrose, which, in the familiar version by Ellerton and Hort, begins:

> O strength and stay upholding all creation.

To attribute such a function to Christ, and to speak of him as the impress made by the seal which is God's *hupostasis* is to come very near to an ontological Christology.

Like the prologue to Hebrews, the 'great Christology' of Col. 1: 15ff contains a description of Christ in terms of cosmic functions:

> He is the image of the invisible God, the first-born of all creation; for in him all things were created, in heaven and on earth...all things were created through him and for him. He is before all things, and in him all things hold together.

Whether or not this is a Christian adaptation of some pre-Christian hymn,[6] as it stands now the passage places Christ on the side of the Creator[7] over against creation. In or by him the sum of things was created; he is both their means and their end; in him (as in the Stoic logos) everything finds its coherence. In the same vein, Col. 2: 9 declares that in Christ the sum of God's divine personality dwells (*en autō(i) katoikei pan to plērōma tēs theotētos*); and E. Schweizer points out[8] that this is not exactly paralleled by references in pagan literature to mortal men filled with *theiotēs* (so Plutarch, *De def. or.* 10 (II 415 c), rather than *theotēs*). *Theiotēs*, meaning the divine properties, is to be distinguished, says Schweizer, from *theotēs*, the divine personality itself. For this, Augustine (*De civ. D.* 7.1) introduced the word *deitas*.[9]

Already 1 Cor. 8: 5f is moving in the same direction when it assigns a cosmic function to Christ – '...one Lord, Jesus Christ, through whom are all things and through whom we exist'. But this, of course, need mean no more, in itself, than that Jesus, like the personified Wisdom of Prov. 8, is the Creator's medium: it does not, so decisively as Colossians and Hebrews, place Christ on the Creator's side over against creation. One should possibly add Rev. 3: 14 to the 'cosmic' descriptions of Christ. There he is called *hē archē tēs ktiseōs tou theou*, which J. P. M. Sweet, among others, interprets as 'the origin and principle of creation'.[10]

Whatever may be said of this, or of the early epistles, it can hardly be denied that at least Heb. 1 and Col. 1, like John 1, use virtually ontological language with reference to Christ. (Col. 2: 17, as will be observed shortly, may present another instance.)

Returning to St John's Gospel, there is one other passage in it, besides those already discussed, which claims attention. This is 8: 58, where, in conflict with Jewish opponents, Jesus declares: 'Before Abraham was, I am.' A great deal has been written about the Johannine uses, not only in 8: 58 but elsewhere also, of *egō eimi*, with special reference to the divine declaration, 'I am He', in such passages as Isa. 41: 4; 43: 10, 13, 25; 46: 4; 51: 12; 52: 6.[11] But whatever may be made of those other occurrences of *egō eimi* (and at 9: 9, on the lips not of Christ but of the man born blind, it demonstrably means no more than 'I am the one'), here at 8: 58, the discord of tenses is so violent – 'before Abraham *was*, I *am*' – that one is practically compelled to conclude that this 'I am' is an ontological statement about Christ's eternal being as an existence transcending time. It contrasts with the more characteristically Semitic and unphilosophical language which, in Rev. 1: 4, describes God (in blatantly ungrammatical Greek) as 'he who is and was and is to come'.

At this point, a further observation must be made about the Epistle to the Hebrews. It cannot be said, despite its prologue and its other flashes of philosophical language, that it adheres consistently to any considered philosophical system. It is well known that the classic contrast, derived from Plato's 'theory of ideas', between invisible, immaterial reality and visible, material unreality – between the absolute and perfect 'idea' or form and the relative and imperfect copy – is exploited in the Epistle to the Hebrews, as it is also by Philo. In the interests of the argument that Christ is superior to Moses, and that Christians, so far from being deprived of the apparatus of religion, have a sanctuary, an altar, a sacrifice, and a Priest transcending and superseding those of the old covenant, the writer to the Hebrews speaks of the real tabernacle in the heavens in contrast to the mere copy made by Moses, and of the entry of Christ, as the ultimate and absolute High Priest, into the real and eternal sanctuary in the heavens after offering the ultimate sacrifice of his own self. To this, the Levitical system is as mere shadow to substance: the realities are invisible, in the heavens; the visible sacrifices are but pale reflections of them. These metaphors drawn in spatial dimensions – that which is above, that which is below; that which is three-dimensional, that which is only its two-dimensional shadow – are used in Heb. 8: 5; 10: 1–9. (It should be observed, in passing, that Col. 2: 17 is plausibly interpreted as using the same 'model' of shadow and substance.) But, side by side with them, the writer does not hesitate to use the less philosophical and more characteristically Semitic language of time. Of course we know (could we forget Professor James Barr's trenchant critique?)[12] that it is foolish and unrealistic to draw sharp lines between 'Greek' and 'Hebrew' thinking. Of course, we know that such time-metaphors as contrast the temporary with the permanent are as much at home with Plato as with Paul. But it remains true that, broadly speaking, biblical writers are more prone to attribute reality and importance to a history which is conceived of as moving along the line of time towards a goal than to a static model of absolute reality or to a purely cyclic notion of history; and it is in its acceptance of this serious teleology and in its refusal to work consistently with static space-metaphors that the Epistle to the Hebrews breaks away from what at first might seem to be an identifiable metaphysic. The Old Testament heroes are waiting until the Christians' destiny is consummated (11: 40). Christians are looking forward to the coming of the end (9: 28; 10: 25, 36–39), or, as the case may be, they have already 'arrived' and are at their heavenly destination when worship foreshortens time (12: 22–24). The heavenly city turns out to be also the city of the future (11: 10 with 13: 14).

In other words, this writer's Platonism is a Platonism of convenience, not a consistently held philosophy.[13] In the presentation of his earnest and moving appeal to his readers, the telic time-image runs concurrently with the static space-image: there are the pure 'form' and the mere approximation; but there are also the 'now' and the 'not yet'. Consequently, for all his sophistication, this writer cannot be claimed as the philosopher of the New Testament. The philosophical terms appear fitfully and disappear again. However, this does not alter the fact that of Christ he does use terms which, as we have seen, are virtually ontological in character. The well-known phrase 'in the form of God' in Phil. 2: 6 (*en morphē(i) theou*) must be passed over here, because it is not unanimously believed to be necessarily different in meaning from the description of man as in the image of God. There are exegetes who think otherwise, and it might, thus, constitute a more specifically philosophical use of language: but the case had better be left open.

The words and phrases discussed thus far all concern the understanding of Christ. There are three other possible instances of philosophical language, two with direct reference to God, one with reference to human destiny. In Acts 17: 29, *to theion* (the only occurrence in the New Testament of this adjective used in the neuter as a noun) is virtually a synonym for *theos*, 'God'. But since strictly speaking it means 'that which is divine' – in English we might say 'the Deity' – it does carry the nuance of emphasizing the nature of God, as though to say not merely, 'God ought not to be likened to material things', but, '*Since God is divine*, he ought not...'. In Rom. 1: 20, God's *theiotēs* is referred to, that is, his divine properties. This is the only occurrence in the New Testament of this word, as distinct from *theotēs*, 'deity', as in Col. 2: 9, already mentioned.

The phrase referring to human destiny is in 2 Pet. 1: 4: *hina genēsthe theias koinōnoi phuseōs apophugontes tēs en tō(i) kosmō(i) phthoras*, 'that...you may become sharers of the divine nature, escaping the corruption that is in the world'. This is notoriously out of line with the main thrust of biblical thinking, which likes to use the language of personal relationship and intercourse rather than of 'natures', and which tends to maintain a sharp distinction between the human and the divine, between the creature and the Creator. J. N. D. Kelly, commenting on the passage, speaks of 'the affinity of these notions [of escape from the world and sharing in divine nature] with Greek mystical philosophy, with its dualist presuppositions', and of 'the substitution of a metaphysical terminology for the earlier language of sonship and fellowship'.[14] Thus, the passage is cited here not because it is typical, but to complete a review of philosophical and quasi-philosophical phrases in the New Testament.

So much for the limited use in the New Testament of the language and ideas of the philosophers. But what must be said about the implications of what the New Testament reflects in its largely unphilosophical writing? If its own use of philosophical language is sparing and unsustained, it need not follow that what is implied by the religious experiences which it reflects can be adequately defined without the help of such language. It is not the *métier* of the New Testament to define its doctrines. But it is a part of the business of the philosophy of religion to attempt this task. Can it do so without the language of divine substance?[15]

It has been maintained by some that New Testament Christologies are exclusively functional: they describe Jesus in terms of his 'work',[16] and nothing may be deduced about his 'being'. But if one examines what is implicit in the descriptions of his 'work', this is questionable. Even the Synoptic Gospels – the last place where one would look for philosophy – confront the reader with the question: 'Who and what is this, who, while genuinely human and apparently making no explicit claims (or, at most, speaking with the utmost reserve) about his status, nevertheless acts with a native authority which is nothing other than the authority of God, and who seems to identify himself as the *locus* of God's sovereignty?' Of course it is impossible to prove that such a person is one with God in an ontological sense; but, together with other phenomena, this provides a body of evidence pointing in that direction. Again, were the soil of New Testament thought a polytheistic one, the titles 'Lord' and 'Son of God' might in themselves reflect no more than an understanding of Jesus as (to use C. H. Talbert's term)[17] an 'immortal', that is, a human hero who, in course of time, had come to be deemed a demigod. Were this the case, it would have legendary rather than ontological implications. But this is not compatible with the monotheistic convictions behind the New Testament. If one takes account of the date, provenance, and circumstances of these documents, the reasons for their applying such titles to Jesus cannot plausibly be sought in the world of the Hellenistic saviour-cults. Yet, the most obvious alternatives, namely, to interpret these titles as merely honorifics for a great rabbi or a great prophet or a messiah, will not work either. The titles are used, from the earliest times to which we have access, in contexts and in ways which make it singularly difficult to believe that they are no more than titles of respect for a merely human leader. The title 'Lord', except in the vocative (which is not significant for this purpose), is too intimately associated with scriptural passages referring to God for it to be explicable as a merely human honorific; and 'Son of God' is used in ways conspicuously deeper than and different from the human, messianic usage. And there are other christological phenomena which cannot be pursued here but which point in the same direction:[18] here is a person such that, often only half-consciously, his earliest followers found themselves driven to say things of him which imply an estimate not only of his function but of his being; that is, an ontological estimate of the 'person' of Christ, not only a functional estimate of his 'work'. To put the same conclusion in other words, it is that the religious experiences reflected in the New Testament are not adequately described in terms simply of the noble example or lasting influence of a great, human leader. If and when it comes to attempting some definition of their implications, it is necessary to speak of Jesus as himself divinely creative, and to put him 'on the side of the Creator'; and that means indeed reaching the borderlands of ontology.

This is particularly well illustrated by the narratives of the appearing of Jesus to his disciples after his death. There is no question but that the disciples came to believe Jesus to be alive with an irreversible, absolute life – the life of the age to come. This is demonstrable. Without this belief, there would have been no Christian movement and no New Testament. The question is whether their conviction was justified – whether it corresponded with reality; and that is a metaphysical question. Does the conviction that Jesus lives correspond with ultimate reality? Is Jesus to be called one with God in his being? Is his life the life of God? One's answer to this metaphysical question is, in part, dependent on how one understands the relation between history and religion. History is commonly understood today (at least in the West) as concerned with the recording and interpreting of exclusively human affairs. The historian may say that soldiers on the battlefield of Mons believed that they saw angels. As a historian, he will not say that angels were there – even if he believes it. History (in this current sense) may, however, lead the investigator to the borderlands. It shows him men and women convinced of the aliveness of Jesus. If, at the same time, it shows him no plausible source of this conviction within its own territory of purely human affairs, then the investigator is driven to carry his quest across the frontier. Beyond the frontier as a historian he cannot go. But it is by his investigations as a historian that he is caused to look beyond the frontier, since, as a historian, he gets nothing but perplexity if he tries to stay within his own territory, finding within it no way of giving a satisfactory account of the phenomena. Thus it is that the New Testament interpreted as historical evidence may conduct us to the borderlands and point us across them to where the creative aliveness of Christ implies that he is 'on the side of the Creator', and so leads to an ontological account of him. However sparingly the New Testament borrows the language of that country beyond the frontier, students of the New Testament discover themselves to be in some sense its citizens. The New Testament is no island.

Notes

1 B. Lindars, *The Gospel of John* (London, 1972), p. 370; and, for patristic speculation, M. F. Wiles, *The Spiritual Gospel* (Cambridge, 1960), pp. 118f.
2 So, again, Lindars, *John*, p. 370.
3 Augustine, *Confessions* VII.ix.13, 14. Translation by W. Montgomery in *Selections from St Augustine's Confessions* (Cambridge, 1910).
4 E.g. Athanasius, *Contra Arianos* III.30, *PG* 26, 388A. For this reference, as for valuable advice on the whole essay, I am indebted to C. M. Jones of St Peter's College, Oxford, and Ridley Hall, Cambridge. B. Hebblethwaite also was kind enough to read and comment on an earlier draft.
5 See M. J. Suggs, *Wisdom, Christology, and Law in Matthew's Gospel* (Cambridge, Mass., 1970).
6 See E. Schweizer, *Der Brief an die Kolosser* (Neukirchen-Vluyn, 1976), pp. 50–5 and n. 105.
7 Schweizer, *An die Kolosser*, p. 58.
8 Schweizer, *An die Kolosser*, p. 58; cf. C. E. B. Cranfield, *The Epistle to the Romans*, I (Edinburgh, 1975), p. 115.
9 *Hanc divinitatem, vel, ut dixerim, deitatem; nam et hoc verbo uti iam nostros non piget, ut de Graeco expressius transferant id quod illi* theoteta *appellant*...
10 J. P. M. Sweet, *Revelation* (London, 1979), *in loc.*
11 The Hebrew phrases represented by 'I am he' or by 'I, I am he' are rendered in the LXX by *egō eimi* or *egō eimi, egō eimi* or *egō eimi autos*. It is usually assumed also that there is an allusion to the great 'I am who I am' of Exod. 3: 14 (LXX *egō eimi ho ōn*). See P. B. Harner, *The 'I Am' of the Fourth Gospel*, Facet Books, Biblical Series 26 (Philadelphia, 1970).
12 J. Barr, *The Semantics of Biblical Language* (Oxford, 1961).
13 For a careful examination of this question, see A. S. Browne, 'An examination of the relation between the believer and Christ as understood by the author of the Epistle to the Hebrews', unpublished dissertation for the degree of Ph.D. in the University of Cambridge, 1979.
14 J. N. D. Kelly, *The Epistles of Peter and of Jude* (London, 1969), pp. 303, 304.
15 For an important study of this language, see G. C. Stead, *Divine Substance* (Oxford, 1977).

16 One of the best known 'functional' Christologies is O. Cullmann's *Die Christologie des Neuen Testaments* (Tübingen, 1957), ET *The Christology of the New Testament* (London, 1959). See a critique in H. Ridderbos, *Paulus: Ontwerp van zijn theologie* (Kampen, 1966), ET *Paul: an Outline of His Theology* (Grand Rapids, 1975), pp. 68f.

17 C. H. Talbert, *What is a Gospel?* (Philadelphia, 1977), e.g. p. 52, n. 106.

18 For a discussion of some of these, see C. F. D. Moule, *The Origin of Christology* (Cambridge, 1977).

2

Athens and Jerusalem: Joint Witnesses to Christ?

G. W. H. LAMPE

The notes to this essay will be found on pages 36–8

Dies irae, dies illa,
Solvet saeclum in favilla,
Teste David cum Sibylla.

To the medieval Church it seemed in no way surprising that the scriptural Psalms and the pagan oracles should jointly witness to the truth of the eschatological hopes and fears of Christian believers. It was not generally realized that those Sibylline oracles, which apparently ranked alongside the utterances of the Psalmist and the canonical Prophets as divine proclamations of the Gospel before the event, were in fact Jewish and Christian compositions in imitation of the classical oracular hexameters. They were believed to be genuine, and the necessary inference was drawn that God could make use, and had made use, of the cultic apparatus of paganism, as well as his normal instrument, the Bible, to communicate the Christian revelation to the world.

This was not an easy conclusion to reach, although in time it came to establish itself as an accepted part of the Christian tradition. Even Constantine, when introducing the famous acrostic poem on the word *ICHTHYS*, showed some diffidence. He wanted, so he told the 'assembly of the saints', to adduce extraneous (that is, non-Christian) testimonies to the divinity of Christ. This oracle, declaring in the acrostic the name and titles of the Lord (Jesus Christ, Son of God, Saviour), had been delivered by the Erythrean Sibyl. She was priestess of Apollo, and lived in the sixth generation after the Flood (hence possessing all the credentials of remote antiquity which the Greco-Roman world required of alleged sources of revelation). That cult was certainly undesirable; it was the source of unseemly passions. Nevertheless, within the inner recesses of that superstition, she was filled with divine inspiration and prophesied the things of God which were to come to pass, showing in an acrostic the story of the coming of Jesus. The Emperor considered her blessed, for the Saviour chose her as the prophetess of his providence on our behalf. He had to admit, however, that most people, while agreeing that the Erythrean Sibyl was a real prophetess, suspected that some Christian, not destitute of the poetic muse, had composed these verses and falsely attributed them to the Sibyl. His answer to this charge is weak: it cannot be shown to be true; Cicero had read the poem, translated it into Latin, and incorporated it in his writings (there is confusion here with an acrostic referring to the possibility of kingship for Julius Caesar); and its authenticity is supported by the fact that Virgil ascribed the undoubted prophecy of Christ in his *Fourth Eclogue* to the authorship of a Sibyl, in this case the Sibyl of Cumae.[1]

I shall return to the *Fourth Eclogue*. For the present I only wish to notice that Constantine was prepared to believe that authentic divine inspiration could be received by a pagan priestess so as to become a true prophetess of Christ. In presenting this belief to the Christian public, however, Constantine had to be very careful to disavow any intention of conferring respectability on the cult of Apollo itself. To claim that the pagan gods or their servants might be called as witnesses on the side of the Christian Gospel was to use a double-edged weapon. There was the possibility that if Christians asserted that the oracles had actually on occasions spoken the truth, pagans might ask them to allow that they had spoken the truth at other times as well. To concede that the true God had inspired the priestess of Apollo to prophesy the coming of Christ could open the door to a more general admission that she might be a source of revelation, and to allow this would be to place her potentially on the same level as the Hebrew Prophets and the other inspired teachers whose words were contained in canonical scripture. It might, indeed, be almost tantamount to a recognition that the Christian God might speak through Apollo, even, conceivably to an identification of Apollo with the word of God. The same danger was attached to the Christian use of Greek poets and philosophers as allies in the missionary enterprise. To persuade thinking pagans that their own intellectual and spiritual leaders pointed the way to Christ as the true fulfilment of their highest ideals and the full revelation of a reality which they had already perceived dimly themselves was an effective missionary strategy. It had to be balanced, however, by an uncompromising refusal to allow the possibility that there might be more than one ultimate source of divine revelation. To show the pagan world that its own philosophers, poets and oracles gave supporting testimony to the truth of Christian belief and the excellence of Christian moral principles was to build a bridge between Hellenism and the Bible; but the Church made it perfectly clear that this bridge was constructed for one-way traffic only.

Intellectually, spiritually and morally the conflict between Christianity and paganism in the Roman Empire was remarkably one-sided. The most formidable opposition to the Christian movement was generated by the popular belief that its adherents were *atheoi*: essentially bad citizens, disloyal to the ancestral traditions which bound the family and society together in an accepted way of life, subversive of ordinary decent morality, openly disrespectful towards the authority of local and imperial government and towards the gods who guarded and protected that authority and ensured the peace and safety of society. The solid cultural, social and political structure of the empire, to which pagan religion gave both outward expression and inner cohesion, was not easily destroyed. In the end it was taken over by Christianity rather than replaced by a new order, and its capture became possible when the Church, through effective apologetics, the public example of its members' mode of life, and, more especially, the witness of its martyrs, had succeeded for the most part in refuting the popular charge of 'hatred of the human race'. On the intellectual level, however, (involving also the spiritual and ethical) Christianity as a system of belief entered upon its campaign to conquer the Greco-Roman world with an enormous advantage: that of possessing the authority of divine revelation.

The theological revolution of modern times is centred upon changes in the Christian understanding of revelation and, in particular, upon the widespread abandonment of the traditional belief that revelation is communicated by God to man in the form of propositions, so that it is possible to speak of revealed doctrines. In the long perspective of Church history it is only a short time since it was generally held that revelation consists in, or at least includes, the disclosure by God of a body of information, directly communicated by him and guaranteed by his own authority to be true for all men at all times – an upper tier, as it were, of a single structure of knowledge, the lower tier of which is accessible to the natural process of rational human enquiry. This body of revealed knowledge, consisting of 'formulas, true before God' containing 'the mysteries of the Spirit, the great mysteries of Christianity', had, in the words of Archdeacon G. A. Denison's gravamen presented in the Lower

House of the Convocation of Canterbury in May, 1890, against Charles Gore and *Lux Mundi*, 'been delivered into the keeping of the Church on behalf of "all sorts and conditions of men"' for their 'implicit, simple and humble acceptance'. That consensus has now been broken down and can never be put together again. Doctrinal statements, that is, propositions about God and his relation to the world and to ourselves, are not commonly believed today to be communicated directly by God in such a way that somewhere, in the Bible or the creeds or the authoritative teaching of the Church, they are accessible to us as a store of unchanging and guaranteed truths.

There is, so Christians believe, revelation; but it never comes to us except as mediated, not only in human words, not only through human forms of thought, but in human experience and through human thinking and imagination and emotions, whether our own or those of other people, present and past. It is essentially mysterious and elusive, for it is given in fragmentary and transient experiences of the transcendent, moments of awareness of an extra dimension, as it were, in our apprehension of love, truth, beauty, judgement, claim, demand, vocation. Paradigmatic examples of such experiences are given in the stories of the call of Moses at the burning bush and Isaiah's vision in the Temple. In such moments of awareness of encounter with transcendent personal reality revelation evokes a response of awe, penitence, and personal commitment, trust, and obedience to a calling and a claim. This is the response of faith, which is really not so much a distinct reaction from the human side to a personal approach from beyond the human self as an essential and inseparable aspect of the revelatory experience itself. Revelation and faith represent two ways of looking at the same awareness of encounter, or rather of being encountered. The natural and proper desire to articulate the meaning and implications of revelation/faith so as to offer a rationale of it to the experiencing subject himself, and to enable it to be communicated intelligibly to others, leads, by a process of analysis, reflection and comparison, to the articulation of a system of beliefs or doctrinal formulations, 'the Faith'. The relation between faith and 'the Faith' is exceedingly complex and hard to define; the initial experience of personal encounter and of responding with faith usually takes a particular form in the case of each individual, determined by his own presuppositions, that is, by the system of beliefs which he already holds: Moses would not have experienced the encounter at the burning bush in that particular way had he not been a believer already in the God of Abraham, Isaac and

Jacob. Nevertheless, a fairly clear distinction can be drawn between the primary insights or awareness of faith and the doctrinal constructions, closely akin to the models used by the scientist, which serve more or less adequately, and always subject to revision or replacement, to analyse and articulate that awareness. The creeds belong to the latter category; the Bible is a record of certain human revelatory and faith-evoking experiences, and of attempts to articulate them intellectually, which have proved, through their effects on other people through the centuries, to be uniquely significant.

The early Church, however, made no such clear distinction. It believed that the content of its system of beliefs had been directly revealed by God. The essence of the idea of apostolic succession, as it was held in somewhat different forms by Clement of Rome, Irenaeus, Tertullian and even Origen, was that Christ communicated a body of teaching, authenticated by his own divine authority – no less than that of God's uttered and communicated Reason and Wisdom – to his chosen apostles, from whom it was transmitted to each generation of believers in turn through the succession of duly accredited teachers in the apostolically founded episcopal chairs. That teaching had been embodied in the writings of the apostles and their immediate followers which the Church had come to recognize as a 'New Testament', continuous with the corpus of revealed truth which it had inherited in the Jewish scriptures. In the Bible the Church possessed a revealed and infallible source and norm of belief and conduct; its task was to interpret the sacred scriptures correctly, and, according to such theologians as Irenaeus and Tertullian, the 'rule of faith', itself a 'breviarium' of the main tenor of scripture, had been handed down from apostolic times to serve as a guide to, and a criterion of, scriptural orthodoxy.

Paganism had no revealed system of belief with which to confront the Church's scriptures and the credal orthodoxy which was derived from them. The cults were not concerned with credal formulations, nor with ethical principles in the sense in which these were inculcated and practised in the Church. The concept of divine inspiration was familiar in the Platonist tradition of philosophy and played a prominent part in Hellenistic religion, but there was no equivalent to a holy book or to divinely authorized successions of teachers to expound that book. Hence the one-sidedness of the conflict of Christianity with intellectual paganism. In the last resort the philosophers and poets were speculating, using the resources of human wisdom to try to attain knowledge of the truth, or, as the Platonist tradition increasingly interpreted this, to arrive at an encounter with God; the Christians declared or proclaimed authoritatively truth which God, taking the initiative, had communicated to them through the prophets in the Old Testament and the apostles in the New. In a contest between those who believe that they possess absolute truth in the form of 'God's word written' and those who hope to reach a closer approximation to absolute truth through philosophical enquiry there can be only one outcome, so long as the basic claim of the former to possess a divinely guaranteed body of revealed truth is not effectively challenged. In the early centuries the opponents of Christianity generally confined their effort to picking holes in the content of this alleged revelation: the Bible contained unseemly and absurd stories, internal contradictions, much, especially in the Gospel narratives about Jesus, which was obviously unworthy of a son of God (he showed unheroic fear in his prayer in Gethsemane, folly in his choice of Judas, and so on), and in many respects it was unacceptable as a corpus of divinely revealed wisdom. Such attacks, even when delivered with the accuracy and shrewdness of a Celsus, were not very difficult to repel; skilful exegesis could produce quite convincing counter-arguments. What was not attempted was an assault on the strong-point on which the defence of the whole Christian position depended: the concept of a sacred book of infallible truth, whose real author was not its human writers but God.

It was not argued that what the Bible actually contains is not God's own words, but a record of the belief of certain human beings that God had spoken to them, and that the rightness of their belief is a matter for investigation and critical appraisal; it cannot be assumed *a priori*. If the subject-matter of the Bible is human experience, albeit human experience of God, then, if it does convey a faith-evoking revelation to those who read it, this comes about only through their understanding and evaluation of the ideas and emotions of the people whose beliefs and hopes and fears and ideals and errors and shortcomings the Bible records. If by 'the Bible' we really mean the experience of certain people, then it will be read in the first instance, as B. Jowett recommended in his contribution to *Essays and Reviews*, 'like any other book'. It may be that the experience of those people will prove supremely, even uniquely, revelatory of God to those who study it. The existence of the Canon represents the extent to which, during the centuries, this has been found to be the case; but the formation of the Canon, on this view, cannot be seen as a miraculous act by which this particular body of literature was singled out for all time from the rest of human thought and recognized as God's unmediated word. Its content therefore stands, in the first instance, on the same footing as the writings of the philosophers and the poets, and, indeed, as the sacred books of other religions. Any, none, or all of them may mediate divine truth in so far as human reason and imagination can apprehend it.

Such a view of the Bible, however, belongs to the post-Enlightenment age of historical and literary criticism and comparative study. In the early centuries the idea that the Christians might actually possess direct divine authority for their teaching was not itself repudiated; the objections were rather to the claim that this or that particular element in their teaching carried the divine guarantee of truth. The general possibility being admitted, it followed that there was no effective opposition to the Christian assertion that their doctrines stood on a different level from that of the philosophies. These were at best human attempts to search for God, relying on 'the wisdom of this world'. The Christian teaching was God's own address to mankind.

As Christians saw the matter, there was only one revelation and it had only one source: God. Nowadays a Christian believer who accepts a liberal theology of the kind sketched above can envisage the possibility of many revelations. All originate in the one God, but this one God may lie behind, as it were, the various theistic faiths and express himself through them all, it may be in different degrees according to the receptivity of their adherents. The God of Islam, the God of Judaism, the God of Christianity may be understood as alternative ways of conceiving the one God, or perhaps as aspects, or modes of self-communication, of the same one God. The early Church entertained no such possibility. The one and only God was the God of Christians. He was, indeed, the God of Jews as well, but the differences between Jews and Christians were due simply to the fact that the former misunderstood his revelation. If they came to a right understanding of their own scriptures they would recognize that their God was the Christians' God, that is to say, the God whose Logos is Jesus Christ. Hence the Christian dialogue with Jews, when seriously engaged in, as by Justin with Trypho, consisted chiefly in bandying contrary exegesis of texts of what both sides recognized to be inspired scripture.

There was no one God behind the many faiths, and no God but God who was incarnate (hence the vigour of Tertullian's repudiation of Marcion's dualism). The Logos of God was, according to the Apologists, none other than the reason in which, because they have been created as rational beings, all men participate. On the basis of this understanding of the Logos Justin was able to adapt Stoic theory to his missionary purpose. The idea of an immanent principle of rationality which gives order to the cosmos, and to live in harmony with which must be the aim of the wise and virtuous man, leads Justin to make his famous claim that 'those who have lived with Logos are Christians, even though they may have been regarded as "atheists", such as Socrates and Heraclitus among the Greeks and Abraham and Elijah among the barbarians',[2] and the still more far-reaching assertion that 'whatever among all men has been well said belongs to us Christians'.[3] This enables Justin to develop a two-pronged apologetic: Christianity is the fulfilment of the Hebrew scriptures, as Trypho must realize after their true meaning has been unfolded to him; it is also the fulfilment of the partial and incomplete, but nevertheless, so far as they go, valid insights and aspirations of Greek philosophy. Yet, again, the Logos in whom all rational beings have a share, and with whom Socrates and Heraclitus and other philosophers lived, is not a Word or Reason standing, as it were, behind both the Bible and the philosophers and revealing truth through Christianity and paganism alike as through two parallel channels of communication; for the Logos is *Jesus Christ* and Jesus Christ *is* the Logos – solely and exclusively. Without the revealed truth which Christianity possesses and offers, the 'germinal' or 'seminal' Logos implanted in rational creatures can communicate only an indistinct and inadequate apprehension of the truth, even though it is itself a partial and incomplete manifestation of Christ.

The witness of Hellenism to the truth of Christianity was therefore always subservient to, and strictly controlled by, the biblical revelation and the doctrinal tradition derived from it. Within the limits of the authoritative God-given body of truth, the testimony of philosophy and of the natural knowledge of God implanted in, or accessible to, all men is valuable supporting evidence, particularly as a source of useful arguments *ad homines*; but it plays a subordinate role and is never allowed to stand on an equal footing with the biblical tradition as a source of revelation. In this way Christianity was in the enviable position of being able, on the one hand, to advance the exclusive and uncompromising claim to offer infallible truth (the strength, or apparent strength, of all fundamentalism) and at the same time to assimilate Greco-Roman religious and philosophical thought, ideals and practice and use them in the furtherance of the revealed Gospel. Again, the process of assimilation was virtually one-way.

This double apologetic required the maintenance of a delicate balance. The Greek Apologists had to conduct a difficult operation in respect of pagan philosophy: on the one hand to use it as supporting testimony to their biblically-based witness and, on the other, to deny it any value in its own right as a source of truth independent of the Christian revelation. Thus Justin sets off the fragmentary character of the philosophers' grasp of the truth, demonstrated in the disputes and contradictions that are inherent in the philosophical schools, against the recognition that they, or some of them, did apprehend in part what Christ reveals fully,[4] and Tatian devotes much of his *Oratio* to a vehement and contemptuous attack on the schools of philosophy. Athenagoras fills his *Legatio* with allusions to classical literature, and takes a favourable view of philosophy, but never with any suggestion that these sources offer more than supporting evidence, useful for breaking down pagan prejudices. His attitude foreshadows that of Basil[5] and the church historian Socrates[6] in the fourth and fifth centuries: pagan literature, as Basil maintains, is useful because it furnishes examples of moral conduct which is laudable by Christian standards, and, according to Socrates, because it can teach Christians how to use the weapons of paganism in argument against paganism.

Tertullian is a good example of the way in which this balance was maintained. His attitude, though expressed more forcibly and memorably, does not seem to be essentially different from that of the Greek Apologists. On one side, Tertullian appeals to the evidence for the doctrine of creation afforded by the order and beauty of nature,[7] making use of the familiar Stoic argument employed by Christians from Clement of Rome onwards and adumbrated by Paul in Rom. 1: 20 and by Luke's speeches in Acts 14: 17 and 17: 24. In a more original way he also cites the testimony of the 'naturally Christian' soul; in moments of stress even a pagan will use monotheistic language (exclaiming 'God' rather than 'Jupiter') and will 'look to the heavens, God's throne, and not to the Capitol'.[8] He owes a great deal in his own thought to philosophy, especially Stoicism (including his belief, set out in his *De Anima*, in the corporeality of the soul). In his *Apology* he says that the philosophers acknowledge the Logos as creator of the universe. Zeno speaks of him as the creator who formed all things according to a plan, and calls him 'fate' and 'god' and 'mind of Jupiter' and 'universal necessity'. Cleanthes attributes all this to 'spirit' which pervades the universe. We Christians ascribe to the Word and Reason and Power, through which God made all things, Spirit (that is, deity) as their proper substance, in which Word utters the fiat of creation, Reason gives order to it, and Power (*Virtus*) perfects it.[9] The revealed truth of Trinitarian theology is thus supported by evidence from philosophy. Similarly, philosophers and poets acknowledge the reality of demons; the testimony of the soul witnesses to the existence of Satan when a heathen person utters a curse (apparently the expletive *malum*); Plato attests angels; and magi affirm both angels and demons.[10] Socrates denied the existence of pagan divinities, and so had a glimpse of the truth.[11] Plato, he says elsewhere, held commendable views on immortality.[12]

On the other hand, this appeal to the witness of non-Christians has to be offset by demonstrations of the inferiority of philosophy to revelation. Socrates, in spite of his enlightened attitude, ordered a cock to be sacrificed to Aesculapius.[13] The vices and weaknesses of philosophers, contrasted with Christian morality, make him exclaim: 'So where is there any likeness between the Christian and the philosopher, between the disciples of Greece and of heaven?'[14] Alternatively, he has to insist that what they hold in common with Christians was derived by the philosophers from the scriptures; for example, their ideas of final judgement, heaven (Elysium) and hell (Pyriphlegethon) were all borrowed from the Christian body of revealed truth.[15] Here Tertullian is using the familiar Christian argument, taken over from Judaism, which, by demonstrating the greater antiquity of the Old Testament writings and claiming that when pagan thought coincides with Christian teaching this is due to plagiarism, enabled the Church to deny to Hellenism the status of an independent source of revelation by virtually taking over its insights and incorporating them into the Bible.

Philosophy altogether exceeds its legitimate function as a secondary and subordinate witness to Christian truth when it attempts to reverse these roles and determine the content of Christian teaching. This is what Tertullian believes has happened in the case of the heresies, and philosophers are 'the heretics' patriarchs'.[16] Philosophically dominated heresy seeks to change the substance of revealed truth, especially the doctrines of God's wrath, creation *ex nihilo*, the virgin birth of Christ, and the resurrection of the flesh.[17] Valentinus derives his characteristic teaching from Platonism, Marcion from Stoicism, and heretics and philosophers join in asking the same questions about the problem of evil, the origin of man, and 'whence is God?'. The essential difference between orthodox Christianity and the philosophies is that 'we have no need of *curiositas*, after Christ Jesus, nor of enquiry, after the Gospel; since we believe, we have no desire to believe further'. 'What then has Athens to do with Jerusalem, the Academy with the Church, heretics with Christians?'[18] It is true, of course, that the attitude of Clement of Alexandria is much more positive. He denies that philosophy seduces Christians from the faith[19] and he cannot think that Paul was attacking Greek philosophy in 1 Cor. 2: 6–8; the philosophers did not offer insult to the Lord at his appearing, and Paul is inveighing against the wise among the *Jews*.[20] Clement is glad to take Plato as a fellow searcher in the quest for God, which in the *Timaeus* (28c) he had truly described as difficult; for in all men, and especially in those engaged in *logoi*, a divine effluence has been infused, compelling them, even against their will, to acknowledge the existence of the one eternal and ingenerate God.[21] Cleanthes presents not a poetic theogony, but a true theology, and truly teaches what God is like.[22] Those Christians who do not think fit to touch philosophy or dialectic or natural science, but only demand bare faith, are like people who want to harvest grapes without first tending the vine. The truly learned man brings everything to bear on the truth, gathering what is useful from geometry and music and grammar and philosophy for the defence of the faith.[23]

At times Clement, whose readiness to engage in a search for God would have displeased Tertullian, seems to come close to suggesting that philosophy is a co-ordinate source of truth, rather than the handmaid of the Christian revelation. Christ's words, 'Jerusalem, Jerusalem, how often would I have gathered your children, as a bird her young ones' (Matt. 23: 37; Luke 13: 34), signify, since 'Jerusalem' means 'vision of peace', that those who engage peacefully in contemplation have been trained in many different ways for their calling. The phrase 'how often' shows that wisdom is manifold and 'by all means saves some', 'because the spirit of the Lord has filled the world'.[24] Generally, however, even Clement is cautious in his commendation of philosophy and insists on assigning it a subordinate and propaedeutic role. In the first place, not all philosophy is acceptable; 'there are many thyrsus-bearers but few *bacchoi*', and Plato's 'genuine philosophers' are those who delight in contemplation of the truth.[25] The 'philosophy and empty deceit' of Col. 2: 8 refers to Epicureanism which denies providence and deifies pleasure, and Stoics, too, are wrong in holding that God is corporeal and pervades the vilest matter.[26] By 'philosophy' Clement tells us he means 'not the Stoic or Platonic or Epicurean or Aristotelian, but whatever has been well said by each of these schools, teaching righteousness with pious knowledge, and this eclectic whole I call philosophy'.[27]

Secondly, philosophy is only preparatory for the Christian revelation. It was formerly a means of justification for the Greeks, but it could not bring them to that complete righteousness for which it is an assistance, like the first and second steps to one ascending to an upper room and like the grammarian as a helper of the philosopher.[28] It was the *paidagogos* who brought the Greek world to Christ, as the Law did the Hebrews. It is a preparation for the man who is to be perfected by Christ. The way of truth is one, but into it, as into an ever-flowing river, the streams pour from every direction. Yet, when Prov. 5: 20 says 'Be not much with a strange woman', it admonishes us to use worldly culture (*paideia*), but not to stay and spend time with it, for it is propaedeutic for the Lord's word. Wisdom is the mistress of philosophy as philosophy is of *propaideia*.[29] Greek philosophy does not comprehend the greatness of the truth, and it is too infirm to carry out the Lord's commands; yet it prepares the way for the supremely royal teaching, moderating and moulding the character and fitting him who believes in providence to receive the truth.[30] Paul, claims Clement, shows by his quotation from Aratus in the Athens speech that he approved of what had been well said by the Greeks, and he intimates by what he says concerning the 'unknown God' that the Greeks honoured the Creator in a roundabout way, but that it was necessary for them to apprehend and learn him by the knowledge mediated through the Son.[31]

Christian writers show the same mixture of approbation and caution in respect of pagan prophets. The supposedly heathen oracles of the Sibyls were widely accepted as revelation, though Constantine, as we have seen, realized that there were many hesitations about this. It may be significant that Hermas mistakes the old lady in his vision, who really represents the Church, for the Sibyl.[32] Lactantius quotes Sibylline oracles enthusiastically, while believing them to be pagan. They are 'sacred responses and predictions' by prophetesses who 'all proclaim one God'. He adduces the Sibyl as a witness to the certainty of the Day of Judgement: 'For then there shall be confusion of mortals throughout the whole earth, when the Almighty himself shall come on his judgment seat to judge the souls of the living and the dead'[33] ('teste David cum Sibylla'). Augustine is by no means so sure. He recognizes that, since Virgil apparently ascribes his prophetic *Eclogue* to the Cumaean Sibyl, it is possible that she had actually heard in the spirit something about the one Saviour which she had to acknowledge,[34] and he is prepared to offer a theological exegesis of lines 13–14 of that poem.[35] Having been shown a Greek codex of the

ICHTHYS acrostic, he acknowledges that the Sibyl did write about Christ.[36] On the other hand, he believes that when Paul said that the Gospel had been promised by God 'by his prophets in the holy scriptures' he was making a distinction. Paul knew that some prophets who were not '*his*' had heard and uttered things concerning Christ, 'as it is said of the Sibyl'. 'I would not easily believe this', adds Augustine, 'had not the most noble poet in Latin, before speaking of the new age in a manner which harmonizes sufficiently with the Kingdom of the Lord Jesus Christ, prefixed a verse: "Ultima Cumaei venit iam carminis aetas"'.[37] Paul showed at Athens that he realized that testimonies to the truth were to be found in gentile books; he therefore says 'through *his* prophets', lest anyone should be seduced into impiety by false prophets who may occasionally confess the truth, and he further adds 'in holy scriptures' to show that gentile literature is very full of superstitious idolatry, and must not be thought to be holy because references to Christ may be found in it.[38]

In the light of the cautious patristic handling of 'Athens' as a witness to Christ, and the general insistence that it must always be heard only as a useful but strictly subordinate supporter of 'Jerusalem', it is remarkable that the two are placed almost on the same level in the Gospels themselves. If 'Athens' is interpreted broadly enough to symbolize not only pagan philosophers, poets, seers and prophets, but also representatives of the Roman Empire, each Gospel contains an element of 'Athenian' testimony. In Mark the beginning of the Gospel of 'Jesus Christ, the Son of God'[39] is attested by a combination of two 'Jerusalem' witnesses, prophetic utterances from the scriptures; but the first direct affirmation of the truth of the Gospel by a human person (as distinct from the demons) is made by the 'Athenian' centurion at the Cross: 'Truly, this man was the Son of God'.[40] The Fourth Gospel presents a similar picture: the truth that Jesus was the King of the Jews is proclaimed in Greek and Latin, as well as in Hebrew, by the Roman governor, who, as Chrysostom observed in commenting on John 19: 19–22, thereby ascribed to Jesus the kingdom and the *universal* worship prophesied of the Son of man by Daniel,[41] and, by writing the *titulus* in the three languages, created the firstfruits of the confession of Christ's Lordship by 'every tongue'.[42] Augustine associates the witness of the gentile Pilate with that of the gentile magi. The latter came from the East, the former from the West, fulfilling Jesus' prophecy that many should come from the East and the West, and, by witnessing respectively to the birth and the death of the King of the Jews, they enter the Kingdom and sit down with the ancestors of the Jews, being 'grafted in' by their faith.[43]

Luke develops this theme much more fully. His concern is to direct a two-pronged apologetic towards Jews and Gentiles, proving to the former that Christianity is as old as Abraham, to the latter that it is 'as old as the Creation'. His chief object is to show that the Gospel is the fulfilment of, and is continuous with, God's revelation to Israel, Israel now being seen to include all men, whether Jews or Gentiles, who accept that Gospel. There are, indeed, two traditions in Israel, as the speech of Stephen tells us: the one, a tradition of faithful response to God's revelation, comes down from Abraham through Moses and the prophets to the Messiah and those who now preach and heal in his name; the other, a tradition of rejection and disobedience, extends from the brothers of Joseph and those who refused to accept Moses, through those who worshipped the golden calf and persecuted the prophets, to those who killed the Messiah and to the Sanhedrin that murders his witness. Jesus is therefore presented by Luke as one who followed the Law while deepening and correcting the manner of its observance; Luke's Paul, as a Christian, is the ideal Pharisee, 'saying nothing but what the prophets and Moses said would come to pass'.[44]

To show the world, even if he cannot convince contemporary Judaism, that the Church is the real Israel as originally called and constituted by God is Luke's principal aim. He pursues it throughout the two volumes of his work, from Jerusalem to Paul's final debate with the Jews in Rome. In the great controversy as to who are the authentic Israel and who are the false and apostate Israel the witnesses are the Old Testament scriptures. At the same time Luke has to show the Gentiles that their proper place is within the genuine, Christian, Israel. Apologetic directed towards them has to prove that the answer to the question why they should come in, that is, why they should believe in the Christian Israel's God, is given by their own religion. Christianity is the fulfilment of the right tradition in paganism, just as it is of the right tradition in Israel, the right tradition in this case being that of monotheism. So Luke uses familiar Jewish arguments from natural religion (God's works in creation) for the gentile apologetic which he concentrates in the Lystra and Athens speeches.[45] But in the Athens speech he goes much further. The inscription to the Unknown God is made to show that the God preached by Christians is the God whom the Greeks actually worship already, though hitherto in ignorance. Of pagans and Christians alike it is true that the one God 'is not far from each one of us, for "In him we live and move and have our being"' (Acts 17: 28), and, whereas the apologetic to Judaism rests on the testimony of the Hebrew scriptures, the appeal to the Greeks is similarly supported by 'Athenian' proof-texts from 'your poets'. Aratus' line, 'For we are also his offspring' really does seem to be treated by Luke as a testimony to the Gospel in parallel to, and co-ordinate with, that of the scriptures.[46] Certainly Luke's use of this Hellenic witness alarmed some later commentators, among them Chrysostom who warns his readers that the poet was speaking of Zeus and Paul of God the Creator, not meaning the same god as the poet (God forbid) but ascribing the quotation to him to whom it should properly belong; Paul made it clear, too, that the altar belonged to God, and not to him whom the Athenians worshipped.[47]

More shocking than Luke's appeal to pagan poets was Matthew's astonishing introduction of the magi into his story. For if Luke's poets exemplify the religion of 'Athens' at its highest, magi represent its seamy side. Today Christmas carols, cards and plays have turned Matthew's magi into the highly picturesque but totally respectable 'three kings of Orient'. In Matthew, however, they are not kings, though the echoes in his narrative of Isaiah 60: 3, 6 and Psalm 72: 9, 10, 15 made the later identification of the magi with Arabian or other Eastern kings easy (Ps. 72: 9 is directly applied to the magi by Tertullian;[48] at least from the time of Caesarius of Arles they have become three kings, on account of their three gifts).[49] They are simply magi, not disguised in the respectability of the Authorized Version's 'wise men'. Magi were far from respectable. They were diviners by means of astrology, and therefore practitioners of an art which Christians were never weary of denouncing as dangerous superstition and exposing as ridiculous and self-contradictory. *Magi* and *mathematici* were constantly in trouble with the police from the early days of the Julio-Claudian principate when they were expelled from Rome to the rule of the Christian emperors when they were hunted down with especial savagery, as Chrysostom's story reminds us; as a young man he, with a friend, fished a book out of the river at Antioch during a major police drive against *biblia goetika kai magika*; they realized it was a book of magic just as a soldier approached, but were providentially able to jettison it without being caught in possession.[50] It is true that Philo speaks of magi as natural scientists, recipients of revelations about divine prodigies in silent contemplation,[51] but generally they represent a shady and unsavoury aspect of paganism.

In Luke magi play a prominent part as obstructors of the apostolic mission,[52] and have to be met or threatened with the full force of miraculous power. In Matthew, on the contrary, these gentile astrologers enact the role which Luke assigns to the angel Gabriel. For although Matthew's readers already know that Jesus has been divinely revealed as saviour, and as the one who fulfils the Emmanuel prophecy of Isaiah, it is the magi who first tell them directly that he is the Messiah, the King of the Jews. What was announced to Mary by the angel in Luke 1: 32–33 ('he will reign over the house of Jacob for ever' on 'the throne of his father David') is disclosed first, according to Matthew, by magi to whom it has been revealed by their study of the stars. They know that the King of the Jews has been born, for they have seen his star – much in the manner of the magian interpretation of stars at the birth of Alexander.[53] Accordingly, they travel to Jerusalem to worship him with gifts. The idea that they follow the star from the East to Judaea has no support from Matthew's story: the star which they saw in the East reappears on their way from Jerusalem to Bethlehem and guides them to the house of Joseph and Mary. By that time the witness of the star that the King of the Jews has been born has been supplemented by the testimony of scripture (Micah 5: 1–3 conflated with 2 Sam. 5: 2) that the destined birthplace is Bethlehem. It looks very much as though, in this instance, the roles of 'Jerusalem' and 'Athens' are reversed and the prophets act as secondary supporting evidence to assist astrology.

Matthew's magi worship Christ; there is nothing here of the later suggestions that this implied that they abandoned their profession and surrendered to him the tools of their craft. They are bona fide witnesses to, and worshippers of, the Christ. They return, as magi, to their own land, having been granted a revelation from God in a dream, not to return to Herod at Jerusalem.

One may suppose that the impact of this story on the Evangelist's readers would be somewhat like the effect on readers of *The Daily Telegraph* of a report in that paper of a visit to Mrs Thatcher, shortly before the British General Election of 1979, of a delegation from the high command of the Provisional I.R.A. to assure her of their enthusiastic support and their confidence that she would soon become Prime Minister – and, further, to offer her some souvenirs of the Troubles to exhibit in Number Ten when, as they hoped and expected, she soon moved in.

Patristic commentaries bear out this supposition. They handle the story very uneasily. The gifts presented no problem. Clement of

Alexandria explains that gold symbolizes kingship;[54] Irenaeus already holds that all three are christological in their significance (myrrh that he was to die for mankind and be buried, gold that he was the king whose kingdom would have no end, incense that he was God, 'made known in Judaea' as Psalm 76: 1 had prophesied);[55] Origen tells us that gold, incense and myrrh show Christ as king, as perfect God and perfect man, and as about to die on our behalf.[56] Hilary varies this conventional interpretation with his triad, king, God, man, 'summing up the whole meaning of the mystery: death (as man), resurrection (as God), judgement (as king)'.[57] Soon the gifts receive moralizing interpretations. Chrysostom tells a congregation: 'They brought gold, you must bring temperance and virtue; they brought incense, you must bring pure prayers; they brought myrrh, you must bring lowliness, an humble heart, and almsgiving.'[58] The *Opus imperfectum in Matthaeum*, a Latin version of a Greek, probably Arian, work of the early fifth century, equates gold with faith and wisdom, incense with prayer, myrrh with the good works which keep Christ crucified for ever in man's memory. Caesarius of Arles has, similarly, gold for wisdom, incense for prayer, myrrh for perfect mortification.[59]

Nor did the fact that Matthew's magi represent gentile believers cause difficulty. Augustine works out an application to them of Eph. 2: 14–15: the shepherds and the magi show that Christ is the corner-stone who joins the two walls represented by the shepherds from Judaea and the magi from the East; of the two Christ makes one new man.[60] Less edifying is the tendency to use the gentile magi as a stick with which to beat the intransigent Jews. Jerome is only one of many commentators who think that the whole episode was designed to show up Jewish unbelief, contrasted with the recognition of Christ by Gentiles (and magi at that).[61]

The difficulty was to tone down the effect of Matthew's narrative. It could be done in several ways. One way was to suppose that the story indicates the overthrow of heathen magic at the appearance of Christ on earth. This notion was already found in the quite different account given by Ignatius of the appearance of a star and the cessation of sorcery and magic.[62] It was taken up in the exegesis of Matthew. Origen says that magi are people in communion with demons, and that they can invoke and constrain them by spells until the appearance of something more divine and potent than either the demons or their spells. At the birth of Jesus the effect of the appearance of the heavenly host was to cause demons to lose their strength and the power of magic to be overthrown by the angels and by the divinity in Jesus. It was because the magi found that their magic no longer worked that they set out to discover why, and went to see what might be indicated by the star which they recognized from Balaam's prophecy to be a portent of the advent of someone superior to the demons.[63] Tertullian had already suggested that the magi's offerings to Christ indicated that sacrifices were to cease, and that their return home by 'another way' symbolized their abandonment of their previous way of life. After the coming of the Gospel all diviners, Chaldeans and magicians are punished by God, like Simon Magus and Elymas.[64] According to Gregory of Nazianzus the moment when they joined the angels in worshipping Christ was the time when all skill in the astrologer's art came to an end.[65] Sometimes this defeat or conversion of the magi is taken as a fulfilment of Isa. 8:3–4; they are the 'power of Damascus and the spoils of Samaria', captured by Christ.[66]

Another method of taking the sting out of the story was to make out that these particular magi were reputable philosophers rather than shady astrologers. Jerome says that magi are commonly identified with *malefici*, but among their own people, Chaldeans, they are highly regarded as philosophers, and their art is patronized by kings and princes.[67] An interesting variation on this theme appears in the *Opus imperfectum in Matthaeum* already mentioned. It quotes an uncanonical (but 'innocuous') scripture to the effect that among a people in the extreme East next to the Ocean there was handed down a writing under the name of Seth concerning the star mentioned by Balaam. Twelve of the more studious among them, devotees of heavenly mysteries, constituted themselves watchers for that star. Sons or relatives took the places of those who died. They were called in their tongue 'magi' because they glorified God in silence. Every year after harvest they went up on Mons Victorialis which has a cave and pleasant springs and trees. There they washed, prayed and praised God for three days. After many generations the star appeared, descending over that mountain in the form of a child surmounted by the likeness of a cross. It told them to go to Judaea, and it preceded them as they journeyed for two years. When they returned after the events recorded in the Gospel, they worshipped God more zealously than before, and preached and taught many of their people. After the resurrection the apostle Thomas went to that province and they were baptized by him and assisted his mission.[68]

The connection with Balaam was developed by many commentators. This enabled the magi to be brought within the sphere of the

Old Testament, and at least partly 'depaganized' and transferred from 'Athens' to 'Jerusalem'. Origen maintained that Balaam was one of the Persian magi, and that they kept his prophecy, expecting a great king to be born to the Jews.[69] According to Ambrose the magi were actually descendants of Balaam and 'heirs of faith'. They recognized the star which Balaam had seen in spirit, knew that it denoted one who was man and God, realized that their arts had ceased, and confessed a stranger.[70] Jerome, commenting on Isa. 19, says that the Lord entered Egypt (signifying this world) and all divination and idolatry knew itself to be broken, so that magi from the East, either taught by demons or knowing from Balaam's prophecy that the Son of God was born who would destroy all their arts, came and worshipped the child.[71]

Another obvious line to take was to use the magi as an example of the divine condescension which accommodates revelation to the capacity and the situation of the recipient of it. It is no more surprising, says Chrysostom, that God should call the magi by means of a star than the Jews by means of sacrifices, purifications, new moons, ark and Temple. He allowed the magi to be brought to the manger by a star, so as to lead them to better things, and after they had come to Bethlehem he no longer spoke to them through a star but through an angel (that is, in a dream).[72] God's action in leading them by a star rather than by an angel, a prophet, an apostle or an evangelist is like that of a human father who speaks to his children in baby talk, 'not using Greek words for food and drink, but a kind of barbarian language for children'.[73]

The real difficulty, however, was to explain away the star and the association of divine revelation with astrology. The *Opus imperfectum in Matthaeum* is content to issue a warning. The text, 'We have seen his star...' may encourage unbelievers to think that everyone lives under the control of his own star. But this is unthinkable; it would deprive us of free will and moral responsibility, and nullify God's commandments and exhortations by fastening the responsibility for human wickedness on him, as the maker of the stars that determine our conduct. A more positive approach was to assert that the Epiphany star was not a natural star at all, and hence not part of the subject-matter of astrology. In Clement's *Excerpts from Theodotus* there is the suggestion that the strange new star was the Lord himself, come to transfer those who believed in Christ from the sphere of fate to that of providence. His birth delivered us from *genesis* and fate; so baptism delivers us, and although fate is true until we are baptized, thereafter the astrologers no longer speak the truth.[74] Origen thinks the star was new, unlike any ordinary star, but to be classed with comets which do signify great events in history. Elsewhere he maintains that it was a heavenly power in the form of a star, guiding the magi by travelling at a low altitude; the fact that it stood over where the child was shows that it was no ordinary star.[75]

Some authors introduce a scientific discussion of this problem. The homily on the birth of Christ dubiously ascribed to Basil contains a warning, 'Let no one introduce the apparatus of astrology into the rising of this star'. It was not one of the existing stars from which astrological inferences might be attempted. It was new. All stars are either permanently static or constantly mobile, but this one possessed both properties, first moving, then standing still. It is a mistake to suppose that it resembled the comets, which seem to appear specially to signify the successions of kings; for these, too, are generally static, being an eruption of fire in a circumscribed locality. Comets and meteors have the same origin: when the air around the earth becomes excessive and overflows into the ethereal region, and its thickness and turbidity as it rises provide material for combustion, it presents the brilliant appearance of a star. The magi's star, however, alternated between being visible and invisible, so that they might learn whose it was, whom it served, and for whose sake it had come into being.[76]

Chrysostom admits that enemies of the truth use the episode of the magi to argue for the validity of astrology. He replies, first, that the magi did not really learn very much from their star. That Jesus was King of the Jews? But he was not; he told Pilate that his kingdom was not of this world. Then their conduct was quite different from that of astrologers. The latter try to predict from the known time of birth what a man's future will be; but these magi knew neither the place nor the time of birth. This star told them that someone had been born and they came to see him, at the risk of such great danger, and with the certainty that they would gain so little material advantage, that at the human level the whole story is absurd. The solution of the difficulty begins with the star. It was not, says Chrysostom, in my view a star at all, but an invisible power which took on that appearance. No star travels like this one. Sun, moon and stars all move from East to West, but this one went from North to South, for that is the direction from Persia to Palestine. Nor did it appear at night, but at midday when the sun was shining. No star has such power, not even the moon. Its appearance, disappearance and reappearance indicate a highly rational power. Nor could a star point out a little hut or the body of a small child. To show so small a spot a star would have to come right down and stand over the baby's actual head; which is just what the evangelist says it did. It is not, therefore, one of the stars that appear in the ordinary course of nature.[77]

The boldness with which Matthew set Athens, in its less creditable guise, beside Jerusalem as joint witnesses to Christ has evoked apologiae on these lines from the second century onwards. In fact, the anxiety with which the early Fathers approached Matthew's Epiphany story has not yet been allayed. The latest expression of it to come to my notice is the article 'Christianity and Astrology' by Canon Harold de Mel in the Christmas 1979 issue of *Darsana*, the journal of the Anglican church in Sri Lanka.

He writes as follows:

> The star seen by the Magi was therefore something unique, a star seen once, only once, and once for all...Nobody else saw it, not even the shepherds...It was not a known or identifiable heavenly body, a conjunction of planets or a comet or a meteor...God created a wonderful star to guide the astrologers who believed in stars. God always comes down to the level of men...At the same time he lifts them up to a higher level, and so these astrologers were lifted up above petty superstition. The first point we have to note is that the star was supernatural and not a heavenly or supernal body which we can ever identify. The second point...is that the coming of astrologers to worship Jesus does not signify any correct prognostications based on their astronomical studies. God guided them to the manger not to promote or perpetuate superstition, but to disclaim and destroy superstitious practices...Accordingly, the Magi gave up their witchcraft, black magic, belief in astrology and faith in horoscopes. They also offered to the Holy Babe all the specific substances used by them...frankincense to caste out devils, myrrh to prepare potent potions, and the profits they had made in gold. The common interpretation of these gifts (to represent priesthood, death and kingship) is fascinating but far-fetched...Nowhere in the New Testament is astrology accepted or upheld. St Matthew...wrote his Gospel for Jews who would not have misunderstood the purpose for which the coming of the Magi was included in his narrative. It was to

> proclaim the triumph of Christ over Gentile abominations. We in the East, living in an environment full of superstition, and those in the West who...study horoscopes in the daily newspapers...are apt to misinterpret this incident to suit their predilection due to lack of faith. That is why they ask, 'If astrologers came to Jesus, why shouldn't we go to them?'

Canon de Mel would have been applauded all the way from Tertullian to Augustine. But would Matthew himself have agreed? It scarcely seems likely. We need not doubt that his story of the appearance of the star has its roots in the Old Testament – in Balaam's oracle, 'I see him, but not now: I behold him, but not nigh: a star should come forth out of Jacob, and a sceptre shall rise out of Israel' (Num. 24: 17), linked with the prophecy of Isa. 60: 3, 'And nations shall come to your light, and kings to the brightness of your rising'. Nor is it improbable that Matthew was acquainted with Jewish traditions, reproduced later by the Christian Fathers, which connected the magi of Chaldaea and Persia with Balaam, the Gentile whom God had made, against his own will, a channel of prophetic revelation. He gives no hint, however, that he expects his readers to be familiar with such traditions and to realize that through the link with Balaam magi from the East might be regarded almost as honorary prophets of Israel rather than as heathen astrologers. Nor is there any ground for supposing that Matthew thought that this star was a unique creation, perhaps not a physical object at all, and therefore no part of the subject-matter of astrology. Neither Matthew himself nor his Old Testament background offer any support for the idea that the gifts offered by the magi represent the surrender of the tools of their wicked trade and their conversion from 'belief in astrology and faith in horoscopes'. There is no parallel here to the collection and burning (not the presentation as acceptable gifts to the Lord) of their books by the magicians of Ephesus who were converted by Paul.[78] On the contrary, taken at its face value, Matthew's story tells us uncompromisingly that the birth of the King of the Jews was revealed, like that of Alexander, by a star which was observed by magi in the regular practice of astrology, and that, after they had communicated this revelation to the people of Jerusalem, these heathens were led to the Messiah by the joint guidance of their star and the scriptural prophecy of Micah, worshipped him, presented him with their treasures, and were favoured with a special divine revelation to enable them to return safely to their own country.

The relationship between this simple but startling narrative and the fantastic and allusive rhetoric of Ignatius is hard to determine. The latter passage runs as follows in Lightfoot's translation:[79]

> And hidden from the prince of this world were the virginity of Mary and her child-bearing and likewise also the death of the Lord – three mysteries to be cried aloud – the which were wrought in the silence of God. How then were they made manifest to the ages? A star shone forth in the heaven above all the stars; and its light was unutterable, and its strangeness caused amazement; and all the rest of the constellations with the sun and moon formed themselves into a chorus about the star; but the star itself far outshone them all; and there was perplexity to know whence came this strange appearance which was so unlike them. From that time forward every sorcery (*mageia*) and every spell was dissolved, the ignorance of wickedness vanished away, the ancient kingdom was pulled down, when God appeared in the likeness of man unto newness of everlasting life; and that which had been perfected in the counsels of God began to take effect. Thence all things were perturbed, because the abolishing of death was taken in hand.

It is possible, and it has often been thought probable, that the above passage represents a tradition, independent of Matthew, of the star of the Nativity; conceivably it could be the earlier of the two. This, however, is unlikely. The idea seems to presuppose an actual historical appearance of a 'star of Bethlehem' underlying both the Matthaean narrative of the magi and the poetic imaginings of Ignatius, and this, despite the many attempts to reconcile the Epiphany story with scientific astronomy, is scarcely worth serious consideration. Short of that possibility, it seems extremely improbable that two independent traditions about a star should arise independently of each other, especially since Ignatius shows little sign of having derived his imagery directly from the oracle of Balaam, the original root of the idea. It is still less likely that Matthew developed his story out of the myth used by Ignatius.

It is much more probable that Ignatius is dependent upon Matthew for the idea that the realization of the counsels of God in the opening events of the Gospel was announced by the appearance of a star, and that he is deliberately substituting a poeticaly conceived but essentially more conventional picture for the bold assertion by Matthew that astrology had revealed the birth of the Messiah. Ignatius certainly seems to have known the First Gospel. Close parallels to Matthew occur at *Epistola ad Trallianos* 11.1; *ad Philadephenses* 3.1; *ad Smyrnaeos* 1.1, 6; *ad Polycarpum* 2.2, and rather more distant echoes at *Epistola ad Ephesios* 5.2, 6.1, 17.1; *ad Polycarpum* 1.2–3; *ad Magnesios* 5.2, 9.3; *ad Romanos* 9.3; and there are other possible Matthaean allusions. In Ignatius' legend of the star three essential components of Matthew's narrative reappear in a different guise: the appearance of a star, a connection between this star and the art of the magi, and the inauguration of a new kingdom (by implication, since the appearance of God in the likeness of man brings about the destruction of 'the ancient kingdom'). These components, however, have been reassembled in a way which anticipates three elements in the later patristic anti-astrological exegesis of Matthew. The star is altogether new and strange, and quite unlike the ordinary constellations; the star is a manifestation of Christ himself; its, or his, appearance signalizes the abolition of all heathen *mageia*. It looks, then, as if Ignatius may have constructed his myth on the basis of Matthew's story, going to the dream of Joseph in Gen. 37: 9 for the central idea of the supremacy of the new star over the sun, the moon, and all other stars, and to the Pauline Epistles for the notions of a revelation hidden in the silence of God and now manifested (Rom. 16: 25, Col. 1: 26, Eph. 3: 9. Ignatius alters the Pauline sense while using the Pauline language, and, in a Gnosticizing fashion, makes Paul's 'aeons' the actual recipients of the revelation), and of the purpose of the coming of Christ as the inauguration of 'newness of life' (Rom. 6:4). By the use of these materials Ignatius seems to have transformed the Matthaean Epiphany into a much more innocuous, if also more fanciful, myth and established a foundation on which the later Fathers could build their anti-astrological exegesis of the star.[80]

Matthew may, as Canon de Mel remarks, have written his Gospel for the Jews, but he was at least as anxious as Luke to promote and vindicate the mission to the Gentiles. The commission of the risen Lord to make disciples of all the nations (or Gentiles), apparently solving the problem of their relationship to the Mosaic Law by substituting for it the new Law of Christ's teaching,[81] is foreshadowed by several important passages in the earlier part of the Gospel, such as the comment that the move of Jesus from Nazareth to Capernaum fulfilled the prophecy of the coming of light to those in darkness in the land of the Gentiles;[82] the insertion of Jesus' own prophecy concerning the admission of Gentiles to the heavenly feast (and the expulsion from it of the 'sons of the kingdom') into the story of the centurion;[83] the use made of the 'Servant Song' of Isa. 42: 1–4, with its strong emphasis on the salvation of the Gentiles, in connection with Jesus' Galilaean ministry.[84] In his narrative of the magi he has given a strong hint that Gentiles will have already been prepared for the coming of the Gospel by a revelation given in their own terms, and a clear indication that he was prepared to acknowledge gentile sources of revelation, not only, like Luke in Paul's speech at Athens, as testimonies to monotheism against idolatry, but even, in parallel with the Prophets, as witnesses to Christ.

Notes

1 Constantine, *Oratio ad sanctorum coetum* 18–20.
2 Justin, *1 Apologiae* 46.
3 Justin, *2 Apologiae* 13.
4 Justin, *2 Apol.* 10.
5 Basil, *De libris legendis gentilium.*
6 Socrates, *Historia Ecclesiastica* 3.16.
7 Tertullian, *Apologeticus* 11.
8 Tert., *Apol.* 17; *De Testimonio Animae, passim.*
9 Tert., *Apol.* 21, citing Diogenes Laertius, 7.174.
10 Tert., *Apol.* 22, citing Plato, *Symposium* 28.
11 Tert., *Apol.* 46.
12 Tert., *De Resurrectione Carnis* 3.
13 Tert., *Apol.* 46.
14 Ibid.
15 Tert., *Apol.* 47.
16 Tert., *Adversus Hermogenem* 8.
17 Tert., *Adversus Marcionem* 5.19.
18 Tert., *De praescriptione haereticorum* 7.
19 Clement of Alexandria, *Stromateis* 1.2.20.
20 Clem. Al., *Strom.* 5.4.25.
21 Clem. Al., *Protrepticus* 6.68.
22 Clem. Al., *Protr.* 6.71.
23 Clem. Al., *Strom.* 1.9.43f.
24 Ibid. 1.5.77ff.
25 Ibid. 1.19.91ff.
26 Ibid. 1.11.50–51.
27 Ibid. 1.7.37.
28 Ibid. 1.20.99.
29 Ibid. 1.5.28–30.
30 Ibid. 1.16.80.
31 Ibid. 1.19.91.
32 Hermas, *Visiones pastoris* 2.4.
33 Lactantius, *Divinae Institutiones* 1.6, 7.24.
34 Augustine, *Epistulae* 258.5.
35 Augustine, *De civitate Dei* 10.27.

36 Ibid. 18.23.
37 Augustine's attitude here resembles that of Constantine, who supported the claim that the Sibyl had prophesied Christ by appealing to the *Fourth Eclogue*, his translation of the latter having already been doctored so that the line 'iam redit et virgo, redeunt Saturnia regna' read 'the Virgin returns, bringing a beloved king (*eraton basilea*)'.
38 Augustine, *Epistola ad Romanos inchoata* 3.
39 But note the variant reading.
40 Mark 1: 1–3; 15: 39.
41 Dan. 7: 14.
42 Phil. 2: 11.
43 Augustine, *Sermones* 201.
44 Acts 26: 22.
45 Acts 14: 15–17; 17: 22–31.
46 Whether or not 'in him we live...' is also cited from the poets need not be discussed here.
47 Chrysostom, *Homiliae in Acta Apostolorum* 38.3; cf. *Homiliae in Epistulam ad Titum* 3.
48 Tertullian, *Marc.* 3.13.
49 Pseudo-Augustine, *Sermones* 13.
50 Chrysostom, *Hom. 38.5 in Ac.*
51 Philo, *Quod omnis probus liber* 11.74; cf. *De specialibus legibus* 3.18.
52 Acts 8: 9ff; 13: 6ff.
53 Cicero, *De Divinatione* 1.47.
54 Clement of Alexandria, *Paed.* 2.8.63.
55 Irenaeus, *Adversus haereses* 3.9.2.
56 Origen, *Fragmenta in Matthaeum* 2: 1–21.
57 Hilary, *Commentarius in Evangelium Matthaei* 1.5–6.
58 Chrysostom, *De beato Philogonio* 6.
59 Pseudo-Augustine, *Sermones* 139.
60 Ps.-Aug., *Serm.* 199.
61 Jerome, *Commentarius in Evangelium Matthaei* 2.
62 Ignatius, *Epistola ad Ephesios* 19.
63 Origen, *Contra Celsum*, 1.58–61.
64 Tertullian, *De Idolis* 9.
65 Gregory of Nazianzus, *Carminum libri duo* 1.1.5.53ff.
66 Cf. Justin, *Dialogus cum Tryphorie Judaeo* 77.4, 78.1, 2, 9–10; Tertullian, *Ad Judaeos* 9; Peter of Alexandria, *Epistula canonica* 13; August., *Serm.* 202; *Opus imperfectum in Matthaeum* hom. 2 (Migne, *PG* 56.637).
67 Jerome, *Dan.* 2.
68 *Opus imperfectum in Matthaeum.* On this story see J. Bidez and F. Cumont, *Les Mages Hellénisés* (Paris, 1938), 2, p. 120.
69 Origen, *Fr. in Matt.* 2: 1–21; cf. *c. Cels.* 1.58–61; *Hom. 13.7 in Num.*
70 Ambrose, *Expositio in Evangelium Lucae* 2: 45.
71 Jerome, *Isa.* 19; cf. Pseudo-Basil, *In Christi generationem* 5.
72 Chrysostom, *Homiliae in Matthaeum* 6.
73 Chrysostom, *Hom. 3 in Tit.*; cf. Origen, *Fr. in Matt.* 2: 1–21.
74 Clement of Alexandria, *Excerpts from Theodotus* 74–78.
75 Origen, *c. Cels.* 1.58–61; *Fr. in Matt.* 2: 1–21.

76 Pseudo-Basil, *Chr. generat.* 6; cf. Gregory of Nazianzus, *Orationes* 5.5, *Carm.* 1.1.5.53ff.
77 Chrysostom, *Hom. 6 in Matt.*
78 Acts 19: 18–19.
79 Ignatius, *Eph.* 19; J. B. Lightfoot, *Apostolic Fathers* (London, 1889), II, II, p. 549.
80 Direct use of Ignatius is made by *Protevangelium Jacobi* and Clem. Al., *Exc. Theodot.* 74.
81 Matt. 28: 19–20.
82 Matt. 4: 13–16.
83 Matt. 8: 11–12.
84 Matt. 12: 17–21.

3

The Concept of Mind and the Concept of God in the Christian Fathers

CHRISTOPHER STEAD

The notes to this essay will be found on pages 53–4

In his treatise *On Prayer*, Aristotle is said to have declared that God 'is either Mind or something beyond mind' (*ē nous estin ē epekeina ti tou nou*). Our sole authority for this Aristotelian dictum is the sixth-century pagan philosopher Simplicius, and it is impossible to tell whether earlier Christian writers were acquainted with the treatise *On Prayer*; but one can hardly imagine Christians objecting to this cautiously-worded statement. Yet it seems to have gone almost unremarked that there is no biblical authority, in either Old or New Testament, for describing God as Mind. The Bible speaks in more concrete terms of God as living and active and responsive to the needs of his children, especially in contrast with the dumb and insensate images of the pagan cults. But from the second century, at least, it was taken for granted by Christian apologists that the Greek word *nous* provided a convenient shorthand term to express their conviction of God as living and personal, and to link that conviction with the theism which was developing on its own lines among contemporary Greek philosophers.

In practice, of course, the early Fathers differed a good deal in the confidence and consistency with which they characterized God as Mind. Wolfhart Pannenberg has noted some second-century writers who used this title without embarrassment: Aristides, Athenagoras, Minucius Felix.[1] The great Alexandrians of the third century, Clement and Origen, present a more complex theology; sometimes they describe God as Mind, in other passages they declare that he is something more than mind, and yet again they acknowledge, like Aristotle, that either opinion is possible. In the fourth century Eusebius and Athanasius seem to be noticeably reluctant to characterize God as Mind; but later in the century, as Karl Holl observed, Gregory of Nazianzus applies this predicate with some freedom and some confidence.[2]

We can assert, without much fear of contradiction, that both the concept of mind that is here assumed, and the doubt over its applicability, derive in the main from the tradition of Platonism. To take the latter point first: the most influential text is certainly the famous passage from the sixth book of Plato's *Republic*, 509 b. In this immediate context, to be sure, it is being or substance, rather than mind, with which Plato compares his supreme principle, the Form of the Good; it is not a being, he says, but beyond all being (if these are at all adequate renderings); *ouk ousias ontos tou agathou, all' eti epekeina tēs ousias presbeia(i) kai dunamei huperechontos*. But the setting of this pronouncement is an analogy projected from the sense of sight and the visible world, on the one hand, to the mind and the intelligible realm, on the other. The Good has a function in the intelligible world, towards the mind and its objects (*en tō(i) noētō(i) topō(i) pros te noun kai ta nooumena*, 508 c) such that it both transcends them and makes them possible, just as in the visible world the sun gives both existence and clarity to vision itself and to visible things. Plato's thought is therefore correctly represented by the text-book statements that God is not only beyond being, but also beyond mind and intelligence;[3] and one implication is that when God is described as 'either Mind or something beyond mind', the words 'either' and 'or' convey a true disjunction. In this tradition 'beyond being' implies 'not being'; hence God cannot be described as an intelligent being who, however, possesses some further character which outweighs or redirects his intelligence so that it is no longer his distinctive attribute; God's transcendence is not like that of man, who is indeed an animal, but has the further and distinctive attribute of being rational. Those thinkers – and some Christians among them – who took Plato literally, were forced to the conclusion that either God is intelligence, or else he gives intelligence to other beings but does not possess it himself.[4]

By way of amplifying this point, let us note in passing that two principal alternatives to the doctrine of God as Mind also probably stem from the Platonic tradition, or at least from eclectic philosophies open to Platonic influence. There is first the theory, clearly stated by Clement and by Novatian amongst others, that *no* predicate adequately represents the divine nature; we can only fall back on a list of predicates which taken together give us an indication of it; in Clement's phrase, *athroōs hapanta endeiktika tēs tou pantokratoros dunameōs*.[5] Secondly there is the theory that all the predicates we can apply to God in fact refer to the same reality, since God's nature is a perfect unity which cannot tolerate any differentiation. This theory has a long history, which ultimately goes back beyond Plato to Xenophanes; but it is most energetically and forcefully stated by Irenaeus, who gives it what became its classical form, as an identity of the divine attributes: God is 'wholly Mind and wholly Spirit and wholly Thought...and wholly the source of all good things'.[6] These two theories do not, to my knowledge, occur together as a pair of alternatives, though some Christian writers, including both Clement and Novatian, enunciate both; but it is not, I think, fanciful to see here the influence of the first two theses of Plato's *Parmenides*, in which it is argued, first that the perfect unity refuses all predicates, and secondly that it accepts all predicates indifferently.

We proceed, then, to the concept of mind as it was developed within the Platonic tradition; and I shall try to identify some assumptions about the mind which passed from Plato to the Christian Fathers, and thus entered the common stock of orthodox Christian theology. If this seems a larger and more abstract topic than is usually presented by patristic scholars,[7] I can plead that it will be in part a survey of some very familiar ground; but also that a fresh survey is called for in the light of our modern study of the mind and of the descriptive terms we apply to it. It is for this reason that I have chosen a title for this essay which incorporates the phrase 'The Concept of Mind', this being the name of an influential work by an Oxford philosopher, Gilbert Ryle, published in 1949, which advises us not to think of the mind in terms of conscious acts of intelligence, of knowing this and deciding that; or at least, not primarily so; but rather in terms of intelligent performance, in which the conscious review of our undertakings plays a much smaller part than commonly-accepted theory suggests. At some points this proposal squares with Plato's assumption; one remembers Socrates' repeated comparisons between knowledge and practical skills like weaving or shoe-making. At some points it conflicts most sharply; and I shall argue that the conflict becomes extreme when we pass from Plato himself to the later Platonism on which philosophizing Christians so largely relied.

(1) In terms of its later influence, much importance attaches to Plato's division of the soul into three parts or faculties, *nous*, *thumos* and *epithumia*, which might be rendered as 'intelligence, spirit (or spiritedness) and desire'. In Plato himself, it is fair to point out, this triad is not put forward as 'a complete outline of psychology', but is meant to indicate the factors involved in responsible behaviour. Nor

does it hold the field exclusively; some of Plato's observations employ the simpler two-part division between intelligence and emotion, just as his four forms of cognitive experience are compressed (as they commonly were by later summarizers) into a simple contrast of intelligence and sensation. But in later Platonism the tripartite division came to have distinctive authority, partly no doubt because the rather tentative suggestions made in the *Republic* were more confidently repeated in the *Timaeus*.[8] Posidonius reintroduced the tripartite scheme into Stoicism, which even in its earlier forms had embodied some of Plato's characteristic assumptions. Indeed one can hardly exaggerate the long-term importance of this tripartite scheme, if I am right in thinking that a continuous line of tradition connects it with the Kantian division of our mental faculties into knowing, willing, and feeling, which has been influential until very recently.

Plato himself, as we have said, is by no means bound to a scheme of just three elements; but it is instructive to compare his three-part analysis of the soul with two other triads outlined in the *Republic*; namely, the three orders in the state, worked out in Book III, 414ff, and the three classes of men, recognized in Book IX, 580, with rough parallels elsewhere. Let us ask the question, How sharp are the divisions within these triads? In the case of the imagined society, Plato clearly envisages an absolute partition; a man is assigned to one class or to another for life, according to his qualifications. His qualifications might be a matter of degree, but the function assigned to him is distinctive and unchanging.[9] Now what about the three classes of men? Here it seems evident that the division is less sharply drawn. Plato does indeed sometimes differentiate his types of character by saying that they are 'governed' by one part of the soul rather than by the others; but this should be interpretable as a mere relative predominance; indeed Socrates' whole educative activity seems to presuppose that the dominance of reason in men's lives can be strengthened; men are not absolutely predetermined, in the way the Gnostics later supposed; in some cases at least, moral influence can make reason predominate where passion ruled before.

The division within society, then, is exclusive; the distinction among characters is not. What shall we say about the distinction within the soul? I cannot discover that this problem was raised in antiquity, though it is perhaps presupposed in the question whether the soul's various operations should be attributed to its various parts (*merē*) or to its powers (*dunameis*). 'Parts' suggests an exclusive division; 'powers' could suggest various exercises which the whole soul performs; just as seeing or hearing each engage one particular sense-organ, whereas running or swimming employ the whole body. However, Christians at least seem not to have developed the argument in this way. Plato himself, I think, perceived that no complete separation is possible. He says explicitly that dispositions apparently opposed can be combined, and that *some* impulses at least incorporate an element of reason; thus he playfully alludes to the dog who 'shows a fine instinct, which is truly philosophical' by recognizing and attacking intruders. More seriously he suggests that it is precisely the man of spirit who will peaceably accept a just rebuke. Again, Plato sees that intelligence has to be motivated, and can be wrongly motivated, as it is with dishonest men whose vision has been forced into the service of evil.[10] Intelligence should be motivated by love of knowledge, and genuine knowledge involves acquaintance with the timeless world of ideal Forms, which enriches every part of our nature. The sensuous attractions of that vision are of course most powerfully expressed in the *Symposium*, which develops the theme of 'a constant passion for knowledge' already mentioned in the *Republic*.[11]

But can the Platonic image of the tripartite soul really accommodate the fact that our emotional nature is amenable to reason? It may seem difficult to allow this without suggesting that 'the *epithumētikon* in a just soul harkens to the *logistikon* in that soul through itself possessing an extra little *logistikon* of its own' – a suggestion which has very properly been derided by Bernard Williams.[12] The absurd consequence can be avoided, I think, if we recognize that words like *pathos* and *epithumia* do double duty; they may stand for a pure product of analysis, such as *to epithumētikon*, the appetitive element in our make-up; or they may stand for actual movements of the psyche in which this element is conspicuous. However, the myth represents both cases by complete personalities – if for the moment we can allow that horses are persons[13] – which would then have to possess all three elements in some degree, though in terms of the myth each of them stands for one element. When this is seen, the paradox is resolved, and we can allow for possibilities that are familiar to us all; the case where reason is in control; and the converse case, in which a desire overcomes our moral principles, and possibly our common sense as well, though the intellect is not really inactive, since we intuitively recognize that an opportunity for sensuality has come about; or the quite different case in which intellect does its work coolly and reflectively, but does it in the service of sensual desire; as, to take Augustine's example,[14] when we deliberate whether to commit adultery or to go to the theatre.

The subtleties and nuances of Plato's imagination are by no means recalled in the later Platonism which influenced the Christians, based as it was on a selective anthology of texts which retained many traces of Stoic intervention. Where Plato had presented the philosophic character as a mean between the over-impressionable and the over-rigid,[15] the Stoics opted for rigidity. Where Plato had insisted that our impulses should be controlled by intelligence, Chrysippus adopted a purely intellectualist theory of moral decision, as being in every case a calculation, a *krisis*; though it is not clear to me how far this was conceived as a psychological theory, applicable to all men, as against an ethical ideal attainable only by the sage. When the Platonic image of three departments in the soul was revived by Posidonius, it was partly reinterpreted on Stoic principles. In certain contexts it could now be assumed that for an action to be controlled by intelligence was a sole and sufficient criterion of its rightness. This assumption worked both ways; it affected both the notion of right action and the notion of intelligence. 'Intelligence' had now to be understood as intelligence governed by the intellectual grasp of right values, the 'intelligibles'; attention centred on the definition and interrelation of the virtues, rather than on their concrete, experienced uniqueness; and the theory left no room for, what was a commonplace of ordinary observation, the intelligent man whose motives are selfish; he has to be classed, paradoxically, as a fool.

More important, in the Platonic revival there seems to have been little sense that emotional and instinctive reactions may embody their own unreflective and useful logic, besides being such as the well-motivated intelligence can approve.[16] They are now constantly described as *pathē*, 'passions', a word which suggested unsought interference with the normal current of life, which could indeed convey suggestions of unnatural vice, and which at best connoted morally neutral occurrences whose justification depended upon their being controlled by intelligence. The influential debate centred on whether the *pathē*, so understood, were allowable at all; whether moderation or absence of passion should be the ideal. But this controversy by-passed the vital point, namely the question-begging use of the word *pathos*, which represented every emotional response as an irrational disturbance, as something potentially vicious and anarchic; for though a distinction existed in theory between the morally neutral *hormē* (impulse) and the morally suspect *pathos*, this distinction was constantly overlooked. The ideal of *metriopatheia* – of being 'moderately passionate' – also embodies ambiguities in the word *metrios* which even Aristotle had failed to remove, as if the conditions of right action could be wholly expressed in arithmetical terms. But it is clearly a truism to say that *vicious* passions should be suppressed; but it is not obvious at all that emotional responses as such should be only moderately intense.[17] We would call them 'excessive' or 'uncontrollable' only if we had already decided that they needed to be checked; no sane person would speak of an 'ungovernable' passion to do the will of God.

As a result of such confusions, both *nous* and *pathos* were impoverished by their antagonism. To put the point in terms of Plato's chariot-myth, the two horses are not seen as healthy animals exercising their senses and their real if limited intelligence; instead, they gallop along blindly; it is the merest chance if they take the right course; and the charioteer can never give them their head, but crouches, vigilant and anxious, incessantly monitoring their every footstep. And so, quite naturally, the mind of God has no horses; it is a horseless carriage, a locomotive! In terms of the theory, God's motivation can only be an intellectual appreciation of the absolute beauty which he himself displays; there is no escape from Aristotelian self-thinking.

It should have been obvious that such a theory can do justice neither to Christian ethics nor to Christian theology. There is no place here for breaking alabaster vases of precious ointment; or again, to put the point in coarser and contemporary terms, the most ineffective theologian – myself, for instance – could claim a higher dignity than, say, Mother Teresa; since he is, however inadequately, directing his intelligence towards spiritual truths. This inference could be supported with quotations, especially from Clement and Origen, if time allowed. Such Christians did not, of course, suppose that every use of the intelligence is laudable; they were alive to the dangers of sophistry and idle curiosity, and had St Paul's authority for recognizing the 'depraved reason', the *adokimos nous*. But such vices are treated as something different in kind from the normal use of the intelligence. And their theory could not allow that some pieces of rational reflection, even though perfectly innocent in themselves, may be fairly trivial, and ought to give way to deeply-felt impulses; still less, that in some cases our heart may be wiser than our head!

And as regards the doctrine of God, the theory shows its clearest and best-known consequences in Origen's embarrassments in dealing with God's responses to human necessities, which the Old Testament so freely describes in emotional terms. To his credit, Origen the exegete occasionally wrings a concession out of Origen the philosopher, as in his Sixth Homily on Ezekiel, where he says 'the Father himself...is longsuffering, merciful and pitiful. Has he not then in a sense passions? The Father himself is not impassible. He has the passion of love.' But this pronouncement is an exception, and is contradicted elsewhere. Origen can go to great lengths to describe precisely God's abstraction from the world, using the Platonic term *periōpē*, which implies a place of detached observation, and the Aristotelian image of God's self-contemplation. It seems difficult to reconcile this apotheosis of withdrawal with even a knowledge of human suffering.

There is therefore no effective bridge between the Platonic psychology and the biblical doctrine of a God who loves and cares and provides. Origen for one has no equivalent of the theory adopted by the Platonist Albinus and the Christian Tertullian, in which there are divine counterparts of the human *thumos* and *epithumia* in God's attributes of authority and affection;[18] or even of Philo's theory, which I think derives from the same source, of two subordinate divine powers of severity and benevolence. The nearest Origen comes to this is in teaching that the biblical anthropomorphisms all indicate spiritual truths; God has spiritual sense of seeing and hearing, just as he has, spiritually speaking, a head and a heart.[19] But the weaknesses of this theory are plain; we may believe by faith that such biblical language is applicable; we cannot conjecture how it applies. We may believe that God knows what human beings see and hear; but is it allowable to postulate two distinct senses, analogous to our seeing and hearing, in one who needs neither eyes nor ears? After all, an influential theory declared that God's seeing was identical with his hearing. Perhaps, after all, the nearest we can get to a coherent hypothesis is to postulate some species of direct cognition analogous to our own self-knowledge; in a modern idiom, it is of course telepathy that springs to mind.

But if the Platonic psychology sits awkwardly with biblical theology, it has of course embarrassments of its own. It combines badly with the view, derived from the *Symposium*, by which precisely the lowest and most disorderly *pathos*, our sexual desire, can be transferred from human loves to the divine beauty. Plato never wrote a companion piece to the *Symposium* in praise of *thumos*, and Christian mystics, who so constantly speak of divine *erōs*, cannot appeal to him to enrich the language of their asceticism by expressing its motive in terms of courage and generosity.

In saying all this, I have admittedly been describing a strand in early Christian theology which is not wholly representative. It was however influential, since it was adopted by able and reflective divines. Admittedly, also, Christian practice often clashed with this theory; the intellectuals were also masters of the arts of persuasion; they sought to *move* their hearers, to rouse them to passionate desire to perform those works of mercy in which less articulate Christians were already engaged; they sought, indeed, to arouse a passion for the passionless life.

Some idea of the dominance of the Platonic image of the tripartite soul can be got from a section of the dialogue between Gregory of Nyssa and his formidable sister Macrina, the *de anima et resurrectione*.[20] Macrina has been speaking of the rational nature of the soul, and Gregory objects that the soul also contains affective elements, namely 'spirit' and desire, *thumos* and *epithumia*. In reply, Macrina concedes that they exist, though she adds some disparaging comments on Plato's chariot-myth and on the art of dialectic. These impulses, she explains, are things which we share with animals; they are not distinctively human, any more than the sense or the digestion. She appeals to Moses as a man who was not given to anger or acquisitiveness, suggesting thereby that he actually lacked both 'spirit' and desire; and she inveighs against human feelings, one-sidedly exemplified by rashness and cowardice, fear and arrogance, which she says are excrescences, *murmēkiai*, which have wrongly attached themselves to the rational soul. At this point the doctrine of our animal inheritance, which is reasonably consonant with the creation-story of Genesis, gives place to a distasteful version of the Platonic theory of accretions (*prosartēmata*) which derives from Plato's image of the sea-god Glaucus and enjoyed a popularity among the Gnostic sects which Macrina should have found disquieting.[21]

Gregory now very naturally objects, alleging that virtuous characters like Phineas and Daniel were moved to do good precisely by 'spirit' and desire.[22] (The defence of *epithumia*, we have seen, is not unexpected, since language borrowed from the *Symposium* as well as the Song of Songs has deeply penetrated the expression of Christian mysticism; the defence of *thumos* is a little less usual, though it can be found, for instance, in Gregory's *De Virginitate* 18, where he develops Plato's image of the watch-dog from *Republic* 375–6.) Gregory, then, persists in his defence, and Macrina promises a more considered reply. But the one really new point which emerges is a disavowal of Gnostic pessimism. Man's impulses (*hormai*) are not bad in themselves – to say this would discredit our creator – but become passions (*pathē*) when they escape from rational control.[23] In all other respects, this speech is even more deeply coloured by Platonism than the last. The Genesis creation-story is paraphrased in terms of a scale of being reminiscent of Aristotle; and the criterion of right action, similarly, is seen in what is peculiar to man. Man's rationality, his *logikē kai dianoētikē dunamis*, is distinctive and imitates the divine character; and only this rationality belongs to the essence of the soul. The doctrine of impulses as external accretions is discreetly reintroduced.[24] Even the chariot-myth, which Macrina has so recently denounced, proves too useful to be jettisoned, and we are told that 'if reason lets go the reins, and like a driver entangled in his chariot is dragged along behind it, carried along by the irrational movement of his horses, then the impulses are converted into passions'. Macrina thus repeats Aristotle's mistake of regarding man simply as an animal with reason added on as an extra capacity, instead of seeing that in all men, whether bad or good, the impulses are necessarily modified by superior intelligence. Thus 'reason' is exempted from moral evaluation, and all wrongdoing is assimilated to sensuality. The Christian ideal so presented consists in the apprehension of the divine glory; but it cannot see the manifestation of that glory in outgoing love. At the last judgement, when Christ exclaims 'I was hungry and ye gave me no meat', Macrina's disciples could reply with assurance 'Yes, it was our duty to exercise our logical and intellectual powers'.

(2) From time to time in the later Greek world one encounters the view that there is nothing mysterious about the gods; they are in fact exactly what the popular cults and legends take them to be. But a far more influential view, which was taken for granted by Platonists, Jews and Christians, was that divinity is mysterious and unknowable to man. It then became natural to support this doctrine by claiming that there is something inherently puzzling about the mind itself. This opinion is found in Philo, and can be paralleled in Gregory, who explains that the mind, as the image of God, must be mysterious; it cannot be conceived as either compound or simple.[25]

In practice, however, two analogies imposed themselves very early, and came to influence Christian thought. The first of these is the analogy of vision. It was an ancient commonplace that sight is the most valuable of the senses; and in Plato – if not earlier – the mind is metaphorically described as 'the eye of the soul', *psuchēs omma* (*Rep.* VII, 533 d, cf. 519 b). We sometimes find sight coupled with hearing as the best, the most eminent, and most philosophical of the senses;[26] but generally sight is preferred, though often by a misleading argument which associates sight with first-hand perception, but hearing with indirect reports;[27] misleading, in that if I want to know, for instance, whether it thundered during the battle, it is my sense of *hearing* that has the best claim to be reliable, rather than any visible record. More to the point, sight gives us clear and detailed information, as St Basil observes; it is immediate in its action, like the light which makes it possible; and it can traverse great distances, though (to follow St Basil again)[28] its power is partly exhausted in so doing, so that distant objects appear small.

But of course there are limitations to the sense of sight, some of which were not noticed by ancient writers. The eye cannot see itself, says Philo, just as the mind cannot understand itself.[29] The eye sees things from a certain view-point, so that at any moment some things are unseen behind it; others are obscured by intervening objects; everything, unless it is transparent, has a hidden side; and some things are in principle invisible. And even the real advantages claimed for vision are sometimes only relatively valid; sight is not in all cases immediate, or infallible, or independent of teaching, as anybody knows who has had to puzzle over a complex diagram. The Fathers, when they describe God's perception in terms of seeing, imagine a perception which is immediate, unhindered, and penetrating; God observes the acts which we perform behind closed doors and the thoughts which are hidden within our hearts; but even God has a certain perspective. 'The Lord looked down from heaven upon the children of men'; there can be nothing to which he looks up.

The parallel between thinking and seeing is of course especially persuasive when applied to *immediate* acts of cognition; one can grasp certain logical relations, for example those of arithmetic, with the same kind of intuitive certainty as one can grasp relationships between objects presented to the view. But some mental operations require a space of time and a series of operations which a man may have to formulate to himself in words or other symbols. Plato expressed the contrast between immediate and indirect cognition as one between *noēsis* and *dianoia*, or between *nous* and *epistēmē*, comparing *nous* with the number one and *epistēmē* with the number two;[30] the underlying thought presumably being that *nous* establishes an identity between the knowing mind and its object, whereas *epistēmē* works by some form of representation; it is like a line joining two points.

It seems to me that this very important distinction between intuitive and discursive thinking was soon obscured, in Christian theology, by a quite different distinction between the spoken word and the unspoken thought on which it was supposed to depend. The concept of the *spoken* word of God is of course primitive and biblical; the concept of an *unspoken* word which prepares the way for it is a philosophical elaboration, which our experience in some degree supports; for we do sometimes conduct unspoken rehearsals of the speeches we mean to make and the orders we intend to give. This distinction, developed in the Stoic phrases *logos endiathetos* and *logos prophorikos*, was taken over and applied to God himself with some confidence by Athenagoras, Theophilus, and Irenaeus; and Tertullian experiments with the notion that such an internal divine discourse already in some sense implies an interlocutor, who is later to emerge as a distinct *persona*.[31] A century later, Marcellus of Ancyra puts the opposite case,[32] perhaps with some elements of teasing humour; at the creation, God can be compared to an artist, who 'wishing to form a statue, first considers its form and features within himself, then imagines a suitable breadth and depth . . . and prepares an appropriate quantity of bronze', and finally 'being conscious that his reason, by which he normally reasons and does everything, is assisting him . . . addresses himself as if he were addressing another, saying, "Come, let us get to work! Come, let us make a statue!"'

Christian theologians sometimes criticized the concept of *logos prophorikos*, the spoken word, arguing that it suggested a mere transient utterance, and was inadequate to characterize the eternal, all-controlling Word of God. Its counterpart, the *unspoken* word, they took for granted. But without doubt we do quite commonly speak *without* unspoken rehearsals; indeed the New Testament urges us to do so;[33] and modern philosophers add the point that unspoken words require just as much explanation as spoken ones; they cannot help us to understand the problem of how thought gives rise to any kind of expression, or indeed any behaviour at all. Gilbert Ryle moreover insists that we are misconceiving the problem if we think of thought as a process on which behaviour is causally dependent; we should rather think of intelligence as a quality which can characterize both our silent reflections and our public performances. We might think of dismissing these comments for the moment, as too remote and abstract for theologians to consider. But we can hardly ignore the point that the whole notion of discourse, whether unspoken or uttered, seems to depend on human limitations, from which, so far as we can see, an unlimited intelligence could be exempt. Why should such an intelligence be bound to proceed discursively, step by step, rather than take in the whole complex of facts in one sweep of attention? And why should he be bound to use symbolic representations, such as words, when his cognition does not need to be simplified or facilitated? To pursue these questions might lead us towards a radical criticism of patristic theology in some of its central departments; as a first conjecture, we might be led to think that the Word of God must be understood exclusively in terms of his self-communication; which of course would lead us further away from the Alexandrian logos theology, and might engender an unexpected sympathy for the ingenious Marcellus.

Perhaps, as a partial amends for these subversive thoughts, I may add this point. Reflecting on the concept of *nous* and *epistēmē*, we may perhaps think that a faulty analogy lies behind the observation that the knowing subject must *necessarily* be distinct from the object known. Yet this observation has not been without influence. Several of the Gnostic sects sought to answer the question why anything has ever existed besides the supreme God by postulating that God must form some knowledge or idea of himself, and that this knowledge must be a distinct reality at a lower level of perfection, which in turn has led to a series of emanations in which the divine nature is ever more imperfectly reflected. Plotinus, on the other hand, starting from similar premisses about the perfect unity of the supreme Being, argued that such a being could not have knowledge of himself; he must remain in the undisturbed enjoyment of his perfect felicity; a secondary operation of monitoring or reporting this experience would constitute a distraction.[34] Neither type of solution will be attractive to Christians, who in any case cannot give this kind of uncritical allegiance to the doctrine of divine unity without nullifying their more central convictions of God's providence and God's love. We have to think of an intelligence responsive to the needs of endless myriads of creatures. The fact that *we* may experience self-consciousness as some kind of distraction will be without significance if we try to imagine an intelligence even on the cosmic scale.

(3) Our discussion so far has been concerned with intelligence, conceived initially as a distinctively human faculty, and also largely dissociated from other human capacities and impulsions and provided

with its own peculiar motivation. Intelligence was valued as providing access to the realm of *noēta*, the ideal Forms which are the source of both knowledge and goodness. The Forms compose a structure or hierarchy which it is the task of dialectic to apprehend; but they culminate in a supreme principle to which any notion of structure is inappropriate. It is seen in the *Symposium* as inexpressible beauty, in the *Republic* as the Form of the Good, and elsewhere it is described as undifferentiated unity. Aristotle's God, when pictured as a mind which contemplates only itself, makes much the same impression. At a more accessible level, Plato conceives beauty in terms of symmetry or of harmony, that is to say, in the interrelations of Forms that can be mathematically described; and he tends to see human qualities in the same way; the virtues are ideals of inner harmony and adjustment. To appreciate this kind of beauty, our minds must be capable of taking in an ordered complexity, which in practice, for creatures limited as we are, has to be apprehended piecemeal, by moving from point to point. But in either case our intelligence has a role which is essentially receptive, if not passive, for which indeed Plato adopted the term *anamnēsis*; it is the vision, attained by being recovered, of a beauty and order which is independent of ourselves.

As is well known, Plato himself cannot be described as a consistent theist; in the *Timaeus*, at least, the divine Craftsman contemplates a world of Ideas which he has not made and which is the pattern for all the goodness which he tries to achieve in his work. In later Platonism, as again is well understood, the Ideas are reinterpreted as thoughts of God. The point I now wish to make in conclusion is that this doctrine was accepted by Christians without making the proper adjustments to the concept of mind, whether in God himself or in us human beings. Accordingly, *nous* is still seen as a detached power of contemplation, sometimes assimilated to a mystical absorption in inexpressible beauty, sometimes described as the reflection on concepts, theorems or reasoning processes, so that even God himself is endowed with *noēmata*, *theōrēmata* and *logismoi*.

I do not wish to exaggerate this tendency. Of course many of the Fathers were largely untouched by Platonism, and even the most philosophically minded of them do reproduce the biblical image of God as a being who is active in outgoing love towards his people. But these conceptions were not effectively combined with the Platonic inheritance, which was the main resource of Christian theologians in organizing their theology and commending it to cultivated pagans. Within this tradition, the mind is conceived as directed towards realities independent of itself; and the value of its apprehension depends on the value of the realities it contemplates. The best minds look upwards, indeed upwards by an infinitely ascending scale, according to Gregory of Nyssa; and their only conceivable activity is that of assimilating themselves to the beloved and adored reality whose fullness lies for ever beyond their grasp.

It must be clear that, however imperfectly we conceive it, the Godhead cannot be pictured in this fashion. God is himself the source of all perfections; and it seems precarious to say that these are limited in number, so that God sets up a system of just so many timeless patterns, and judges human actions and character in terms of their conformity with the human exemplar. It is surely legitimate to say, with Augustine, that God may require a different obedience from different generations. It is still more evident that God does not look towards such patterns, or engage in theorizing or ratiocinating about them, in such a manner that he draws inspiration from them. By his very nature as the source of all goodness, God can only look downwards; but he looks down with creative love and authority, seeing in men both the reality of what they are and the possibility of what they may become; his life-conferring generosity restrained only by his care to preserve in each of his creatures their own authentic self-determination. The study of the Fathers can bring us only to the threshold of that vision.

Notes

1 W. Pannenberg, *Basic Questions in Theology*, vol. 2 (London, 1971), p. 148 = *ZKG*, 70 (1959), 21–2.
2 See my *Divine Substance* (Oxford, 1977), p. 169, n. 27; K. Holl, *Amphilochius* (Tübingen and Leipzig, 1904), p. 163.
3 Albinus, in *Platonis Dialogi*, ed. C. F. Hermann (1851–3), vi.164.18; see J. Whittaker, 'Epekeina nou kai ousias', *VC*, 23 (1969), 91–104.
4 Plato, *Republic* 509 b, 'not a being'; cf. Aristotle, *Ethica Eudemia* viii.2, 1248 a 27, *logou de archē ou logos alla ti kreitton*... *theos*, Albinus 165.22, *ou gar ōn hoper estin hē noēsis* (but contrast 163.29), Celsus in Origen, *Contra Celsum* VII.45, Whittaker, *VC*, 23 (1969), 102–3.
5 Clement of Alexandria, *Stromateis* v.82.1; cf. Novatian, *De Trinitate* 2.
6 Irenaeus, *Adversus haereses* ii.13.3, cf. i.12.2 *al.* (W. W. Harvey, i, pp. 111, 282). (Cambridge, 1857)
7 This essay is based on an address to the International Patristic Conference at Oxford on 7 September 1979.
8 In the *Republic* the tripartite scheme is suggested with some hesitation; see vii. 439 d, 440 e.
9 The exception is demotion for cowardice, 468 a.

10 See *Rep.* 375 c–d; 375 e–376 a; 440 c; 519, where cf. Cicero, *De Natura Deorum* iii.66–71, wrongdoing implies intelligence.

11 *Rep.* 484 b; cf. 376 e.

12 *Exegesis and Argument: Studies in Greek Philosophy presented to Gregory Vlastos*, ed. E. N. Lee, A. P. D. Mourelatos and R. M. Rorty (Assen, 1973), p. 199.

13 In the *Phaedrus*, where the three elements are pictured as two horses and their charioteer, Plato describes the horses' appearance, but also their behaviour, introducing psychological terms; see esp. 253–4.

14 Abbreviated from Augustine, *Confessions* viii.10.

15 *Rep.* 410–11.

16 Cf. e.g. Posidonius fr. 31: *en tois alogois tēs psuchēs dunamesin epistēmas ouk egginesthai*. Sextus Empiricus mentions an opposite and equally simplistic view: intellect and passions are coextensive! – *Adversus Mathematicos* vii.359, cf. 307 (*SVF* ii.849).

17 Aristotle, *Nichomachean Ethics* ii.6, 1105 b 27ff, proposes a quantitative treatment; but this does not square with the more complex conditions noted at 1106 a 21, 1109 a 27, 1115 b 15. Posidonius, fr. 31, says that to be amenable to rational discipline, the 'horses' must be neither too strong or too weak (!).

18 Albinus 178.32–4, Tertullian, *De Testimonio Animae* 16.3–5.

19 Origen, *De Principiis* II.8.5, *Commentarii in Evangelium Joannis* XIII.22, and cf. *c. Cels.* VII.33–4, *Dialogus cum Heraclide* 154ff.

20 *PG* 46, esp. 48 A ff.

21 *PG* 56 C, cf. Plato, *Rep.* 611 c–d and e.g. Albinus 172.9, Numenius, *Fragments*, ed. E. Des Places (Paris, 1973), fragment 43, Plotinus i.1.9, and for Gnostic use, Basilides in Clem. Al., *Strom.* ii.113.3.

22 *PG* 56 C–57 A, cf. Num. 25: 7 and Dan. 10: 11, where the Greek has 'man of desires' for 'man greatly beloved'.

23 *PG* 61 A.

24 *PG* 57 C, *exōthen epigenesthai*, cf. 61 B, *tōn exōthen epeiskrithentōn*.

25 Philo, e.g. *De Legum allegoriis* i.91; Gregory of Nyssa, *De hominis opificio* 11, *PG* 44.153–6.

26 Philo, *De specialibus legibus* i.29, 193, 337–9.

27 Philo, *De confusione linguarum* 148, *De Abrahamo* 60, and cf. Job 42: 5.

28 St Basil, *Homiliae in hexaëmeron* ii.7, vi.9, *PG* 29, 45 A, 140 B.

29 Philo, *Leg. All.* i.91.

30 Aristotle, *De Anima* i.2, 404 b 22.

31 Tertullian, *Adversus Praxean* 5.

32 Marcellus of Ancyra, fr. 58 (52), in Eusebius, *De ecclesiastica theologia* ii.15.

33 Matt. 10: 19, Luke 21: 14.

34 See e.g. J. M. Rist, *Plotinus, the Road to Reality* (Cambridge, 1967), pp. 38 ff and refs.

PART TWO

Theological enquiry after Kant

4

Kant and the Negative Theology

DON CUPITT

The notes to this essay will be found on pages 66–7

Donald MacKinnon has described Kant's religious thought as standing in the tradition of the negative theology.[1]

There is an obvious truth in this. By the negative theology we usually understand the doctrine that so emphasizes God's transcendence as to remove him beyond the reach of descriptive language. God cannot be characterized directly but only indirectly, by saying that he is not subject to the limits that make other objects capturable in language. Thus it is said that God is not-limited, not-dependent, not-bodily, not-temporal, not-spatial, not-complex and so forth.

Sometimes the doctrine is misunderstood as asserting that all judgements about God must be negative in their grammatical form; and then the objection is made that every negation implies a corresponding affirmation, so that the doctrine defeats itself. For surely, to *deny* that God is complex and temporal is to *affirm* that God is simple and eternal. However, this is not quite the point. The main emphasis is not upon grammatical negatives, but rather upon the necessarily indirect character of all language about God. The motive was originally reverential. The ancient Jews evolved a great variety of periphrases and similar constructions to avoid speaking directly of God, and the negative theology is simply a hellenized version of the same practice.

An analogy may help to make the point clear. A short list of categorical negative commandments is a rather generous ethical code, for it leaves a great deal of scope for creative choice in positive action. By contrast, a short list of categorical affirmative commandments leaves much less choice. Somewhat similarly, a habit of speaking of God in an indirect or veiled way leaves a great deal of logical space for God to move in. It does not pretend to restrict God, but preserves a decent reticence. The obliqueness of the language bears witness to the transcendence of that to which it alludes.

The Greek goes beyond the Jew only in that he says in rather more express terms that it is not merely religiously presumptuous to try to pin God down in human language, but logically impossible. For God is strictly ineffable or incomprehensible.

Many of the Greek Fathers quoted texts from Plato which they took to support this view, such as the assertion in the *Republic* (509b) that the Good is 'beyond being'. Since Being was commonly thought to be the most general of the categories and that in which all the others inhere, to describe the Good as beyond being is to imply that it eludes all the categories, and therefore altogether transcends human comprehension.[2] Kant's doctrine is rather similar, for he holds that the categories of the understanding are simply rules for ordering experience. Within the world of experience we can define criteria for applying these rules so as to generate objective knowledge; but the categories cannot have any proper transcendent application beyond the bounds of possible experience. Apart from experience and the criteria for applying them in experience, they are empty. So the categories of substance, causality and so forth cannot profitably be extrapolated beyond the world. There can be no valid causal inference from the world to its unknown ground, and there is no way of enlarging our knowledge of the unknowable world-ground by analogical reasoning. For Kant, David Hume had exposed the arbitrariness and futility of that kind of anthropomorphism.

Hume himself had ended with a theism reduced to vanishing-point: 'The cause or causes of order in the universe probably bear some remote analogy to human intelligence', but that proposition is not capable of any further elaboration, and can have no practical consequences.[3] Kant took a different view. He still held a form of the old belief that the idea of God is innate in human reason. The mind is naturally oriented towards God, spontaneously generates the idea of God, and needs that idea. Yet on the speculative side Kant's view of God is if possible still more austere than Hume's, for he holds that there is no way at all of moving from our idea of God to God's actual being. His solution was to say that *our idea of God* (the Ideal of Reason) has a valuable regulative function to perform both in guiding theoretical reason and as a postulate of practical reason, always provided that we fully recognize its speculative inadequacy. So, unlike Hume, Kant certainly did not wish belief in God to become inoperative and practically insignificant. He believed it was essential to retain it, and held that the idea of God can indeed be kept provided that we use it merely as a rule for guiding our thought and action within this world, and do not pretend to gain thereby any speculative knowledge of the unknowable world-ground. Yet in a strange way the very strenuousness with which Kant strives to remain within the limits of thought, and his insistence on our inability to know God as God is, may itself be seen as an indirect or 'negative' witness to the Transcendent.

So in these two respects there is a real resemblance between what Kant is saying and the old tradition of the negative theology, though we are already beginning to notice some differences emerging. Kant is himself, and not a Greek Father. When we enquire in more detail into just what is meant by the negative theology, complications arise. Kant actually seems to *contradict* many of its main tenets, and though there will remain a broad truth in the claim that we who live after Kant must walk the negative way, it will certainly not be quite the same way as it was for the classical theologians. Many of the old landmarks have gone.

What, then, was the negative theology? The best reply is that it was a set of doctrines, a temper of mind, and a style of spirituality very widespread among theologians (including Platonists, Christians, Jews and, eventually, Muslims also) for over a thousand years. Understood in a broad sense, it is still an essential feature of mainstream orthodox theism, especially in the Greek Orthodox tradition because of the special authority that tradition gives to the Cappadocian Fathers, the Pseudo-Dionysius and St John of Damascus.

In this old high-orthodox theism one of the most commonly recurring assertions runs as follows: it is certain that God exists, but the nature or essence of God is unknowable. The mystery may be invoked by speaking of it indirectly, or in negations, or by affirming symbolic 'names'; but in the end it is ungraspable by the mind, as the eye is dazzled by the sun.

A few examples of this assertion may be quoted. Philo, writing about A.D. 20–40, says that God 'is not apprehensible by the mind, save in the fact that he is. For it is his existence which we apprehend, and of what lies outside that existence nothing'.[4] In the fourth century, St Basil says, 'That God is, I know; but what is his essence I hold to be above reason.'[5] Thomas Aquinas, in the thirteenth century, discusses the nature of God under three headings; his existence, 'what manner of being he is, or rather, what manner of being he is not', and his activity.[6] As late as the eighteenth century we still find Hume's *Dialogues* being conducted upon the premiss formulated by Pamphilus and Demea: God's existence is certain, but his nature is at least problematic and for Demea it is 'altogether incomprehensible and unknown to us'.[7] It is still Demea, not Cleanthes, who is described as orthodox.

Modern philosophy, having been to school with Hume, Kant and Frege, finds this old doctrine empty and foolish. The basic objection was clearly formulated by the deist John Toland: 'Could that Person justly value himself upon being wiser than his Neighbours, who having infallible assurance that something call'd *Blictri* had a being in Nature, in the mean time knew not what this Blictri was?'[8]

Toland is surely right. The affirmation that God exists has no content unless something can be said about what God is. From the modern point of view, Thomas Aquinas seems in the following text merely to be striving after vacuity: 'In this life our minds cannot grasp what God is in himself; whatever way we have of thinking of him is a way of failing to understand him as he really is. So the less determinate our names are and the more general and simple they are, the more appropriately they may be applied to God.'[9] Surely this amounts to saying, the vaguer the better, even unto perfect emptiness?

Kant of course fully accepts that the old doctrine has collapsed, and for him it is God's *existence* rather than his nature that is unknowable. God's *nature* is not mysterious, for we have a clear, unproblematic and useful *idea* of God immanent within our reason. Kant is very bold on this point. In *Prolegomena*[10] he says that many things given to us in experience, such as gravitational attraction, are utterly mysterious to us; but when we step outside nature we deal with mere concepts generated by our own reason, and they are not mysterious at all, for Reason can certainly explain its own products. It spontaneously produces the idea of God and uses it to guide the understanding towards the ideal of the completest possible systematic unity in our scientific explanation of the world. As for the use of the idea of God in ethics, Kant says in the *Religion*[11] that 'every man *creates a God* for himself, nay, must make himself such a God according to moral concepts'. For if someone presents us with something and urges us to worship it, we must refuse. Kant insists on the insufficiency of any empirical or inductive approach to theology, warns against the danger of heteronomy, and holds that what God is for us and what faith is must be purely rationally determined. It would be idolatry to acknowledge any other God than the God who is immanent in practical reason.

It sounds as if at this point Kant is deliberately setting out to contradict the element of authoritarian appeal to mystery in the old negative theology. On the contrary, he says, the nature of God must be comprehensible, for the concept of God is generated by human reason. It guides the understanding and inspires moral endeavour. But of course for Kant the actuality of God can never be given in experience, and we can therefore never be theoretically justified in asserting either God's existence or God's non-existence. On Kant's account God's existence is problematic, but God's nature *as the Ideal of Reason* is explicable; and he adds that the ultimate world-ground must remain unknowable.

Thus although Kant does continue some of the themes of the old negative theology, he alters it considerably in order to make it intellectually and morally more acceptable. The old doctrine asserted that God's existence is certain but his nature unknowable. For Kant the proofs of God's existence fail, and the old doctrine is in any case empty and morally objectionable. In his view, acceptance of a positive revelation of supra-rational truth would subject us to an odious *despotism of mystery*. The Ideal of Reason is an available God who is intellectually and morally acceptable, and we must preserve strict agnosticism about the real God.

In retrospect we find ourselves asking the question, 'Why did not the old theologians see that they were talking nonsense in asserting both that God's existence is certain and that we can know nothing of what God is? For seventeen centuries this assertion was copied from one writer to another, and they all thought it was true until Toland came along and showed it to be empty in one sentence. Why?'

The answer is surely that in prescientific culture, before the Enlightenment, the universe was commonly perceived as a hierarchy of powers or energies. To say that a thing existed was to attribute to it a certain degree of activity, life or power, and therefore a certain status in the cosmic hierarchy of powers. So the Old Testament prophets typically say of pagan gods that they are *weak*. It was not usual to say that Bel or Nebo did not exist. It was sufficient to say that Bel and Nebo did not have the power-rank their devotees misguidedly attributed to them.

With this view of existence as the most general descriptive predicate went the doctrine of degrees of being, and the various maxims about causality. Everything in the universe is empowered, energized and caused to exist by something else that is above it in rank. Every effect has a cause, the cause (since it is something of higher rank in the order of being) has in itself in a more eminent way all the qualities that are found in the effect, and so on.

The universe was therefore conceived as a descending power-hierarchy. Everything comes down from above. Such a system, it was thought, clearly must have an apex, and the purpose of the ancient emphasis on God's transcendence was to insist that the apex was not the Heavens, nor astral deities, but a God enthroned above the Heavens who transcended the cosmos altogether. To speak of God in negations was not to empty the concept of God but rather positively to affirm the plenitude of God's sovereign unlimited freedom and originating power.[12] Similarly, to call God pure act, or pure existence, or He Who Is, did not seem empty: on the contrary, it was to affirm his supreme omnipresent power and activity.

The old negative way belonged with, and was intelligible in terms of, a certain view of the universe which has now passed away. It is not difficult to show, as Anthony Kenny does,[13] the emptiness of its slogans in terms of the modern analysis of existence as the exemplification of a concept. The modern negative theology, after Kant, has to endure objective uncertainty about the existence of God. There are many ways of trying to cope with this but, however one copes with it, it is a new situation.

When we turn to the related question of causality, we again find that Kantian theism is somewhat different from the old tradition.

The earliest Jewish monotheism said something like this: the reality of God is undeniable and inescapable. God is a massive and dreadful concentration of pure sacred power by which society lives and on whose favour its well-being depends. God is too terrible for any but the most outstanding holy men to be able to approach him directly. It is either forbidden or impossible to see God: but though God cannot be grasped directly, his intentions and his will are revealed in the word of law and prophecy.

As these ideas were formalized in the theology of much later times, they were expressed thus: God certainly exists, God is equally certainly unknowable, but there is an indirect knowledge of God through his works of Creation, Revelation and so on. In some modern theology it has been claimed that God reveals himself; but this was not usually said in earlier times, for if it were said it would violate the basic principle of the negative theology. It is not himself that God reveals, but his will and purposes, what we are to do, how creatures depend upon him, and so on. Thus Aquinas says: 'From divine effects we do not come to understand what the divine nature is in itself, so we do not know of God what he is.'[14]

This last point is important. The traditional theology was, or was usually, cautious in its claims. Put at its most cautious, it was *not* claiming that beginning from worldly events you could reason back (by analogy and the causal maxims) to gain a real knowledge of the divine nature: but it was claiming that the world itself and some particular events in the world can be *recognized as God's effects*.

However, even that minimal claim is still somewhat more than Kant will allow. He vetoes any attempt to enlarge our knowledge by causal inference from the world to God; and although he does have a place for analogy, he always interprets it as a way of ordering our worldly knowledge and action, and not as in any sense describing God. There may be some thought-guiding value in regarding certain features of the world *as if* they were God's effects, but we are not entitled to say flatly that they *are* so.

In the *Prolegomena*[15] Kant makes the point by distinguishing between dogmatic and symbolic anthropomorphism. When we say that God is the world-maker we are saying something about how we are impelled to regard the world, namely, *as if* it were the work of a highest understanding and will. Such symbolic anthropomorphism has regulative value, but we must not pretend that it adds to our knowledge of God as he is in himself. The analogy of God as world-designer is a way of ordering our understanding of the world, and no more.

In the *Religion*[16] Kant makes the same point by distinguishing between a schematism of analogy and an analogy of objective determination. To understand a biological organism I must think of it as if it had been designed. Given the limits of human understanding, I cannot fully reconcile mechanistic and teleological methods of explanation; perhaps only God can know the world in a way that synthesizes them. What I have to do is use mechanistic explanation, supplemented by a purely regulative use of teleological explanation. But this is a fact about how my mind works, and it does not justify me in positively asserting that the unknown world-cause itself must possess intelligence. To say so would lead at once to the anthropomorphism that Hume has so effectively attacked. Again, Kant allows our talk of God an intra-mundane use, but he will not allow it an extra-mundane reference.

The same is also true of Kant's discussions of the distinction between a discursive and an intuitive understanding. The object of making the distinction is to reveal the character and the limits of the human understanding, not to gain speculative knowledge of the Divine Mind.[17] Kant is so fascinated by the idea of an intuitive understanding that we might even say that for him the human mind cannot become fully conscious of itself except by measuring itself against an idea of the Divine Mind. That may be true, but it is still only a fact about *us*, and cannot for Kant be made the basis of an epistemological proof of God's existence, or of claims to an innate knowledge of God.

Thirdly, we may consider Kant's attitude to another theme of the traditional negative theology, which goes back to Philo and perhaps even to Plato. It was said that God is the One, the Monad beyond all distinctions, like a point which has position but no magnitude. God is unknowable by the ordinary apparatus of human understanding. In short, God can only be known by an ecstasy of reason. Various examples of this ecstasy of reason may be quoted: revelation, prophetic inspiration, or the receptive and passive unknowing of the mystic.[18]

It scarcely needs saying that Kant's whole theory of knowledge and temper of mind are unfriendly to such an idea, but there is a brief passage in the *Religion*[19] where he says something about mysticism. Interestingly, the subject provokes him to one of his very rare recognitions that the principles governing the objectivity of human knowledge need to be established publicly or communally. In so far as mystical experience is private, it is mysterious and of no theoretical or cognitive import, for to have such import 'it would have to be capable of being shared with everyone and made known publicly'. 'Feelings are not knowledge', says Kant, reminding us of the way Russell and Wittgenstein were later to distinguish between science and mysticism.[20]

Kant does recognize that there is indeed a holy mystery at the centre of religious faith. It is a private matter, and not of public or theoretical value; but it is more than just a matter of feeling, for since it is holy it must be moral and so an object of reason. It must be thought of as emerging from our inner moral predisposition. And so Kant is led back to the postulates of practical reason, to the mystery of freedom, to our duty to pursue the highest good, and to our need to believe in God as the condition of the attainability of the highest good. In the end, 'this belief really contains no mystery'.[21] By this Kant means that rational faith in God as Lawgiver and Judge, rightly understood as being merely regulative and as derived from reason itself and not from any external authority, is unmysterious.

Kant continues to say that there remains a mystery beyond our grasp. There is much we cannot know; but we must not be *seduced* by the unknowable. Awareness of the limits of thought must strengthen, not weaken, our resolve to live autonomously by the light we actually have. Thus, we know nothing at all about God's providential government of the world, and cannot conceive how God may be able to bring nature into line with the demands of morality. But we can safely leave that problem to look after itself: 'it may well be expedient for us merely to know and understand that there is such a mystery, not to comprehend it'.[22]

This rules out theodicy as an enterprise that is both beyond our powers and morally unnecessary. Joseph Butler, fifty years earlier, had still believed that we can point out some empirical signs of God's moral government of the world. Belief in providence is to some extent confirmed in our moral experience, even though the whole scheme is very imperfectly comprehended. Butler, an honest man, had spun the argument very fine, but nevertheless he still claimed that the workings of providence are empirically detectable.[23] Kant abandons that claim, and as he does so we can see him once again separating religion into two halves. There is the part that concerns us, which is unmysterious, rational and moral; our duty, practical reason and its postulates: and there is the part that does not concern us because it is a mystery into which we cannot penetrate. It is sufficient to acknowledge the mystery. In Kant's view we must not allow ourselves to heed the siren voices of those who say that because the ultimate is mysterious we must therefore accept the claims of revelation, church authority, religious irrationalism and mysticism. Instead he offers a way of faith that makes no concessions to such things.

At this point what Kant is saying is strikingly different from the older negative theology, which had always been closely allied with mysticism. The Greek Fathers, for example, invoke a sense of the mystery of the divine transcendence in order to awaken heavenly longings. Their language is designed to *attract*, whereas Kant's language is designed to *repel*. Kant wants us to renounce impossible and futile aspirations and be content with doing our duty. Do not aspire after the real God, he says, for that will only end in anthropomorphism and fantasy. Be content with the available God postulated by practical reason – fully recognizing his non-descriptive character – for that is sufficient. The nearest you can come to the real God lies in your very recognition of the merely regulative status of the notion of God with which in fact you must operate. It is vain and morally harmful to ask for more.

The old negative way was speculative and mystical, whereas Kant's purpose is to eliminate speculative and mystical theology. In this life the only way to God is the path of duty, and the traditional task of theodicy, to

> ... assert Eternal Providence.
> And justify the ways of God to men,

is ruled out as impossible.

This reminds us of another context in which the phrase 'negative theology' is used, and one that is well known to be of interest to Donald MacKinnon. To many of his early readers Kant seemed pessimistic and sceptical. An interesting case is that of the writer Heinrich von Kleist, who was overwhelmed by what he learnt of the Kantian philosophy in the years 1800–1. It broke his faith in the possibility of steady progress by self-cultivation towards the ideal of absolute knowledge of the whole truth of things. Kant seemed to have destroyed the optimistic world-view of the Enlightenment. It appeared that all we can ever know is the truth as constructed by us from appearances. We can never know the truth absolutely. By asserting that the pure ego was unknowable Kant had set impassable limits to self-knowledge, and by separating morality from nature he had eliminated any objectively-sustained meaning or moral order in the course of human life as we empirically live it. In a series of eight cold stories Kleist shows a world in which there is no moral providence, life makes no sense, fate is amoral, ironical or malicious, and people cannot understand the truth of their own or other people's behaviour.[24] In a letter Kleist hopes that, in spite of the evidence, the world is not governed by an evil spirit, but merely by one who is not understood. Kleist committed suicide in 1811 at the age of 34.

Kleist, it is said, misunderstood Kant. But Kant himself, after all, had 'found it necessary to deny *knowledge*, in order to make room for *faith*'.[25] Kant allows us no knowledge of God's real existence, nature or action, and no built-in, empirically-detectable and sustaining moral providence in the empirical world. Rejecting the possibility of mystical knowledge of God by an ecstasy of reason, Kant is left with a non-cognitive philosophy of religion which leaves the believer to be sustained in a harsh world by nothing but pure moral faith. Though it can truly be said that Kant's religious views are in the tradition of the negative way, I suggest that our discussion has shown that his position is more bleak and austere than that of any of his predecessors.

In the recent debates in Britain a number of writers, including R. B. Braithwaite, R. M. Hare, T. R. Miles and D. Z. Phillips, have proposed various forms of non-cognitive philosophy of religion.[26] Their views are interestingly varied, and it may well be urged that Phillips in particular is a writer of genuine religious force, who shows what form the negative way must take in our time, and who through Wittgenstein and Kierkegaard stands in the tradition that flows from Kant.

Phillips of course differs from Kant. He does not claim, and few nowadays would wish to claim, that the idea of God is necessary to motivate scientific endeavour; for why should not the ideal of the greatest possible systematic unity and completeness in our scientific theory of the world be an autonomous ideal? For many, it clearly is so. Nor does Phillips agree with Kant's drastic subordination of religion to morality, for he regards religion as an autonomous and irreducible way of speaking, acting, and appraising one's life. On the other hand, those who think Kant's view of religion very impoverished should note that he conserves certain important religious values perhaps better than Phillips does. For Kant has an eschatology, a pilgrim sense of life in which our present endeavours are sustained by the hope of a glorious consummation yet to come.

Still, Kant and Phillips have much in common. Both philosophies of religion are (in the modern jargon) non-cognitive. Both go further, and declare that all objectification in religious thought is a temptation to be resisted. No doubt many people do suppose that religious doctrines describe real invisible beings, occult agencies and supernatural events that both underlie and are interwoven with the world of fact. But if that is what they think, then they are superstitious; and modern philosophy, in exposing their error, purifies faith. Accordingly Phillips, in particular, refuses to go on the defensive and refuses to admit that his view is reductionist.

Phillips' remarkable philosophy of religion may represent one form the ancient discipline of the negative way might take in our time. Donald MacKinnon, though, takes a very different view. He insists on sticking to a descriptivist or realist interpretation of the major themes of traditional Christian theology.[27] He thinks one should stay with and endure the peculiarly intractable intellectual difficulties that such a position involves. He admires such a stark presentation of the problem of evil as Kleist gives in his story 'The Earthquake in Chile'. To face the facts of evil and tragedy and the trial of faith to which they subject us is itself (though in a very different sense from that of Phillips) to walk in 'the negative way'. For MacKinnon, I believe, the true negative way is the Way of the Cross.

Notes

1 D. M. MacKinnon, *The Problem of Metaphysics* (Cambridge, 1974), p. 9; 'Kant's Philosophy of Religion', *Philosophy*, L (1975), 141.
2 G. C. Stead, *Divine Substance* (Oxford, 1977), p. 140.
3 D. Hume, *Dialogues Concerning Natural Religion* (1779), XII; ed. Henry D. Aiken (New York, 1948), p. 94 (italics removed).
4 Philo, *Quod Deus Immutabilis Sit*, 62.
5 St Basil, *Epistle* 234.
6 Thomas Aquinas, *Summa Theologiae* 1a, prologue to Question 2.
7 Hume, *Dialogues*, foreword and part II, *ad init.*
8 J. Toland, *Christianity Not Mysterious* (1696), p. 133. The growth of discontent with the old doctrine that God's existence is certain but his nature unknowable is described in Don Cupitt, 'The Doctrine of Analogy in the Age of Locke', *JTS*, n.s. 19 (1968), 186–202.
9 Aquinas, *ST*, 1a, 13, 11.
10 P. G. Lucas (ed. and trans.), Kant's *Prolegomena* (Manchester, 1953), § 56, pp. 114f.
11 T. M. Greene and H. H. Hudson (trans.), *Religion within the Limits of Reason Alone* (New York, 1960), p. 175n.
12 G. L. Prestige, *God in Patristic Thought* (London, 1956 edn.), pp. 4ff.
13 A. Kenny, *The Five Ways* (London, 1969).
14 Aquinas, *ST*, 1a, 13, 8.
15 Kant, *Prolegomena* §§ 57–58 (Lucas' edn.), pp. 116–28.
16 Lucas' edn., pp. 58f.
17 C. D. Broad, *Kant: An Introduction*, ed. C. Lewy (Cambridge, 1978), pp. 309ff.
18 See H. Chadwick's chapters in A. H. Armstrong (ed.), *The Cambridge History of Later Greek and Early Medieval Philosophy* (Cambridge, 1967).
19 Kant, Lucas' edn., pp. 129ff.
20 E.g., the title essay in Bertrand Russell, *Mysticism and Logic* (London, 1918); and L. Wittgenstein, *Tractatus Logico-Philosophicus* (transl. D. F. Pears and B. F. McGuinness, London, 1961), §§ 6.4ff.
21 Kant, Lucas' edn., p. 131.
22 Ibid., p. 130n.
23 J. Butler, *The Analogy of Religion* (1736), part one.
24 First published, 1810–11; translated by David Luke and Nigel Reeves in Heinrich von Kleist, *The Marquise of O— and other Stories* (Harmondsworth, 1978).
25 I. Kant, *Critique of Pure Reason*, B xxx: translated by Norman Kemp Smith (London, 1933), p. 29.

26 For Braithwaite and Hare, see Basil Mitchell (ed.), *The Philosophy of Religion* (Oxford, 1971), pp. 72–91, 15–19; T. R. Miles, *Religion and the Scientific Outlook* (London, 1959); D. Z. Phillips, *Faith and Philosophical Enquiry* (London, 1970).

27 See D. M. MacKinnon, *Explorations in Theology* 5 (London, 1979), especially papers 5 and 11.

5

Ideology, Metaphor and Analogy

NICHOLAS LASH

The notes to this essay will be found on pages 89–94

Introduction

Theologians are more frequently charged with flight from reality than with strenuous engagement in its obdurate complexity. If 'it is the fault of the idealist always to seek escape from the authority of the tragic',[1] then it must be admitted that much Christian preaching and theological writing, appealing as it does to 'ultimate reality', or to a 'higher truth', in a manner that depreciates or trivializes the urgency and agony of particular choice and particular circumstance, provides ample warrant for Donald MacKinnon's contention that 'idealism remains a besetting temptation of the theological understanding'.[2] 'Idealism', he wrote twenty-five years earlier, 'is always in the end the acceptance of the realm of ideas as somehow self-justifying, of man's spiritual experience as the real motor force of historical change'.[3] It is hardly surprising that one who thus characterized idealism should insist that 'There are deep lessons to be learnt by the contemporary theologian from serious engagement with the Marxist rejection of idealism'.[4] And if, for Marx and for most Marxists, religious discourse is presumed to be inescapably idealist in character, MacKinnon himself is one of many contemporary Christian theologians who would agree with the late Michael Foster that 'Christianity is itself opposed to idealism', and that 'the Christian should agree with almost all the criticism which the Marxist brings against idealism'.[5]

Any such agreement would entail accepting many fundamental features of the Marxist critique of 'ideology'. I have attempted elsewhere to indicate some of the senses in which the practice of Christian belief, and Christian theology, are appropriately characterized as 'ideological'.[6] I suggested that both the practice of faith and theological reflection are 'ideological' in the non-pejorative sense that they are aspects of the general process of the production of meanings and ideas. The practice of faith and theological enquiry are, moreover, frequently more or less 'ideological' both in the sense that they reflect patterns of social relationship and dominance, and in the sense that believers in general and theologians in particular are frequently unaware of or unable to perceive the extent to which this is so, and hence fail to recognize the ways in which their discourse concerning man, the world, and God, is subject to that element of illusion and distortion described, in the Marxist tradition, as 'false consciousness'. And if, from this point of view, the responsibility for the 'critique of ideology' devolves partly upon the social scientist, I would wish to resist his claim to be the sole executant of this critical function, and to insist that it falls to the theologian, also, to seek to make problematic the grounds of religious practice and theological enquiry.

In the present paper, I want to indicate some of the ways in which Christian theological enquiry, or some aspects of that enquiry, might contribute to the 'critique of ideology'. I propose to do this by making some tentative suggestions concerning the relationship between 'metaphor' and 'analogy' in religious and theological discourse. By way of introduction, however, it will be convenient to return to Donald MacKinnon's reflections on the controversy between 'idealism' and 'realism'.

The epistemological dimension of this controversy is indicated by MacKinnon's characterization of Kant's refutation of idealism as 'a necessary part of his subtle and strenuous effort...to hold together a view which treated learning about the world as a finding, with one that regarded such learning as a constructive act'.[7] The complexity of the relationship between 'finding' and 'fashioning',[8] between discovery and construction, may be indicated by reminding ourselves that, in myth, parable, the writing of history and of the novel, *narrative* forms are not the least important of the modes of discourse that we employ in our attempts to 'discover', to lay bare, something of what is the case concerning the world in which we are, and concerning the ways in which we are and may be 'located' in a world that sets objective limits to our attempts to fashion it to our desires and fancies.

Even though Archimedes leaping from his bath could be said to have 'made' a discovery, it would still seem more immediately apparent of narrative than it is of the language of scientific discovery that we *construct* our apprehension of reality, and that in this sense construction (with its attendant risks of fantasy and illusion) is the form of all 'invention'.[9] We should, however, remember Einstein's insistence 'on the extent to which fundamental scientific progress must wait on the development, by spontaneous intellectual creativity, of more powerful branches of mathematics'.[10] Nevertheless, there does seem to be a sense in which narrative construction is more patently a 'work of art' than is the elaboration of scientific theory. And, if this is so, then that sense may be closely connected with the apparently more pervasive presence of the *metaphorical* in narrative than in theoretical discourse.

Already, several questions are suggested which should be of some interest to students of Christian theology; and they are questions which raise issues concerning the 'ideological' character of religious practice and theological reflection. In the first place, there is the question of divine revelation. A form of Christian faith which had surrendered all attempt to speak of our perception of meaning, our apprehension of hope, as fundamentally 'given' in revelation would have surrended, without a struggle, to Feuerbach's perceptive but partial critique. And yet the way is now barred to any theology of revelation which attempts, 'positivistically', to see, in the sources and grounds of Christian hope, exceptions to the rule that it is only in risking the construction of a story that human beings have given content, shape and specificity to their hopes and fears. The narrative that declares our hope to be 'received' and not 'invented' is itself an interpretative and, in *that* sense, a 'constructive' enterprise. And we cannot avoid taking personal responsibility for the tale that we tell, even while acknowledging that the truth of the tale ultimately depends upon a fulfilment of conditions the manner of which is beyond our observation and understanding.[11]

But, with that acknowledgement, is not any possibility of the Christian legitimately laying claim to *knowledge* of the truth of the tale that he tells automatically excluded? This is no new question. Aquinas attempted to tackle it in the first question of the *Summa Theologiae*. Its contemporary exploration would demand the kind of close attention to problems concerning the relationship of 'knowledge' to 'belief' which many contemporary writers, from Christians (cheerfully disclaiming any suggestion that they 'know' that of which they speak) to Althusserian Marxists (arbitrarily restricting the range of use of the concept of 'knowledge' to the products of their 'theoretical practice'), prefer either to evade or disastrously to oversimplify.[12]

In the second place, if, as I propose to argue, there are forms of narrative discourse which have an irreducible centrality in the practice of Christianity, is not Christian religious discourse thereby rendered unavoidably 'ideological' at least in the sense that the 'truthfulness' of a tale told is partly determined by the circumstances of its production – in respect both of the 'point of view' from which it is told, and of the linguistic and imaginative resources available for its construction? In other words, does not narrative discourse lack that aspiration to universality and timelessness of expression which is characteristic of 'theoretical' or 'scientific' discourse?

In the third place, if the Christian wishes to urge that there are tales to be told which, for all the particularity of their production and symbolic content, nevertheless 'embody' or 'signify' 'universal' truths, is he not obliged to consider questions concerning the relationship of myth, history and poetry to metaphysics? Donald MacKinnon has suggested that metaphysics sometimes emerges as 'the attempt to convert poetry into the logically admissible'.[13] In what circumstances could such 'conversion' hope to be successful? And what forms of metaphysical discourse are available, today, that are not fatally infected by idealism?

Brian Wicker, on whose stimulating study *The Story-Shaped World* I shall shortly be drawing, argues that 'Metaphor...raises questions that only analogy...can answer, while conversely analogy can only answer questions that are raised in a metaphorical form'.[14] In the light of my earlier remarks on the epistemological dimension of the controversy between idealism and realism, I suggest that Wicker's proposal might be expanded along the following lines.

The metaphysician traditionally conducts his enquiry along the 'way of analogy'. He supposes himself to be in some sense set on a voyage of discovery, at least inasmuch as only the boldest of bad metaphysicians would cheerfully admit that he was arbitrarily imposing patterns on the world of our experience. However, set on such a voyage, the theological metaphysician is prey to scepticism and discouragement in view of the fact that, appropriately mindful of the interrogative, heuristic character of his analogical extension of familiar usage, discovery is always indefinitely postponed.

The story-teller explores in a different direction. Conscious of his responsibility to help his audience to 'shape' their experience, to 'make sense' of their world, he journeys along the way, not of analogy, but of metaphor. But the attempt to 'make sense' of the world elides with dangerous ease into the attempt to make the world, in our imagination, conform to how we would have it be. The narrator is prey not so much to discouragement as to the illusion that the human quest for meaning and truth is a quest for appropriate construction.

The forms of Christian discourse are set between the poles of metaphor and analogy, of narrative and metaphysics. How, then, may the relationship between these poles be negotiated in practice and characterized in theory? And what steps can be taken to minimize the twin risks of scepticism and illusion? These are some of the issues on which, after this protracted introduction, I wish tentatively to offer some reflections.

Metaphor and autobiography

The tension between the story-teller and the philosopher, between metaphor and analogy, expression and analysis, betwen 'the logic of the heart' and a cooler, more dispassionate set of logical tools, is ancient and intractable. And if, in the nineteenth century, Newman attempted to sustain the tension in his exploration of the relationships between 'real' and 'notional' assent, between 'religion' and 'theology', today, in theological circles in Britain, the tension is in danger of slackening into mutual indifference. It is not that the conflict has been resolved, or even significantly clarified, but rather, as Brian Wicker suggests, that the battleground has shifted from theology to literary criticism.[15]

Wicker illuminatingly contrasts the divergent assessments of the metaphorical in two contemporary traditions of criticism, represented by Norman Mailer and Alain Robbe-Grillet. Both men see their task as 'helping to free the individual from a system of emotional and cultural constraints...rooted in the inherited ideology of their respective societies'.[16] Mailer would free us from the 'one-dimensionality' of technologism through 'a return to an older poetic and metaphorical way of looking at the world'.[17] According to Robbe-Grillet, the anthropomorphism that is endemic to metaphorical discourse perpetuates our enslavement to 'Nature', itself a construct of bourgeois Romanticism. He sees it as the job of the novelist to cleanse our language of anthropomorphism by banishing all metaphor

Epistemologically, a central issue concerns the cognitive status of literary and artistic experience and expression.[18] And if, in philosophy and the social sciences, an ancient rationalism still frequently depreciates the cognitive capacity of metaphorical discourse,[19] Gadamer's study of *Truth and Method* and Ricoeur's study of *The Rule of Metaphor* signal a redressing of the balance.[20] Gadamer has sought to rehabilitate the Romantic recognition that 'art is knowledge and the experience of the work of art is a sharing of this knowledge'.[21]

Mailer would surely agree. But perhaps we should say, more cautiously, that art *may* be knowledge, because 'the recurring temptation to self-indulgence and even dishonesty that goes with a dedication to metaphorical language is far from conquered today'.[22] Robbe-Grillet's attempt to 'cleanse' our language of metaphor represents one form of the struggle against this temptation. 'We need', says Wicker, 'the corrective presence of the not-human...of that which is impervious to linguistic manipulation.'[23] The theological overtones are clear. But how can that which is 'impervious to linguistic manipulation', *sive Deus sive natura*, be brought to speech? Where non-human empirical reality is concerned, the answer might be sought in the quest of scientific discourse for a formal purity as little 'infected' as possible by the anthropomorphism of the metaphorical. Where the mystery of God is concerned, however, it is less clear what linguistic strategy, if any, could meet this demand. We shall return to such questions later on. I have mentioned them at this stage only to suggest that the 'corrective presence' to which Wicker refers cannot make its appearance exclusively *within* the narrative mode of discourse. Narrative without metaphor (in so far as it is possible at all) merely depicts a world devoid of meaning, and to be left alone with one's own meaninglessness is 'an ironic kind of "liberation"'.[24] Are these the only options available: the construction of meaning or the recognition of meaninglessness? Or is there also meaning that is not, in the last analysis, fashioned but found? Even the form of the question is, significantly, metaphysical. Thus it is that reflection on metaphor raises questions which cannot be answered metaphorically (because anthropomorphism cannot be anthropomorphically transcended) and which receive, in narrative discourse from which metaphor has – so far as possible – been banished, only the bleakest of negative responses.

I suggest that the distinction between narrative, metaphorical discourse, and those non-narrative modes of discourse to which reflection on the metaphorical gives rise appears, within Christianity, as a distinction between religious practice and critical reflection on that practice: between 'religion' and 'theology'. This is only a first approximation demanding further specification which I shall try to give to it as the argument proceeds.

The distinction between religious and theological discourse, too often obscured or elided in the work of theologians, philosophers and social scientists alike is, nevertheless, fundamental and irreducible. It is, however, formal and heuristic in character, and to insist that it must be kept in mind is not to issue a warrant for employing it with that insensitivity to the complex variety of particular instances which is the besetting sin of so many attempts at classifying or 'mapping' our linguistic usage.

Having issued that warning against mistaking the map for the countryside, I now want to suggest that the paradigm or 'focal' forms of Jewish and Christian religious discourse are not simply narrative but are, more specifically, autobiographical. They are autobiographical both in the sense that they are 'self-involving' (although this will be shown in their performance, and will not necessarily appear in their grammatical form) and in the sense that, as self-involving, they 'locate' the speaker (or the group of which he is a spokesman) in a particular cultural, historical tradition: 'My father was a wandering Aramean.' Whether the 'audience' addressed is God (in acts of supplication and worship) or other people (in acts of witness), the Christian is the teller of a tale, the narrator of a story which he tells as *his* story, as a story in which he acknowledges himself to be a participant.

From this elementary observation, a number of things follow. In the first place, Christian religious discourse, as autobiographical, will always be shaped and influenced more deeply than we know by the circumstances of its production. However 'truthfully' we try to tell our story, the narrative that we produce is always subject to ideological distortion.

In the second place, Christian religious discourse, as autobiographical, tends to attribute an unwarranted universality to the particular forms in which, in particular circumstances, it finds expression. Convinced that the tale that we tell is truly told, Christians tend to assume that the way they tell it is the way it has ever been and must ever be told.

In the third place, the construction of an autobiography, as of any narrative, entails selection, planning, the imposition of order. We do not 'merely' remember. We seek to construct, to '*make*' sense of our lives and of our history. Unless we construct the narrative, we can make no sense of our temporally ordered existence. But the very fact that the sense has to be 'made', the narrative constructed, threatens the veracity of the tale.

In the fourth place, every narrative has a beginning, a middle and an end. But 'end' ambiguously signifies both conclusion and goal, both terminus and purpose. And the Christian, like any autobiographer, stands in the middle of the history to which he seeks to give narrative expression. He is therefore tempted, for the sake of the coherence of the story (which is the coherence of his human and Christian experience) to claim a clearer apprehension of the 'plot' than the evidence warrants. Living in hope of resurrection, he is tempted to reduce past and present suffering to the status of necessary conditions of a 'happy ending'. 'The temptation of Hegelian and utilitarian alike', says Donald MacKinnon, 'is to find always the justification of the present in the future.'[25] And he adds: 'But the Cross utterly prevents such a trivialising of the past.'[26] The dark facticity of particular deeds and particular tragedy may not be obliterated for the sake of the coherence of the narrative. Not the least insidious of the forms of idealism by which Christian religious discourse is threatened is that which, springing from the conviction that there *is* a sense which it all makes, seeks prematurely to give to that sense unified narrative expression.

I have been trying to sketch some of the ways in which, as autobiographical (and hence as metaphorical) discourse, Christian religious speech is threatened by 'self-indulgence and even dishonesty'. Are there countervailing influences to hand which might discipline and purify faith's tendency to construct a significance which, *as* constructed, is at best distorted and, at worst, illusory? There are, I suggest, at least two such corrective influences.

I have already insisted on the importance of the distinction between 'religion' and 'theology', between the practice of faith, in worship and witness, and critical reflection on that practice. Thus the first corrective influence, or set of such influences, arises from the interaction of practice and reflection. There will be a variety of forms of reflection (or 'theological disciplines') corresponding to the variety of aspects under which the practice of faith may be critically considered. Thus, for example, because Christian religious discourse is *discourse* it demands 'grammatical' or philosophical consideration (in the next section of this essay, I shall therefore consider 'theology as metaphysics'). Because Christian religious discourse is paradigmatically *narrative*, it demands literary–critical consideration. And because Christian narrative is in some sense autobiographical, it demands historical consideration.

The tendency, in contemporary English biblical studies, is to consider literary–critical and historical aspects of theological reflection as sharply distinct and to concentrate on the latter to the neglect of the former. This tendency derives from a period when positivistic conceptions of historical understanding went hand-in-hand with non-cognitive accounts of literary and poetic statement (which carried the implication that the fruit of literary–critical reflection on the biblical narratives could only be 'subjective' in character). But if it has sometimes been assumed (in theology and elsewhere) that there is 'a natural tension between the historian and the literary critic',[27] there is no timeless validity to this assumption. Thus, for example, Gadamer has powerfully argued the case for recovering a sense of the fundamental unity of the hermeneutical disciplines. From such a standpoint, it makes sense to say that 'historical understanding proves to be a kind of literary criticism writ large'.[28] Gadamer, at least as I understand him, is not seeking to obliterate the distinction between historical truth and the truth of metaphorical fiction. He is calling to our attention connections and similarities that have been too long obscured from view. At least, where Christian theology is concerned, it is surely worth remembering that the New Testament historian, for example, is dealing with narratives whose adequate elucidation demands (though it does not always receive) the most sophisticated use of literary–critical skills. And whether what those narratives express is, in the last resort, construction or discovery is, arguably, a question whose resolution is constitutive of the decision of Christian faith.

My first suggestion, then, is that Christian religious discourse is subject to purificatory and corrective criticism from the historian and the literary critic, as well as from the sociologist and psychologist of religion (to mention two other disciplines whose right to be heard is increasingly acknowledged even in the more cobwebbed theological debating-chambers). And if the tensions between practice and reflection are frequently destructive, rather than creative, this is partly because exegetes and historians have sometimes been invited to establish the grounds of belief, rather than critically to reflect upon its past and present performance and, when they have shown themselves incapable of executing this function, it has been concluded that belief has no grounds. But this is to raise questions of verification on which I shall briefly comment later on.

I have said that there are two sets of corrective influences upon the tendency of Christian belief to undergo ideological distortion. I now want to suggest, therefore, that in addition to those external correctives some of which have just been indicated, Christian religious practice also contains *internal* correctives to its own anthropomorphism. If the history of Christian faith and spirituality is a history of exuberant metaphor (verbal, ritual and iconographic), it is – just as insistently – a history of silence, simplicity and iconoclasm: of a sense that what needs to be said cannot be said. Not the least powerful of the pressures generating this apophatic dimension in Christian history has been the experience of suffering. If 'ideology...dulls the tragic vision's alertness to limits',[29] the experience of tragedy can sharpen that vision or (to change the metaphor) can constitute the hard rock on which the exuberance of affirmation is broken. Suffering corrupts and disfigures. And yet, it can also purify. Any description of Christian belief as 'merely ideological', as self-indulgent construction of satisfying narrative, inexcusably ignores the silent witness of that simplicity and realism which has sometimes been the fruit of a practically sustained 'alertness to limits'.

If it is true that one of the most important features of any metaphor is that we must deny its literal truth if we are to understand its metaphorical significance,[30] and hence perceive the truth which metaphor expresses, then it is perhaps not fanciful to suggest that the dialectic of affirmation and denial which is so striking a feature of the history of Christian spirituality amounts to a practical recognition of the metaphorical status of those narrative forms which I have described as paradigmatic for Christian religious discourse.

In the performance of that dialectic, Christians have been motivated by the conviction that they were responding to the 'corrective presence' of that which is 'impervious to linguistic manipulation'. This conviction, married to that unquenchable intellectual curiosity, that 'pure...desire simply to know',[31] which has been one of the hallmarks of Western consciousness, has sometimes provoked Christian believers to forms of reflection, of philosophical enquiry, which transcend the practical dialectic of metaphor and its negation.[32] There are questions which the recognition of paradox and, indeed, silence itself provokes rather than stifles. Metaphorical discourse, I have suggested, raises questions which cannot be answered metaphorically. In various ways, in the past, such questions have been explored along 'the way of analogy', to which we now therefore turn.

Analogy: voie sans issue?

In the previous section I raised the question: how can that which is 'impervious to linguistic manipulation' be brought to speech? When the intended referent of this question is the transcendent mystery of God, there are several reasons for supposing that metaphysical discourse (where metaphysics is conceived as that branch of philosophy the logic of whose procedures focuses on analogical usage of unrestricted generality) cannot provide the answer.

Firstly, there are those who insist that the 'way of analogy' is closed, and that it is only in metaphor that we can hope to speak of God. If this were the case, then there would be no way past the Feuerbachian critique, because we would be unable to discriminate between the 'models' of God that we fashion in metaphor and the discovered mystery signified by such constructions. All that we say of God, affirmatively, is indeed 'projected' from our human experience, is anthropomorphic in character, and we would have no way of showing the sense of such language to be other than 'merely' projective.

Secondly, there are those who, in various ways, assimilate the logic of analogy to that of metaphor, using the two concepts more or less interchangeably.[33] On this account, the 'way of analogy' is apparently open, but the appearance is illusory, because 'analogy' turns out to be either a sub-class of metaphor or the 'common heading' under which 'the family of metaphor' is subsumed.[34]

Thirdly, recent studies of metaphor, standing in varied relations of dependence on Aristotle's *Poetics*, lay the emphasis on dissimilarity. Thus Ricoeur: 'Enigma lives on in the heart of metaphor. In metaphor, "the same" operates *in spite of* "the different".'[35] So far, so good. But not the least of the reasons why I hesitated before deciding to risk using the term 'analogy' in this essay is that it has become increasingly common to lay the emphasis, when speaking of analogy, on *similarity*: as if, along the way of analogy, 'the different' operated *in spite of* 'the same'. This is emphatically *not* the case with Aquinas' use of analogy, although it has sometimes been made to appear so in neoscholastic apologetics searching for a 'direct route', philosophically, to the knowledge of God.

In the fourth place, it could be suggested that the 'No Entry' sign across the way of analogy was most firmly planted by Kant. It is, however, at least worth asking *which* route it was that he blocked in so apparently insurmountable a manner.

According to Donald MacKinnon, Kant 'raised a problem which by dexterous use of Aristotelian analogy [the scholastics] had tried to bypass'.[36] This bypass consisted in exploiting the ontological conviction that, since 'Being...was an analogically participated transcendental',[37] it was possible to move from negation to affirmation, from speech concerning the conditioned to speech concerning the unconditioned ground of all conditions. 'When the schoolmen insist that agnosticism comes before anthropomorphism, we are with them all the time. But, alas, their device for allowing assertion on the basis of negation demands assumptions that we cannot make. For we have to admit in knowledge a kind of intuitive awareness of analogically participated being which we do not seem to have'.[38]

Who are these 'schoolmen', who employ this device? They undoubtedly include many of those seventeenth- and eighteenth-century scholastics against whose views Kant was reacting. But, here as elsewhere, we need to remember the sea-change undergone by late scholasticism in the seventeenth century. Thrown newly on the defensive, proof rather than enquiry became the dominant concern. Theology 'replaced the inquiry of the *quaestio* by the pedagogy of the thesis'.[39]

Nevertheless, even if the conviction that human beings had, or could have, 'a kind of intuitive awareness of analogically participated being' was of considerable assistance to a theology nervously contracting into apologetic, apologetic concerns alone can hardly have accounted for its emergence. Is the presumption of such intuitive awareness to be found further back, in thirteenth-century scholasticism? Or, since that question is impossibly large, is it to be found in Aquinas' treatment in the first thirteen Questions of the first part of his *Summa Theologiae*? For centuries, at least since Cajetan, the answer has appeared to be 'yes', and that affirmative reply is still frequently given in such neoscholasticism as survives even today.[40] In recent decades, however, historical studies of medieval thought on the one hand, and philosophical developments on the other, have made possible a reading of Aquinas that is not filtered through the systematizing transformations wrought in post-seventeenth-century scholasticism. It is beyond my competence to resolve the historical issue. I can only record the fact that I am persuaded by those whose interpretation of Aquinas' procedures, in the text to which I referred, gives us an account of his treatment of analogy which does not involve any recourse to that 'device' against which Kant protested.[41]

One of the central targets of Lonergan's *Insight* is those who persist in assuming that 'knowing consists in taking a look'. On this assumption, terms such as 'essence' and 'existence' are taken to refer to mysterious objects which 'need an extraordinary language to articulate or a superior faculty to apprehend them. Possession of such a faculty then becomes the prerequisite for being a metaphysician. Call it superior insight or the intuition of being.'[42] This model of metaphysical enquiry is in striking contrast to that with which Aquinas worked. For him, 'the mode of metaphysics is not intuitive...but logical'.[43] The metaphysician is distinguished from the logician 'not in possessing an arcane method but simply by the power of his intelligence'.[44] On this account there is a certain irony in H. P. Owen's criticism of G. E. M. Anscombe and P. T. Geach for being preoccupied, in their treatment of analogy, 'with logic at the expense of metaphysics'.[45] And it is significant that Owen, in common with most neoscholastics, supposes that the metaphysician's explorations along the way of analogy can furnish us with a doctrine of God.

To discover what Aquinas is up to in these Questions, it is necessary to attend to his performance, and not to be misled by the fact that the tools he uses are not those which a modern logician would employ. Thus, in spite of Aquinas' insistence that he is concerned to show 'what God is not',[46] generations of commentators have been misled by his use of 'object-language constructions to do metalinguistic jobs'[47] into supposing that he is offering a doctrine of God, at least in the sense that he is constructing a catalogue of divine attributes. In fact, 'Aquinas is not attempting to describe God at all',[48] and 'a perceptive reader would think twice before identifying a deliberate consideration of what God is not with a teaching presuming to say what God is'.[49] His treatment is resolutely grammatical and, 'while a grammatical account cannot pretend to offer a proper account of the subject in question, it can discourage improper ones'.[50] Thus, although in these Questions there are few instances of Aquinas indicating the connections between 'the more austere grammatical discipline of theology'[51] and religious discourse, a view of the relationship between religion and theology is implicit in the procedures he adopts. Theology neither reinforces nor supplants the 'image' of God built up through Christian living – in prayer, work, suffering, relationship – an image which, for the Christian, finds its focus in consideration of the person, words, work and death of Jesus the Christ. The role of theology, as Aquinas conceives it, is to 'exercise critical control' over this image, and over the narratives in which it finds expression, 'now unravelling confusions and inconsistencies that arise from it, now checking it with *praxis* to offset its stereotypical drift, now challenging it as a lazy simplification'.[52] On this account, then, metaphysical theology stands in a critical relationship to religious practice similar to that which I have already suggested obtains between the 'hermeneutical' theological disciplines and the practice of religion.[53]

If Burrell is justified in thus interpreting Aquinas' insistence that he is concerned, by reflecting 'grammatically' on the limits of language, to elucidate what cannot be said of God, then the gulf between Aquinas and Kant is perhaps not so wide, at this point, as has usually been supposed. But if 'we cannot pretend to offer a description of a transcendent object without betraying its transcendence',[54] does it follow that there is nothing which we can truly say of God? It would seem so, for even the discussion, in Question 13, of those predicates which *are* acceptably used of God remains under the rubric of God's 'simpleness', his 'non-compositeness', according to which 'all statements formed of subject and object – that is to say, all discourse – will falsify the reality which God is'.[55] It is at this point that the question of whether or not Aquinas sought to provide the outlines of a 'doctrine of God' is most closely linked with the question of analogy, for it has often been supposed, as we have seen, that the way of analogy provided a route by which the *via negativa* could be transcended, giving rise to a set of positive affirmations sufficiently firm and informative as to constitute the elements of a doctrine of God.[56]

In view of Burrell's insistence that Aquinas' grammatical reflections on language and its limits do not provide us with a 'doctrine of God', it comes as little surprise to find him insisting that, although Aquinas is perhaps best known for his theory of analogy, on 'closer inspection it turns out that he never had one'.[57] And Burrell's comment on Cajetan and, following him, the host of others who have tried to construct such a theory from Aquinas' scattered and unsystematic observations on analogy is somewhat caustic: 'The misunderstanding resulted in the usual way: the philosophical activity of the master became doctrine in the hands of his disciples.'[58]

In fact, the situation is more interesting than that negative comment indicates. Neoscholasticism supposed that, on the basis of a theory of analogy, it was able to construct a doctrine of God. Whereas, if Aquinas *had* had a 'theory' of analogy he would thereby have been prevented from using analogy to speak of God at all. That remark is, I hope, sufficiently provocative to deserve unpacking a little.

Metaphor functions with the recognition of differences: 'the metaphorical statement captures its sense as metaphorical midst the ruins of the literal sense'.[59] Aquinas' distinction between metaphor and analogy stems from this recognition that, if we are to apprehend the truth which metaphor expresses, we must first deny its literal truth. There are, however, some expressions of which this denial is unnecessary, because we do not know and cannot specify the limits of their literal applicability.[60] Thus, for example, to understand what is meant by a 'living' tradition, we have not first got to deny that cultural processes are organisms. Nor, if we describe a friend as having a 'wise expression', do we have hurriedly to add: 'Of course, it's not really his *expression* that is wise'. In both cases, our usage is 'analogical'. In contrast, if we describe a talented gardener as having 'green fingers', it is necessary implicitly to deny the literal truth of the description.[61] Terms like '*wise*, *good* and *living* are used...in contexts so widely divergent that they defy comparison...How are such expressions related? That we cannot say'.[62] We learn how to use such terms appropriately, not by applying a theoretical maxim, but through the practical discipline of developing a sensitive appreciation of appropriate usage. Linguistic usage is an art, not a science. And, if we *were* able theoretically to formulate the way in which the contexts in which we use such terms are related, then we would be unable to use them of 'a God who transcends all our contexts'.[63] It is in this sense that it is true to say that, if Aquinas had had a *theory* of analogical predication he would thereby have been prevented from using analogy to speak of God. Those who have constructed 'theories' of analogy have usually construed 'analogy' as itself a univocal term, whereas Aquinas wisely refrained from making this move: in his hands, the notion of 'analogy' is itself highly analogical.

But what is Aquinas' justification for assuming that even terms such as 'wise', 'good' and 'living' can be applied non-metaphorically to God? The first thing to notice is that the terms selected are 'perfection terms' which occur, as a matter of fact, in the religious activity of praising God.[64] Aquinas' remarks about the applicability of such terms to radically diverse contexts, the limits of which we cannot specify, at least indicate that the believer, in thus articulating his praise of God, is not manifestly talking nonsense. We cannot specify the limits of the applicability of such terms; therefore we cannot specify the limits of their literal applicability; therefore these terms (which believers, as a matter of fact, apply to God) cannot be said to be not literally applicable to God.

At this point, however, it is necessary to notice the part played by those considerations of causality which reflect Aquinas' enduring neo-Platonism. His heuristic definition of God as the 'source' of all things affords 'the formal licence to use [perfection terms] *in divinis*'.[65] As the source of all that is, God is the source of all 'perfections'.[66] It follows, according to Aquinas, that if such terms as 'wise' and 'good' and 'living' *were* to be used literally, they would be used primarily of God and only secondarily of whatever else it is to which they are variously applicable. 'The obvious implication is that we are never in a position to employ these terms literally.'[67] By introducing this hint concerning a specification of the limits of literal applicability, Aquinas, having begun by sharply distinguishing metaphorical from analogical usage, has ended by acknowledging that there is an 'irreducibly metaphorical dimension in analogous expressions'.[68] Or, to put the point anthropomorphically (and thus metaphorically), only God would be in a position to use analogical terms without any touch of metaphor. However, to interpret this recognition as amounting to a concession that, at the end of the day, 'analogy' has been subsumed into 'metaphor' would be to ride roughshod over significant grammatical distinctions which Aquinas was at pains to elucidate.[69] After all, many philosophers of science today would be willing to recognize an irreducibly metaphorical dimension in scientific discourse. But few of them would suppose that they were thereby admitting that all scientific discourse was 'merely metaphorical'.

The philosopher, as Aquinas conceives his task, cannot show the believer *how* to use of God even those terms which are literally (and not 'merely' metaphorically) applicable to God. Just as the philosopher does not *initiate* the quest for God, 'the source and goal of all things', so also the philosopher cannot teach us the appropriate use of religious language. That use will be learnt, in religion as in cookery and politics, by disciplined practice: 'in religious matters, as in others, a philosopher can at best help to discriminate sense from nonsense'.[70]

The way of analogy serves neither as a substitute for nor, in any direct sense, as a confirmation of the way of discipleship. At most, by shedding some light on the logically peculiar character of the linguistic dimension of our quest for God, it may 'help us through the temptation to think that reality is unintelligible'.[71]

Aquinas has often been described as 'agnostic', and my emphasis on the extent to which, in these opening Questions of the *Summa Theologiae*, he resolutely refrains from offering a 'doctrine of God', contenting himself with paying sustained logical attention to what can *not* be said of God, would seem to underline the appropriateness of that description. There are, however, at least two points of view from which the description is misleading. In the first place, Aquinas is not the only great metaphysician to have supposed that there is a sense, however obscure and indirect, in which a disciplined attention to linguistic usage can *show* us something of the character of the objects of our discourse[72] (and therefore, possibly, something of the character of our relationship to God). Of course, grammatical reflection cannot 'directly tell us whether or not there are any such objects',[73] but then it is abundantly clear from the first Question of the *Summa Theologiae* that Aquinas is not concerned to attempt to demonstrate that God exists.[74] It is no business of the philosophical theologian to seek to verify religious truth-claims. It does not follow that such verification is nobody else's business either: 'Wittgenstein did not after all say in his parenthesis "*Religion* as grammar".'[75]

In the second place, I suggest that we need to distinguish between agnosticism as a religious attitude (the practical attitude of one who refrains from worship because of his suspicion that songs of praise are sung not merely into silence but into emptiness) and as a theological policy aimed at insistently reminding the believer of the limits both of his language and of his theoretical understanding. The knowledge born of human love is frequently incapable of finding adequate expression. Lovers, and not only those with weak digestions, have been known to 'sigh and groan'. The lover does not, however, infer from his inability to 'capture the beloved in language' that the beloved is not, after all, known. The 'reticence' of the lover, his continual negation of expressions perceived as inadequate to their object, does not argue nescience, but a more penetrating knowledge than that contained in those 'neutral' descriptions of the beloved that are also available to casual acquaintances, and are found in the files of the family doctor and the social historian. On what *logical* grounds could the possibility be excluded that there is available, within human experience, a 'dark knowledge' of that transcendent mystery of which such neutral descriptions are precisely *not* available (and that they are not is part of the drift of Aquinas' grammatical reflections)? This is, of course, a dangerous line of thought because, if human love is always threatened by illusion, how much more so is man's personal knowledge of the unknown God? If love, any love, is to be responsible, it needs continual submission to a process of verification, of the corrective purification of illusion. But husband and wife do not usually set private detectives (the social equivalent of the 'natural theologian', in the sense in which Karl Barth was rightly suspicious of him?) onto each other, even though there may be circumstances in which resort to this desperate expedient is appropriate. But it is significant that these will be circumstances in which, love having grown cold, personal knowledge has been called radically into question. Burrell nearly captures the sense in which it is and is not appropriate to describe Aquinas as 'agnostic' when he says that 'Aquinas displays his religious discipline most clearly by the ease with which he is able to endure so unknown a God'.[76]

A note on 'verification'

It is fashionable to characterize the strategies available for the testing of religious truth-claims as lying between the limits of 'rationalism' on the one hand and 'fideism' on the other. By 'rationalism', I understand an approach according to which the practice of faith is judged at best irresponsible and at worst superstitious except in so far as its grounds have been established and secured by techniques of verification that are independent of specifically religious considerations. By 'fideism', I understand an approach which, insisting that appropriate criteria of assessment are only available *within* particular patterns of experience, or 'ways of life', refuses to submit the claims of faith to 'external' assessment, whether by the historian, the social scientist or the philosopher.

Christianity has, at one time or another, invested heavily in forms of rationalism in an attempt to ensure its integrity and respectability as an aspect of the human quest for truth. Thus, for example, the burgeoning of 'natural theologies' in the eighteenth century (especially in the form of 'arguments from design') represented an acceptance, by philosophers of religion, of responsibility for securing the theistic grounds of Christian belief. It was not, of course, the theistic grounds alone that needed to be secured. From the eighteenth century onwards, biblical scholars and historians of doctrine came to accept responsibility for securing, by techniques of 'secular' or 'scientific' historiography, the historical grounds of Christian belief.

In our day, both philosophers of religion and historians of Christian origins have increasingly come to admit their inability to fulfil their allotted tasks. But the apparent vulnerability to which their failure exposes Christian belief may yet be beneficial. For the rationalist strategy presupposed that, except in so far as we have succeeded in 'securing' reality *theoretically*, our patterns of action and policy are irresponsible. There is, however, an alternative and perhaps more fruitful strategy which, recognisant of the primacy of action in respect of reflection, of 'social existence' in respect of 'consciousness',[77] supposes that unless we risk seeking responsibly to live and act in the world, any theoretical 'purchase' that we imagine ourselves to have upon reality is fragile and suspect. And if this alternative strategy was put to theological use by Newman, especially in his *University Sermons*, it was put to rather different use, by a contemporary of his, as a central characteristic of Marx's 'materialism'.

The account that I have tried to give, in this essay, of the relation between religious practice and theological reflection – whether historical, literary–critical or metaphysical – is, in this sense, 'materialist'.

To paraphrase Marx, the question whether objective truth can be attributed to Christian believing is a practical question. The Christian must prove the truth, i.e. the reality and power, the this-sidedness of his believing in practice.[78] 'If the Christian faith is true (and unless its truth-claims can be sustained we had better have done with it for ever), its truth is constituted by the correspondence of its credenda with harsh, human reality.'[79] That correspondence eludes theoretical demonstration. It can, however, be practically, imperfectly, partially and provisionally *shown* by the character and quality of Christian engagement in patterns of action and suffering, praise and endurance, that refuse to short-cut the quest by the erection of conceptual or institutional absolutes. The absolutization of contingent particulars is always idolatrous: the denial of divine transcendence.

Thus pragmatically to characterize the practical procedures by which Christian truth-claims are to be submitted to continual 'verification' is not, however, to endorse the strategy of the 'fideist'. For if Christian truth-claims cannot – in any straightforward sense – be confirmed by theological reflection, whether historical or philosophical, they are nevertheless such as to demand continual exposure to *dis*confirmation. Thus, for example, I should wish to argue, firstly, that there are constitutive features of Christian belief which are such as to be permanently exposed to historical falsification; secondly, that the narrative forms in which Christian belief finds primary expression are permanently threatened by that illusory self-indulgence the diagnosis of which is the responsibility of literary criticism; thirdly, that Christian faith in divine transcendence is permanently threatened by that incoherence in its discourse the detection of which is the responsibility of the metaphysician, or 'theological grammarian'.

In brief: the testing of Christian truth-claims occurs, or should occur, in the interplay between their practical verification and their exposure to historical, literary and philosophical criticism.

My justification for offering so outrageously oversimplified a sketch of problems of enormous complexity is that it seemed incumbent upon me to indicate, in however summary a fashion, that approach to problems of verification and falsification which is, I believe, implied by the account that I have offered in this essay of the relationship between theology and religion.

Conclusion

It has sometimes been suggested that Christians both can and should opt either for 'the God of Abraham, Isaac and Jacob', or for 'the God of the philosophers'; either for narrative or for metaphysics; either for 'making sense' of experience or for seeking to discover the truth-conditions of those assertions characteristic of Christian confession. In this essay I have attempted, perhaps too obliquely, to indicate some of the reasons why none of these options is, in fact, available.

To suppose that narrative is an alternative to metaphysics, metaphor an alternative to analogy, is to overlook the fact that 'Metaphor...raises questions that only analogy...can answer, while conversely analogy can only answer questions that are raised in a metaphorical form'.[80] Similarly, to suppose that construction is an alternative to discovery is either, if one opts for construction, to settle for a Feuerbachian account of the 'essence of Christianity' (and there are surely less cumbersome ways of being an atheist than to use the paraphernalia of Christian language and imagery simply to express the form of our alienation?), or to suppose that we have access to the mystery of God other than through the hazardous enterprise of fashioning our human history.

If nothing is gained by attempting partial solutions, neither is anything to be gained by settling back into that benign pluralism ('of course we always need *both*') which mistakes the diagnosis of a problem for its solution. I have suggested that there are two senses in which the story-teller comes first, and two senses in which, if he were left to himself, the integrity and truthfulness of Christianity would be compromised.

Thus, on the one hand, the story-teller comes first inasmuch as Christian religious discourse, as a constitutive element in the practice of Christianity, is paradigmatically narrative (and, more specifically, autobiographical) in form. From this point of view, to 'leave the story-teller to himself' would be to leave Christian practice – unconstrained by historical, literary and philosophical criticism – exposed to the risk, endemic to all autobiography, of 'self-indulgence and even dishonesty'. (And this, even though, as I have indicated, Christian practice also embodies certain *internal* correctives.) There is thus a sense in which the indispensability of theology is the indispensability of criticism for all forms of ideology.

On the other hand, theology's hermeneutical disciplines (historical and literary–critical) also employ narrative, and hence metaphorical, modes of discourse. The historian of Christian origins, and the literary critic, are thus also 'story-tellers' after their fashion. As such, their products invite the logical attention of the metaphysician: in this sense they, too, cannot be 'left to themselves'. But yet, as story-tellers, they 'come first' inasmuch as the metaphysician, proceeding along the way of analogy, can only answer questions that are 'raised in a metaphorical form'.

The picture that emerges, I suggest, is one that would set the dialectic between construction and the disciplined quest for discovery, between narrative and metaphysics, between making sense and assessing the cost of the operation, along not one axis, but two: the 'vertical' axis of the relationship between religion and theology, and the 'horizontal' axis of the relationship between the hermeneutical and philosophical disciplines.

The schematic character of my remarks in these concluding paragraphs may have given the impression that I have sought to construct yet another 'satisfying model' of theological method with which to distract us from the harder task of tackling, both practically and theoretically, the substantive issues. That has not been my intention. Exercises in theological method that lose sight of their essentially heuristic, exploratory character are yet another form in which the temptation of idealism insinuates itself into the theologian's work.

The dialectic between narrative and nescience, anthropomorphism and agnosticism, vision and darkness, autobiographical enactment and the suffering that breaks our constructed identity, is constitutive both of Christian religious practice and of the relationships that obtain between the various patterns of theological enquiry in which that practice is critically reflected. If there are safeguards against illusion and scepticism, they are not, in the last resort, subject to our control. We can, at most, seek to take appropriate precautions.

Notes

1 D. M. MacKinnon, 'The Conflict Between Realism and Idealism', *Explorations in Theology* 5 (London, 1979), p. 164.
2 MacKinnon, 'Absolute and Relative in History', *Explorations*, p. 57. In the same volume, cf. 'Lenin and Theology', p. 22.
3 D. M. MacKinnon, 'Christian and Marxist Dialectic', *Christian Faith and Communist Faith*, ed. D. M. MacKinnon (London, 1953), p. 236.
4 MacKinnon, *Explorations*, p. 57.
5 M. B. Foster, 'Historical Materialism', in MacKinnon, *Christian Faith*, p. 90. The meaning of terms descriptive of philosophical positions or strategies undergoes, in the course of their history, bewildering shifts and diversifications. I hope that, in this paper, the contexts will sufficiently indicate the sense in which the term 'idealism' is being used.
6 Cf. N. L. A. Lash, 'Theory, Theology and Ideology', in A. R. Peacocke (ed.), *The Sciences and Theology in the Twentieth Century*, to be published by Oriel Press.
7 MacKinnon, 'Idealism and Realism: An Old Controversy Renewed', *Explorations*, p. 138.
8 Cf. D. M. MacKinnon, *The Problem of Metaphysics* (Cambridge, 1974), p. 7.
9 The restless ambivalence of that term is not, I think, without significance.
10 MacKinnon, *Explorations*, p. 153.
11 Cf. MacKinnon, *Explorations*, p. 165.
12 It is disappointing to find as sophisticated a philosopher of religion as Anthony Kenny apparently taking for granted a sharp disjunction between 'knowledge' and 'belief': 'I suppose that few people claim to know that there is a God; most believe it as a matter of faith' (Anthony Kenny, *The God of the Philosophers* [Oxford, 1979], p. 127).
13 D. M. MacKinnon, 'Metaphysical and Religious Language', *Borderlands of Theology and Other Essays* (London, 1968), p. 214.
14 Brian Wicker, *The Story-Shaped World* (London, 1975), p. 27. In context, this thesis is far from being as uninformatively abstract as it appears here. It arises from an interpretation of the relationship between the octet and sestet in Gerard Manley Hopkins' sonnet, 'God's Grandeur'.
15 Cf. Wicker, *Story-Shaped World*, p. 7.
16 Wicker, loc. cit.
17 Wicker, *Story-Shaped World*, p. 2.
18 'Mr Moore', said a writer in the first number of the *Westminster Review*, in 1824, '*is* a poet, and therefore is *not* a reasoner' (cited with disapproval in J. S. Mill, *Autobiography* [Oxford, 1971], p. 68). As

Gadamer puts it: 'It is not now said that poets tell lies, but that they are incapable of saying anything true' (H.-G. Gadamer, *Truth and Method* [London, 1975], p. 243).

19 As, for example, in the Althusserian manner of distinguishing between 'science' and 'ideology', according to which only the former can furnish knowledge, or in the epistemological strategy for which Ernest Gellner pleads so eloquently in *Legitimation of Belief* (Cambridge, 1974). For a brief discussion of the Althusserian distinction, cf. Lash, 'Theory, Theology and Ideology', in Peacocke, *Sciences and Theology*.

20 Cf. Paul Ricoeur, *The Rule of Metaphor* (London, 1978). For an historical sketch of the erosion of metaphor from the cognitive to the merely expressive or decorative, cf. Ricoeur's discussion of 'the decline of rhetoric' (pp. 44–64).

21 *Truth and Method*, p. 87.

22 Wicker, *Story-Shaped World*, p. 12.

23 Wicker, loc. cit.

24 Wicker, *Story-Shaped World*, p. 190.

25 MacKinnon, 'Prayer, Worship, and Life', *Christian Faith*, p. 248.

26 MacKinnon, loc. cit.

27 Gadamer, *Truth and Method*, p. 301.

28 *Truth and Method*, p. 304.

29 Alvin W. Gouldner, *The Dialectic of Ideology and Technology* (London, 1976), p. 75.

30 Cf. Wicker, *Story-Shaped World*, p. 26.

31 B. J. F. Lonergan, *Insight* (London, 1957), p. 74. 'Deep within us all, emergent when the noise of other appetites is stilled, there is a desire to know, to understand, to see why, to discover the reason, to find the cause, to explain' (ibid., p. 4). This pursuit of truth 'for its own sake', and the practical and moral dilemmas to which it today gives rise, formed the theme of Professor George Steiner's Bronowski lecture, *Has Truth a Future?* (London: BBC Publications, 1978), which I have elsewhere attempted to 'read' theologically: cf. N. L. A. Lash, 'Christology and the Future of Truth', *Incarnation and Myth: the Debate Continued*, ed. Michael Goulder (London, 1979), pp. 224–32.

32 This is one way of reading the phenomenon of so-called 'hellenization': cf. Wolfhart Pannenberg, 'The Appropriation of the Philosophical Concept of God as a Dogmatic Problem of Early Christian Theology', *Basic Questions in Theology*, vol. 2 (London, 1971), pp. 119–83.

33 This happens even in Pannenberg's interesting essay, 'Analogy and Doxology', *Basic Questions in Theology*, vol. 1 (London, 1970), pp. 211–38; cf. e.g. pp. 212, 228.

34 Cf. Ricoeur, *Metaphor*, p. 260.

35 Ibid., p. 196.

36 MacKinnon, *Borderlands*, p. 209.

37 MacKinnon, loc. cit.

38 *Borderlands*, p. 210. Where the Kantian sources of Barth's rejection of that 'invention of Antichrist' (*Church Dogmatics*, I/1 [Edinburgh, 1936], p. x), the *analogia entis*, are concerned, it is worth comparing MacKinnon's comments with Barth's sketch of Kant's rejection of the

possibility of metaphysics, 'if one understands by it a theoretical knowledge of objects, the concepts of which must be devoid of corresponding *intuitions*' (*Protestant Theology in the Nineteenth Century* [London, 1972], p. 275, my stress).

39 B. J. F. Lonergan, 'Theology in its New Context', *A Second Collection* (London, 1974), p. 57.

40 Thus, for example, according to Professor Eric Mascall, 'St Thomas's doctrine, because it is rooted in the act of being which is analogically common to God and his creatures, gives us a process by which we can transform the *via negativa* into the *via eminentiae* and...can achieve a real knowledge of God in this life' (E. L. Mascall, *He Who Is*, rev. edn. [London, 1966], pp. 225–6). For Mascall, the 'intuition' whereby this achievement is realized is a matter of 'penetrating to the ontological depths' of 'finite beings' so as to 'know them as the creatures of God' (ibid., pp. 91, 85). Armed with this curious metaphor, Mascall elsewhere brings off the most complete misdescription of the 'fundamental thesis' of Lonergan's *Insight* that I have come across: 'knowing always consists in penetrating beneath the immediately apprehended surface of an object into its intelligible *being*. Insight is *in*-sight, seeing *into* the observed object' (E. L. Mascall, *The Openness of Being* [London, 1971], p. 84, his stresses).

41 My justification for relying so heavily, in the following pages, on David Burrell's detailed discussion of this text is, therefore, that – although his reading of these Questions confirms my own impression of what Aquinas was 'up to' – I am less concerned with the historical issue than with sketching an account of the 'way of analogy' which coheres with the general account of the critical function of theological reflection which I am offering in this essay, and which does not entail having recourse to any epistemological theory of 'intuitions' of 'being'.

42 D. B. Burrell, *Aquinas: God and Action* (London, 1979), p. 47.

43 Ibid., p. 48.

44 Burrell, *Aquinas*, p. 6, paraphrasing a favourite passage in Aquinas' commentary on Aristotle's *Metaphysics*: 'Philosophus [differt] a dialectico secundum potentiam' (cf. Burrell, *Aquinas*, pp. 48, 176).

45 H. P. Owen, *The Christian Knowledge of God* (London, 1969), p. 211.

46 'Quia de Deo scire non possumus quid sit sed quid non sit, non possumus considerare de Deo quomodo sit sed potius quomodo non sit. Primo ergo considerandum est quomodo non sit, secundo quomodo a nobis cognoscatur, tertio quomodo nominetur' (Aquinas, *Summa Theologiae*, vol. 2; *Existence and Nature of God*, Ia, 2–11 [London, 1964], p. 18). In other words, the *entire* discussion of God's 'attributes' in Questions 3–11 is under the rubric of what God is *not*, the other two topics being considered in Questions 12 and 13.

47 Burrell, *Aquinas*, p. 17.

48 Ibid., p. 16.

49 Ibid., p. 13.

50 Ibid., p. 22.

51 Ibid., p. 27.

52 Ibid., p. 178.

53 Because 'being that can be understood is language', hermeneutics, according to Gadamer, is 'a universal aspect of philosophy, and not just the methodological basis of the so-called human sciences' (*Truth and Method*, pp. 432, 433). Thus, 'hermeneutics is not to be viewed as a mere subordinate discipline within the arena of the *Geisteswissenschaften*' (H.-G. Gadamer, 'On the Scope and Function of Hermeneutical Reflection', *Philosophical Hermeneutics* [London, 1977], p. 19). I endorse Gadamer's insistence on the universality of 'the hermeneutic *phenomenon*' (*Truth and Method*, p. xi, my stress) and therefore acknowledge that there is a hermeneutical 'aspect' to all linguistic activity. However, by distinguishing between 'hermeneutical' and 'metaphysical' theological disciplines I intend to indicate that there are, nevertheless, distinct tasks to be undertaken not all of which are appropriately described, from the methodological point of view, as 'hermeneutic': cf. B. J. F. Lonergan's comments on 'hermeneutics' in general and Gadamer in particular, in *Method in Theology* (London, 1972), pp. 155, 212. The issue here is closely related to that which is central to the debate between Gadamer and Habermas (on which, cf. T. McCarthy, *The Critical Theory of Jürgen Habermas* [London, 1978], pp. 170–93).

54 Burrell, *Aquinas*, p. 7.

55 Ibid., p. 25. On Aquinas' account, to say that God is radically 'simple' is not to 'name a characteristic of God' but is 'a short-hand way of remarking that no articulated form of expression can succeed in stating anything about God' (Burrell, *Aquinas*, p. 18).

56 The debate between 'Thomists' and those highly critical of 'Thomist' views on these matters is of little interest due to the persistent failure of both parties either to submit Aquinas' texts to detailed and philosophically serious examination or sufficiently to discriminate between the logical and the substantive issues. Cf. e.g., amongst the critics, Keith Ward, *The Concept of God* (Oxford, 1974), pp. 131–58.

57 Burrell, *Aquinas*, p. 55. Burrell's reading is here very close to Herbert McCabe's, according to whom 'analogy', for Aquinas, 'is not a way of getting to know about God, nor is it a theory of the structure of the universe, it is a comment on our use of certain words' (H. McCabe (ed.), *Summa Theologiae*, vol. 3: *Knowing and Naming God, Ia, 12–13* [London, 1964], p. 106).

58 Burrell, *Aquinas*, p. 55.

59 Ricoeur, *Metaphor*, p. 221.

60 'No metaphor is the best possible metaphor – you can always say "I didn't really mean that". But some things we say of God even though they are imperfect cannot be improved on by denying them; their imperfection lies in our understanding of what we are trying to mean' (McCabe, *Knowing and Naming God*, p. 107).

61 There are, I appreciate, problems concerning the relationship between analogy and 'dead metaphor', but I do not think that they affect the point at issue. Cf. Ricoeur's discussion of Derrida, in *Metaphor*, pp. 284–95.

62 Burrell, *Aquinas*, p. 10.

63 Burrell, loc. cit.

64 Cf. Burrell, *Aquinas*, pp. 59–60.

65 Burrell, *Aquinas*, p. 66, commenting on Question 13, art. 5: 'Non enim possumus nominare Deum nisi ex creaturis... Et sic quidquid dicitur de Deo et creaturis, dicitur secundum quod est aliquis ordo creaturae ad Deum ut ad principium et causam'.

66 'It is creative causality, therefore, that establishes between being and God the bond of participation that makes the relation by analogy ontologically possible' (Ricoeur, *Metaphor*, p. 276). Ricoeur rightly insists on the importance of the fact that, in his mature works, Aquinas pursued the enquiry *not* in terms of 'formal' causality, or 'likeness', but of *dependence in act*. Hence it is, also, that Burrell devotes the second half of his study to an elucidation of Aquinas' 'inherently analogous' (p. 116) notion of '*actus*'. For an admirably lucid summary of Aquinas' extension of the notion of causality to God, cf. McCabe's appendix on 'Causes', with its insistence that 'God, for St Thomas, is not a causal explanation of the world... what we know of him does not serve to explain the world, all that we know of him is that he must exist if the world is to have an explanation' (*Knowing and Naming God*, p. 102).

67 Burrell, *Aquinas*, p. 70, commenting on Question 13, art. 6. This implication is far from obvious to Don Cupitt who, contrasting Aquinas and Kant, claims that, according to the argument of Question 13, 'we can transcend our own subjectivity and see the world as it were from God's point of view' (*The Nature of Man* [London, 1979], p. 51). This is grossly misleading. For a more nuanced account of the similarities and differences between Kant and Aquinas on these matters, cf. Karl Rahner, 'Thomas Aquinas on Truth', *Theological Investigations*, vol. XIII (London, 1975), pp. 13–31, esp. p. 25.

68 Burrell, *Aquinas*, p. 56.

69 Cf. Ricoeur, *Metaphor*, pp. 277–80.

70 Burrell, *Aquinas*, p. 69.

71 Ibid., p. 75.

72 Is this not true of Aristotle, Kant and Hegel? Burrell is fond of appealing to Wittgenstein's remark: '*Essence* is expressed by grammar... Grammar tells what kind of object anything is. (Theology as grammar.)' (*Philosophical Investigations*, I, §§ 371, 373), Cf. Burrell, *Aquinas*, pp. 17, 74, 76.

73 Renford Bambrough, 'Introduction', *Reason and Religion*, ed. S. C. Brown (London, 1977), p. 13.

74 This *first* Question is ignored with tedious regularity by philosophers of religion commenting on the second.

75 Bambrough, 'Introduction', p. 16.

76 Burrell, *Aquinas*, p. 67. Two further comments are in order. Firstly, Aquinas sought to moderate the even more radical agnosticism of a 'long tradition of devotion and theology' (T. Gilby, *Knowing and Naming God*, p. xxxii) represented by the Pseudo-Denys (cf. Q. 13, art. 1, 1; art. 3, 2; art. 12, 1) and, in the generation preceding his own, by Alain of Lille (cf. Q. 13, art. 2, c; art. 6, c) and Maimonides (cf. Q. 13, art. 2, c; art. 5, c).

Secondly, although 'Thomist' treatments of the 'doctrine of analogy' have, in their quest for descriptions of divine attributes, supposed themselves to be far less 'agnostic' than the account of Aquinas' use of analogy offered here, it is by no means clear that they succeeded. This I take to be the drift of Campbell's comments on E. L. Mascall's *Existence and Analogy* (London, 1949); cf. C. A. Campbell, 'The Doctrine of Analogy', *On Selfhood and Godhood* (London, 1957), pp. 427–33. For drawing my attention to Campbell's study, and for many perceptive comments on earlier drafts of this paper, I am greatly indebted to J. A. Bradley.

77 Karl Marx, 1859 Preface to 'A Contribution to the Critique of Political Economy', *Early Writings* (London, 1975), p. 425.

78 Cf. Marx's second thesis on Feuerbach, *Early Writings*, p. 422.

79 MacKinnon, 'Lenin and Theology', *Explorations*, p. 21.

80 Wicker, *Story-Shaped World*, p. 27. I find it interesting that this 'slogan' of Wicker's should closely echo the thrust of Ricoeur's more massively learned study, which appeared in the same year.

6

Theological Study: The Nineteenth Century and After

S. W. SYKES

The notes to this essay wil be found on pages 115–18

> At first sight one might be tempted to say that theological study has no place at all in a modern university...The amount of public money available to subvent fundamental research in universities is strictly limited, and one can understand the attitude of mind of those who regard it as little short of scandalous that some part of it should be diverted to the prosecution of a subject so intellectually dubious as theology.[1]

Donald MacKinnon, who penned these words, has always shown himself acutely sensitive to the demand on the theologian to justify himself. 'The theologian in the university today', he writes, 'must live and work as a man who has to establish his right to exist.'[2] 'It should not be easy to be a theologian in a modern university.'[3] 'It is a good thing, even a very good thing, for theology to have to fight for its existence in a university.'[4] 'It is for him to let his worth be proved, and his honesty is in a measure preserved by the fact that he cannot hope to fix his judges.'[5]

This conscious embracing of a perilously insecure position is argued for on a variety of grounds. It is most certainly good for theology itself ('the harder the struggle...the better the work').[6] It is good for theology moreover, not merely in the sense of leading to publications in which the fundamental questions have been deeply probed, but actually in the spiritual impact such a position has on the theologian. His position has radically changed; he cannot any longer speak *de haut en bas*; in his radical insecurity the theologian comes to experience on his own pulse 'the reality of the divine condescension'[7] – the appeal is, of course, to the doctrine of *kenosis*, the self-abasement of the divine Son in his identification with man. Finally MacKinnon allows himself to hint, but no more than hint, that the university itself may be better off for having a theological department. The theologian, despite his critics, will from time to time perceive 'that his self-consciously exposed position equips him for a role that is of genuine, even permanent significance'.[8] Or again, even in his concern for the basic questions of faith, the theologian may be capable of provoking work which is of value to those who do not share the faith in the first place.

> The kind of discoveries that the theologian makes are not immediately shareable; therefore they must establish their import, I had almost said in quantifiable form, by the renewed vitality they bring to critical philosophy, to social science, to historical study.[9]

Behind this last argument, that the relentless prosecution of theology may actually supply a stimulus to other disciplines, lies, of course, a basic cultural assumption which MacKinnon has already expounded. Christianity, its moral and theological ideas, social institutions, art forms, myths and rituals, is, for good or ill, 'a formative element in our culture'.

> It has supplied the language, the conceptual system, in whose terms men and women in these islands have posed and sought to answer ultimate questions. Or if they have sought an alternative idiom, it is as an alternative to the Christian tradition in one or other of its forms that they have sought it.[10]

Referring to the study of persons as various as Bertrand Russell, the young Marx, Lenin, and the protagonists of 'our own gentler liberal humanism', MacKinnon claims the necessity of some knowledge of the Christian tradition, not on a purely superficial level, but rather 'a philosophically critical investigation of a system of belief'.[11] It is by means of that programme of enquiry, in the prosecution of which MacKinnon has made his distinguished contribution, that the theologian has at least some hope of participating in the social tasks of the modern university.

In exploring MacKinnon's view of the changed 'texture of theological existence' – 'changed with the great deliverance that has come to Christianity with the advent of the post-Constantinian era'[12] – we obviously need to examine the impact of the Enlightenment upon the intellectual and religious traditions of Western Europe. In particular, one episode is deeply instructive, namely the attempt to submit the writing of Immanuel Kant to theological censorship, and the response this futile manoeuvre drew from Kant himself. A mere fifteen years after this incident a new university was founded in Berlin, and a newly prominent theologian, Friedrich Schleiermacher, found himself challenged to justify the study of theology as an academic discipline and the presence of theologians in the highest councils of the university, in the face of von Humboldt's opposition.[13] The first part of this essay seeks to expound the arguments of Kant and Schleiermacher respectively concerning the justification for theological study in a 'post-Constantinian era'.

In the second section I seek to respond to Donald MacKinnon's call for a 'philosophically critical investigation of a system of belief' as the ultimate contemporary justification for theology. My response is not, however, that of the philosophical critic, but of one who is provoked by the problems attaching to the idea of studying Christianity as 'a system of belief'. The contemporary study of theology in English universities lacks, I shall argue, that kind of confident self-understanding without which it cannot begin to emerge as 'a system of belief', to which philosophical criticism can be applied.

Both halves of the essay accept the suggestion made by Donald MacKinnon that without struggle and conflict at the very heart of the discipline, theology is an intellectually and spiritually perilous undertaking. How Kant conceived, and Schleiermacher modified, this conflict, and what unrest contemporary theologians in their turn ought to expect, even to provoke – these are the themes that arise from Donald MacKinnon's own profoundly important stimulus to contemporary theology.

I

It might be said that the main impact upon theological study of the era of the European Enlightenment was the incorporation into its subject matter of any kind of relevant conflict that could be rationally sustained. But has that not always been the case with theology? Did not St Thomas Aquinas himself give a remarkable run for their money to all manner of sceptical and heretical views so long as they could be rationally expounded? Indeed he did; and a history of the study of theology could show the extent to which mature and intellectually wide-ranging theologians were fully prepared to test their views against those of sophisticated opponents.

However, theologians have never worked in a power vacuum. Some have been employed by bishops to refute opponents, some have actually become bishops. And with the acquisition by the Church of civil privileges, theological scholarship has been unavoidably embroiled in the trappings and snares of civil power. The destruction of heretical books and the practice of ecclesiastical censorship are merely the obvious outward manifestations of a dimension to the notion of doctrinal and intellectual conflict in Christian theology which cannot be ignored.

It is not, therefore, in any way perverse to open our enquiry into the enlightened study of theology with an example of theological censorship, particularly since it was practised upon one who regarded himself as a self-conscious theoretician of the German Enlightenment, Immanuel Kant. In his well known essay of 1784, 'What is Enlightenment?', we find what to us might be a surprising readiness to allow that the subject matter of theology should be prescribed by the government.[14] Universities funded by the state must necessarily serve the purposes of the state. The three higher faculties inherited from the medieval university, those of theology, law and medicine, are a legitimate expression of the practical concern of a regime for its own well-being and that of its subjects. That essay was written under the kindly eye of Frederick the Great, the doughty supporter of the Enlightenment. Ten years later, in October 1794, Kant was to receive a letter from Frederick William II requiring him to desist from undermining Christianity by his writings on the philosophy of religion. He agreed. But he did so in terms which enabled him, once the King died, to return to the topic of the proper place of theology in relation to other disciplines in his extraordinarily interesting *Streit der Fakultäten*, published in 1795.[15]

What has Kant to say about censorship? It is perfectly clear from his 1784 essay that he regards the state as having a legitimate role to play in relation to the regulation of belief, at least for the time being. He does indeed praise Frederick for his tolerance of diversities of religious opinion; he asserts that public order is the monarch's interest not theological argument, and he finds it admirable that respected clerics are not subject to discipline for openly exposing to examination judgements and insights differing from the received creed.[16] None the less he admits the possibility of conflict between what he somewhat strangely calls a public and a private use of reason; the public use being the arguments a scholar uses before the whole world, the private being the limits he accepts as the occupant of some civic (or clerical) office.[17] Here he clearly has in mind the position of a clerical scholar. *Qua* scholar his use of reason must be absolutely free; *qua* clergyman he may often be quite narrowly limited without impeding the progress of enlightenment. The possibility of conflict between free critical enquiry and the creed of the Church is certainly envisaged, and Kant offers a view on when it would be right for such a man to lay down his office, namely when he discovers that his Church's creed contains matter contrary to 'inner religion'.[18]

Kant's essay is very far from being any kind of definitive statement about the Enlightenment. It is entirely an occasional piece, written with an eye to previous controversies in the *Berlinische Monatsschrift*, and a still larger eye to Frederick the Great. It contains moreover the, to us, comic-sounding sentence, 'There is only one Lord in the world [he means Frederick] who says: Argue as much as you like, about anything you like, but obey!'[19]

His willingness to obey and thus to follow his own prescription was tested under Frederick's successor. The *Wöllnersche Religionsedikt* of 8 July 1788, threatening punishment and dismissal of religious teachers who deviated from adherence to biblical doctrines, put the advocates of freedom to the test. For a period of ten years stricter control of publications was enforced, and Kant was compelled to go to some trouble to evade the suppression of books 2, 3 and 4 of his *Religion within the Limits of Reason Alone*. As soon as they were published Kant received from the King a demand to justify himself, and a requirement that he should not offend in this matter again. It was precisely this situation he had envisaged in his essay on the Enlightenment where he had said:

> It detracts from the King's majesty if he thinks the writings of his subjects worthy of governmental supervision. If he acts from his own supreme insight, he must be reminded that *Caesar non est supra grammaticos*, especially if he supports the spiritual despotism of some tyrants in his State against his other subjects.[20]

These elusive and fragmentary views on the possibility of conflict receive fuller treatment, first in the introduction to *Religion*, where Kant tries to justify his evasion of official censorship by submitting the work to the philosophical faculty of a university,[21] and subsequently in his *Streit der Fakultäten*. Here we find a mature treatment of Kant's own theory of the nature of religion, and thus of the relations of theology and philosophy as disciplines of a university. Needless to say this theory is complex and subtle; and two features of it only have we the opportunity to notice.

The first feature corresponds to his depiction of the possibility of internal conflict within the scholar–clergyman, and consists of a thorough externalization of the conflict. Kant draws a contrast between the respective spheres of operation of the 'biblical theologian' and the 'philosophical theologian'.[22] The former, belonging to the faculty of theology, has a text prescribed for him, namely the Bible, and must work within the limits which that volume lays down. The theologian is, in this respect, no different from the lawyer and the doctor, who similarly have to work within prescribed limits set by the state. The 'philosophical theologian', by contrast, is not subject to such limits. He works by reason alone, and claims the freedom to expand his views as far as the subject takes him. Disputes about the boundary between the two naturally arise – indeed they ought to arise. In the *Streit der Fakultäten* the whole object of the essay is to demonstrate the necessity of an institutionalized rivalry between theology and philosophy, and, though it is of less interest, between law and philosophy and medicine and philosophy. (Here it should be emphasized that by philosophy is meant virtually everything not classifiable as theology, law or medicine; including, of course, the study of language and literature, history, mathematics and the natural sciences as well as what we would call philosophy.) Theology must not be allowed to go on its way undisturbed, without experiencing the conflict provoked by those who claim to be subject to no arbitrary or governmental limitations. Hence Kant's words:

> We may concede to the theological faculty the proud claim that philosophy is its hand maid, though the question remains whether the maid carries the torch in front of the gracious lady, or the train behind her. But the condition is that philosophy should not be chased off or gagged. This very unpretentiousness, merely to be free, but also to be left free to identify truth in the interests of each science and present it for whatever use the higher faculties may want to make of it, ought to commend it to the government itself as above suspicion, yes as indispensable.[23]

Kant presents his views with a certain persuasive charm. He wants, he says, to ensure that the practitioners of the learned trades (priests, lawyers and doctors) should never get away with being regarded as miracle-men by a superstitious public.[24] Conflict, in effect, ensures this; it cuts men down to size. Thus it is not only unavoidable, it is desirable.

However, there is a second observation to be made about Kant's argument. For inside the Trojan horse he has wheeled into the traditional university citadel lies waiting a host of controversial doctrines about the real nature of religion. If we examine the style of *Streit der Fakultäten*, which must surely be one of Kant's most attractive writings, we see an unmistakable irony. In a passage where he is discussing the proposal that the sanction for a particular theological doctrine is aesthetic, that is, based on some pious feeling attributed to a supernatural influence, he asserts: 'The philosophical faculty must be free publicly to test and estimate with cold rationality the origin and content of such an *alleged* basis of information, quite uninhibited by the holiness of the object which is *purportedly* felt, and resolutely to bring this *supposed* feeling to conceptual clarification' (my emphases).[25] The martialling of the resources of the German language for casting doubt on pious enthusiasm provokes admiration as it simultaneously provides evidence of Kant's fundamental conviction that a substantial measure of demystification was in store for Christian theology.

The second feature of Kant's treatment of this issue is, then, that he believed in the progressive nature of the Enlightenment. The evidence is already there in the contribution to the *Berlinische Monatsschrift*: 'Do we live, he asked, in an enlightened age? No, but in an age of enlightenment. We are far from the point where everybody may think about religion without outside guidance.'[26] 'Thinking about religion without outside guidance' is, of course, the theme of the book on *Religion*. And at the end of the section on the nature of the legitimate conflict between the higher and the lower faculties he explicitly envisages a stage in which the last may be first (a pleasant biblical irony), and philosophers be looked to as the appropriate advisers of the men of power, their freedom and growing insight being valued above the obsolete techniques of absolute authority.[27]

Kant's exposure to censorship by one he considered a pious bigot led him to consider quite carefully the precise kind of theological teaching which could ever be sponsored by government.[28] He does not call for the abolition of theology; perhaps he does not ever explicitly envisage it. But when he writes upon the principles of criticism and the pure religion based on the critical work of practical reason, he expresses a deeply held belief that the task of such a philosophical science is the raising of humanity. His view of religion, in other words, is governed by an explicitly formulated hope for mankind, to which Christianity is 'so far as we know' (the words are Kant's) the most convenient guide.

As I have expounded these two features of Kant's later writing on religion, it is plain that he embodies in himself the two tendencies which lie in uneasy tension in the very origins of the Enlightenment, and which were in fact discussed by the Berlin Wednesday Club in the 1780s. In an anonymous contribution to the *Berlinische Monatsschrift*, Johann Erich Biester (1749–1816), one of the magazine's editors, argued in favour of the fusion of state and Church: 'May politics and religion, law and catechism', he exclaimed, 'be one and the same.'[29] Against this explicitly reductionist programme, another contributor, Johann Friedrick Zöllner (1753–1804), wrote bewailing the extent to which the *Aufklärung* was undermining the value of religion and producing confusion in the hearts and minds of men.[30] And it should be noted that Zöllner was prominent in protest against Wollner's edict. What, in any case, is *Aufklärung*, asks Zöllner, thus provoking Kant's reply.

Others among the enlightened were also perceptive of the ambiguity at the heart of the movement. Moses Mendelssohn sees great difficulty in knowing the boundary between the use and the misuse of reason: 'The nobler a thing is in its perfection, says a Hebrew writer, the more hideous in its decay. Misuse of enlightenment weakens the moral sense, and leads to hardness of heart, egotism, irreligion and anarchy.'[31] The dispute can be put like this. There were those who thought that the mere possibility of public discussion was a sufficient index of the presence of enlightenment. On the other hand, there were others who believed that certain beliefs had to yield to the relentless onward march of progressive opinions. Of course, there was no agreement what these were; but you could not get the sense of enlightenment happening if you were unable actually to catch the sound of sacred cows being constantly slaughtered. Mere discussion was not enough.

Kant represents both of these views. On the one hand, he builds into his notion of a university one in which theology and philosophy must conflict, and it seems sufficient if they do; on the other hand, the true religion of humanity begins to outshine the tatty robes and rituals of mere authoritarianism. There is no need to press a contrast, as though the two views are in conflict with each other. They represent different trends in the Enlightenment, but not contradictory ones. The second of the two, the progressive hypothesis, gave birth in due course to the myth of the warfare of science and theology.

But the theory of progressive enlightenment is not to be dispatched with a rhetorical flourish. There is, after all, a progressive element in the very notion of free and open discussion; nothing could be achieved unless governments and churches were actually persuaded to clarify their separate, legitimate spheres of interest. The Christian Churches themselves had to learn through a long and painful series of controversies the proper way to treat internal dissent. There are very good grounds for regarding Immanuel Kant as one of those who prepared the way for the fragile advances of the Second Vatican Council.

I have laboured over Kant because he provides us with an explicit example of a leading figure of the European Enlightenment who reflects on the implications of the Enlightenment for the study of theology. But Kant was no systematic theologian, much though he enjoyed treating theologians who strayed into philosophy in a free and easy manner, 'ruthlessly pulling out their brilliant plumage'.[32] Friedrich Schleiermacher was a systematic theologian who acquired the reputation subsequently for being 'the father of modern theology'. A bare ten years after Kant's *Streit der Facultäten* we find Friedrich Schleiermacher bringing out anonymously, in the context of the planning of the University of Berlin, his *Gelegentliche Gedanken über Universitäten in deutschen Sinn* (*Timely Thoughts on Universities from a German Standpoint*).[33] Schleiermacher was an astute and independent-minded critic of Kant, offering his views on the structure of the university quite specifically with a view to influencing the actual foundation of a university in the erstwhile capital of the German Enlightenment. With this document, and by means of his subsequent appointments to the organizing commission of the university, Schleiermacher moved to the very centre of the German stage as a theoretician of the place of theology in a university. Two years later, in 1810, he published his *Brief Outline on the Study of Theology*, whilst already occupying his post as first Dean of Berlin's Theological Faculty;[34] and this book is still spoken of with respect as one of the finest examples of a plan for a modern theological curriculum.[35]

The comparatively short interval between Kant and Schleiermacher's writing and the knowledge of Schleiermacher's work on Kant's philosophy might lead us to expect a rather direct relationship between the two pieces. But it is not so, principally for the reason that Schleiermacher writes in response to two important lectures, one (a series, 1803) by Schelling, including a lecture on the study of theology, the other by Fichte (1807, published in 1817).[36] The difference of atmosphere is substantial. The movement of transcendental idealism had installed itself as the legitimate heir to Kant's philosophical revolution, and heady blueprints for the reordering of the whole of knowledge had become fashionable. Thus, in particular, Schleiermacher differs radically from Kant in his conviction (which he shared with von Humboldt) that the planning of a university rested on certain explicit views as to the true nature of *Wissenschaft*. Where Kant had been content to make what sense he could of the actual state of affairs in the late-eighteenth-century university, Fichte, von Humboldt and Schleiermacher shared a confidence that they could fashion things anew. And in this new order of things Kant's prophecy of the coming time when the last would be first was speedily fulfilled. For Schleiermacher, the basic presupposition of all higher studies, the unity in the university, was given in the inner unity of all *Wissenschaft*.[37] Following Kant in his subtle depreciation of the learned tradesman's know-how, the mystique of priest, lawyer and doctor, Schleiermacher boldly proclaims the priority of philosophy.[38] Only one who had studied philosophy for a year might be allowed subsequently to specialize in another faculty.[39] More remarkable still, only a lecturer capable of lecturing also in the philosophical faculty ought to be allowed to lecture in one of the specialized departments (a recommendation he assiduously followed in his own career).[40] And directly grasping the thorn of state interference on which Kant had briefly impaled himself, Schleiermacher insists that the corollary of the priority of philosophy in the university is the highest degree of independence from the state consistent with its financial dependency.[41] Schleiermacher perceives it to be a real danger (and one, we may add, no less real with the passage of time) that universities should sink to the level of institutions kept going for state purposes.

The task of a university faced with a generation of young persons is, according to Schleiermacher, to awaken in them the idea of *Wissenschaft*;[42] they are to be concerned with the learning of learning, so to exhibit the totality of knowledge and the outline of what there is to know that each one becomes capable of pursuing each sphere of knowledge on his own.[43] The characteristic productions of universities are, therefore, encyclopedic outlines, text-books and compendia.[44]

Schleiermacher recognizes the objections of those who criticize the pure transcendental philosophy, which, *gespensterartig/phantomlike*, tends to go in for high-flown ideas of knowledge in general.[45] Philosophical study, he believes, requires the special disciplines as much as they require philosophy. Both are to be taken together. But he is in no doubt that there is no outstanding progress in any discipline apart from what he terms the 'speculative spirit'.[46]

What then of theology? It is, in Schleiermacher's understanding, a practical discipline; sharing this disadvantage not merely with law and medicine but also with the natural sciences, none of which von Humboldt was willing to believe helped man to those intellectual heights to which he ought to aspire. Schleiermacher's theory was understandably more positive than von Humboldt's, but it rested on the assumption that in relation to intellectual advance in theology, too, a training in philosophy was indispensable.

Very little, in this outline of theology's relation to philosophy, survives of Kant's model of conflict. The tension, which Kant wanted to locate in the very existence of separate faculties, has been neutralized because the philosopher–theologian Schleiermacher is already a member of both. The impact of *Wissenschaftstheorie* is in the direction of system. Schleiermacher outlines for himself the career of a systematician and then becomes one. It is not that Schleiermacher is unwilling to face conflict; quite the reverse, as his espousal of the discipline of 'polemics' demonstrates.[47] The point is, rather, that in the very comprehensiveness with which he views the task of theology conflicts of style and intention between philosopher and theologian have had to reach the point of resolution before the theologian is able to proceed with his proper task.

Thus theology proper is, on Schleiermacher's account, preceded by certain enquiries. In *The Christian Faith* these are spoken of as studies, three in number, from which Christian theology 'borrows' certain propositions, namely Ethics, Philosophy of Religion and Apologetics.[48] Ethics, in Schleiermacher, is that discipline which elucidates the categories by which human history is understood.[49] The category of 'church' ('a communion or association relating to religion or piety') is, like the category of 'state' or 'art', irreducibly required in the interpretation of human history: 'Unless religious communities are to be regarded as mere aberrations, it must be possible to show that the existence of such associations is a necessary element for the development of the human spirit.'[50] That is what Schleiermacher had set out to demonstrate in his speeches *On Religion*, which are accordingly not to be regarded as an exercise in Romantic religious individualism, but as a defence of the irreducibility of religious communities. 'Ethics' plays in Schleiermacher the role of a particular kind of (non-reductive) sociology of religion. Without any attempt to provide the conventional backing of a natural theology (by proving the existence of God, the immortality of the soul, and the future likelihood of divine judgement) – tasks he explicitly disclaimed[51] – Schleiermacher implicitly acknowledges the necessity of some kind of non-reductive analysis of the phenomenon of human religion.

The term 'philosophy of religion' is reserved for the categorization according to type of the different religions.[52] Here again Schleiermacher is revolutionary, standing at the head of the history of the discipline once called comparative religion, and now not altogether satisfactorily re-named the phenomenology of religion. The point of the discipline is to indicate the 'manner and degree in which one [sc. religious community] may differ from the others, and likewise how the distinctiveness of the various societies of faith which have arisen in history relates to these differences'.[53] By means of such analysis, the distinctiveness of Christianity, when compared with other religions, may begin to emerge. Thus the picture is being built up; first, the general concept of a religious association or church; next, the distinctiveness of the Christian Church in comparison with others.

Thirdly comes 'propositions borrowed from apologetics'. It is the task of apologetics to provide a definition of Christianity in its peculiar essence (*seinem eigentümlichen Wesen nach*).[54] Here there is a certain ambiguity. Is this a discipline external or internal to Christianity? In the *Brief Outline* 'apologetics' belongs, with 'polemics', to the part of Christian theology called philosophical theology.[55] In *The Christian Faith*, however, apologetics is classified with ethics and the philosophy of religion as 'another scientific study';[56] though a few lines earlier it is also called 'a theological discipline'.[57]

Clearly the uncertainty of classification falls far short of formal contradiction. On the one side philosophical theology has to come to terms in its definition of the essence of Christianity with what has been previously specified in philosophy of religion's examination of all the religions; it must, therefore, cultivate a relationship with a discipline ranging more widely than Christian theology. On the other hand philosophical theology according to the *Brief Outline*, includes within it the principles of every theologian's whole theological way of thinking and must be produced in its entirety by himself;[58] it is, therefore, formulated with dogmatics in view. Philosophical theology, in short, is the focus of different interests, which may conflict, though it is the duty of the theologian to make them harmonize. Philosopher and theologian are here to be unified in the systematician.

It is precisely at this point, however, that those who, following Barth (and MacKinnon and many others), are rightly suspicious of the very concept of a 'system'[59] will want to insist on further enquiry. What precisely is being held together in the system, and by what? It is to this question that Schleiermacher addresses himself in his opening definition of theology in the *Brief Outline*: 'Theology is a positive science, whose parts form into a cohesive whole only through their common relation to a particular mode of faith (*Glaubensweise*), i.e. a particular way of being conscious of God (*Gestaltung des Gottesbewusstseins*). Thus, the various parts of Christian theology belong together only by virtue of their relation to Christianity.'[60] As we have shown, by 'positive science' Schleiermacher means one oriented towards practical activity. 'The positive faculties [i.e. law, theology and medicine] each arose from the need to establish an indispensable praxis securely on theory developed out of tradition on the basis of know-how.'[61] The 'praxis' in this case is the 'cohesive leadership of the Christian church',[62] a phrase which one might paraphrase as the practical task of deciding what the Christian Church shall do in the light of what she is. The only 'system' which Schleiermacher desires, in other words, is that sense of unity in all the sides or aspects of Christianity which alone can make possible a cohesive, coherent and harmonious practice of Christianity. Further, this unity of apprehension consists in a judgement about the particular mode of faith (*Glaubensweise*) characteristic of Christianity.[63] Every religion has its own peculiar mode of faith, which is the ground of its inner coherence.[64] What is Christianity's particular mode of faith? What is its essence? Only by attempting to answer this question can incoherence, disorder and disharmony apparently be avoided. Philosophical theology is that discipline which seeks to respond to that question, and in responding to it provides the basis for a 'system' without which cohesive decision-making is impossible.

By so thoroughly relating the study of Christianity to praxis, Schleiermacher unquestionably 'ecclesiasticized' it (as Troeltsch was later to complain).[65] The datum for the Christian theologian is the problem posed by the actual existence of the contemporary Church. The theologian is, therefore, dependent on the Church. But in what sense dependent? Is a theologian supposed to believe in advance the claim of the Christian Church to be a divine society? Is the whole of his activity, as in Schleiermacher's way of seeing the question, directed towards the end of ecclesiastical decision-making? It is not my intention to provide any further discussion of Schleiermacher's proposals, which profoundly influenced the pattern of theological study in German universities for more than a century. It is sufficient to note that Wolfhart Pannenberg, in his major study of the intellectual status of theology, *Theology and the Philosophy of Science*,[66] makes the claim that Schleiermacher, in subordinating the theory of theological study in universities to the training of clergy subordinated it, implicitly, either to the short-term interests of a narrowly conceived confessionalism, or, more dangerously, to the interests and interference of the state. Neither consequence, of course, was any part of Schleiermacher's intention. But the danger in his proposals went unheeded, while at the same time his justification of theological study contained, according to Pannenberg, a major, internal incoherence.[67]

Pannenberg's objection to Schleiermacher highlights the dilemma for the post-Enlightenment study of Christian theology. To what extent is the study of theology an ecclesiastical discipline? Kant's solution was clearly an interim one. For the time being, the unharmonious coexistence of theology and philosophy was a way of cutting theology's tendency towards authoritarianism down to size. But he looked forward to a more prominent position for philosophy in due course. Schleiermacher, boldly grasping the nettle and, at the same time, exploiting the Protestant Church establishment to the full, concealed Kant's conflicts in an apparently ambiguous synthesis. The sheer diversity of the actual practice of modern Western states in the subsidization of Christian theological studies bears testimony to the uncertainty of the arguments upon which either the separation of Christian theology from the university curriculum, or its incorporation into it, is justified.

What follows in the second part of this essay is a reconsideration of modern English practice, in the light of the discussion of Kant and Schleiermacher.

II

It is entirely plain, as Donald MacKinnon argues, that it is as a 'formative element in our culture' that Christian studies appear in the curricula of modern English universities. This carries certain corollaries, for example that English universities can be expected to concern themselves with English Church history. Scottish with Scottish and so forth. Certain choices about a curriculum are made which are relative to a particular region and its history. However the very fact that the cultural justification entails a regional or national bias may raise the question whether the dominant religious group in a region has a kind of natural right to orient the theological curriculum in the direction of its own needs and interests.

The argument against this conclusion has considerable force. Christians are known to be committed to the task of evangelism; and it is because of the (historically evident) possibility of collision between the task of religious persuasion and the task of critical enquiry that religious believers cannot safely be given a *carte blanche* for the pursuit of their own studies at public expense. Universities must be places where the right to the conduct of public conflict is jealously guarded. At the very least immunity from prosecution must be accorded those who publicly dissent from the dicta of a religious authority.

These modern conditions were only securely established in English universities with the overthrow of the Church of England's grip upon the theological faculties. The background history to the foundation of University College, London, is extremely instructive in this respect. A group of Nonconformists desired that the new institution should be in effect a dissenting university, with theological chairs assigned to different denominations. Anglican supporters of Brougham were adamantly opposed to anything other than Church of England dominance or no Church presence at all.[68] Their opposition ensured that in the event theology had no place in the university, its Council declaring in 1827 that it 'found it impossible to unite the free admission to persons of all religious denominations with any plan of theological instruction, or any form of religious discipline'.[69]

What University College, London, found impossible in 1827 was, in other places and in due course, found possible, at least so far as some kind of theological curriculum was concerned. In practice this curriculum had to represent a consensus of *all* the interested parties, and be tolerable to the university as a whole. Inevitably the result was, as we see it today, a variety of differently constructed syllabuses, reflecting the variety of locally negotiated compromises of a pragmatic kind. The universities of Great Britain and Northern Ireland accordingly lack any kind of generally accepted theoretical basis for the conduct or justification of theological study, a confusion which the exponents of 'religious studies' ably exploited in the 1960s.

How far from being satisfactory this situation is can be appreciated when one examines critically the direction in which the syllabuses have drifted, bereft of any coherent justification. Because Christian theology inherently entails the study of a corpus of literature, of history, and of philosophy, the modern theological curriculum currently exemplifies a loose juxtaposition of biblical studies, both literary and historical, of Church historical studies, both intellectual and institutional, and of metaphysics and ethics. The least troublesome way of justifying theological study is by reference to the methods of departments whose existence is universally accepted. But if that is how theological study actually *is* justified, there can be no complaint if the department is simply dismembered. In some universities the dissolution of elements of theological study into departments of classics, ancient and modern history, the history of ideas ànd philosophy has actually been carried out.

How, then, is one to interpret the continued existence of those departments (and even faculties) of theology which so far have successfully resisted dismemberment? One may assume that certain judgements have been made about what is to be retained, and what dropped, in the syllabuses. How have decisions been arrived at? Here again, the simplest explanation of the present situation is to see the modern curriculum as the result of a series of minor pragmatic adjustments to an authentic, denominationally structured syllabus. In early-nineteenth-century England and Scotland, the established Churches imposed a pattern of studies relevant to the preparation of their ordained clergy. In England, for example, biblical studies were regarded as fundamental, because of Article 6 of the Thirty-nine Articles. Patristics (originally called dogmatic theology) and symbolics were justified because of the authority of the early, undivided church. Reformation studies (including the study of the Articles) and liturgy (including the study of the Book of Common Prayer) elucidated the standpoint of the Church of England. Evidences, or apologetics, reflected the Anglican interest in a rational natural theology, inherited from Aquinas.

The necessary adjustment could be made very swiftly. Merely by eliminating the study of the Articles, and slightly adjusting the weight and orientation of the subject matter in other courses, the whole of this syllabus could be apparently deconfessionalized. But the cost to the unity, coherence and sense of urgency of the syllabus was much greater than the slight sacrifice of an already controversial source of denominational allegiance seemed to entail. By abandoning the study of the Articles (the confessional basis), and by failing to find an independent justification for the residual curriculum, English theological study inflicted a grievous wound upon itself, from which it is still manifestly suffering. It has failed, in a word, to find a means of studying the doctrinal substance of Christianity.

Defective though the Articles may have been as a source of denominational coherence (and it is to be remembered that the Book of Common Prayer and the Ordinal also belong, with the Articles, to the foundation documents in the Church of England), they do, none the less, contain treatments of the central doctrinal substance of the Christian faith, the doctrine of God, of the atonement, of justification and of the Church. Because, however, the Articles also contained denominationally committed material, even in their central sections, and because, in the past, persuasion and propaganda had played a larger part than criticism in the way in which this material had been handled, they had to be sacrificed in the interests of the consensus. In short, on the basis of the practical compromises out of which modern syllabuses of Christian theology have arisen, it has been found convenient to omit entirely what, in denominational syllabuses, gave unity and coherence to the whole, namely the convictions of contemporary Christians.

The gap created by this omission is made the clearer when one marks the various surrogates which have taken the place of the study of doctrine. Although the study of the Bible, of the Fathers, or of modern theologians or philosophers is supposed to be justified on the same grounds as any other literary, historical or philosophical discipline, 'biblical theology', 'dogmatics', 'the creeds', 'modern theology' or 'philosophical theology' are, as every modern teacher of these disciplines knows, invested with the urgency and contemporariety of living belief. All too soon students of theology grow impatient when the course of study appear to stray from 'relevant' questions (i.e. matters of immediate interest and concern to contemporary believers) into 'mere antiquarianism' or 'logic-chopping'. My argument is that this regrettable impatience is, in large measure, the product of a falsely aroused expectation that the use of ordinary literary, historical or philosophical methods will contribute directly to the resolution of the central doctrinal problems of Christian believing. The fact that such methods can and should be applied to Christian history, literature and belief is not in doubt; nor that the results of such enquiries constitute *part* of the critical consideration of Christian belief. But what Donald MacKinnon has spoken of as 'a system of belief' cannot be studied in its integrity unless some way is found of examining the nature and implications of the claim that Christian belief constitutes an inner unity. And that means, at least, some approach to that discipline which is spoken of normally as doctrinal, dogmatic or systematic theology.

Here, of course, the question of denominationalism seems to arise again. Dogmatics or systematics figures prominently in the syllabuses of German universities, not least because it is acceptable to the German public that both Protestant and Roman Catholic theological students should be trained at universities in all the disciplines and practical activities of the respective ordained ministry. Practical theology and homiletics are also part of the course provision. Similarly in Scottish universities dogmatic or systematic theology and practical theology are part of the curriculum; and locally negotiated compromises ensure the presence on selection committees of representatives of the Church of Scotland. The question, of course, arises whether or not it is any part of a university's proper activity to assist the Christian Church, or any part of it, in its tasks of clerical training or pastoral care. In England the answer would be likely to be a more resounding negative than in Scotland. But the controversial heart of the question lies in what is considered to be the nature of the subject variously entitled dogmatic or systematic theology (we leave aside the further question of practical theology, though it, too, might be justified in a similar argument). Does the study of dogmatic or systematic theology entail an uncritical or improper commitment to the propaganda of the Christian Churches?

An example will help the discussion at this point, and Christology is the most familiar. For the Christian believer the question, who is Jesus, called the Christ, is among the most personally engaging enquiries of his life. In answer to it he may want to make a series of affirmations, such as that Jesus is Lord, is Son of God, is the Lamb of God, is the future judge of mankind, all of which responses are acutely self-involving. It is indubitable that the study of these affirmations forces upon him other enquiries of a literary, historical and philosophical kind. Inescapably, therefore, he has to grasp the historical problems of the New Testament, the major moments in the history of Christology, and the philosophical problems in the use of metaphor in religious language. Each of these disciplines is likely to figure in a theological curriculum. But is there more?

It is my contention that there is, indeed, more; that the focusing of these various literary, historical and philosophical enquiries is inadequately carried out unless simultaneously the enquirer is learning to understand within what constraints christological thought operates. Christology has never figured as an isolated topic in Christian thought. What Christians mean by Christology is closely influenced by what they have meant in, for example, atonement theology, ecclesiology and sacramental theology, the doctrine of creation, and eschatology. Christology has, in other words, always been part of a larger whole. An enquiry which isolates Christology from that context inevitably distorts it.

But if that is the case, and if one's approach to Christology has been primarily historical (the Christology of the New Testament, of the fourth century, of the fifth century, of the nineteenth century, and so forth), one is at once faced by an impossible task, namely of studying the christological thought of each era of the Christian Church in the context of the whole Christian theology of that period. The sheer quantity of the material at once overwhelms the student. The development of another strategy becomes urgent.

This strategy depends entirely on the simultaneous study of the historical material, and does not replace it.[70] It consists, first, in the attempt to identify the perennial problems with which Christologies have to wrestle successfully if they are to do justice to the constraints within which successive generations of Christian theologians have worked. There are at least four such problems, and there may be more:

(1) The dependence of Jesus on God, his heavenly Father;
(2) The act of God in Jesus, and the implication of the hyphen in the term, God-man, used of Jesus;
(3) The condescension of God in his act in Jesus, his 'coming-down' or 'self-emptying';
(4) The representativeness of Jesus, as man, his Adam-hood.

Each of these problems is rooted in a strand or strands of the New Testament, and simply recurs at every period of the history of christological thought. That they do recur is the justification for speaking of them as perennial problems. Moreover, secondly, the further constraints of christological thought can only be illustrated if *all* the topics of a Christian theology are being subjected to a similar analysis; if, that is, atonement theology, the doctrine of the Church and sacramental theology, the doctrine of creation and eschatology (to name the examples used above) are being simultaneously expounded.

In other words the successful study of the elements which constitute christological belief must involve, in addition to the history of Christology, an analytic study of the constraints in which Christology operates when set in the context of 'the system of belief', or Christian doctrine conceived as a whole. There can be no valid or authentic philosophical criticism of Christian belief which has not taken the trouble to articulate the belief in the first place. The melancholy history of the isolation of so-called 'problems of the philosophy of religion' from their matrix in any particular religion is a further example of the unwillingness to spend time in elucidating what the believer intends by the propositions he utters.

If so much be granted to my argument, then it becomes important to clarify the sense in which I am not now committed to the abandonment of criticism in the interests of propaganda for the Christian Churches. Any theologian who is, as he should be, conscious of the need to struggle for his existence in a modern university ought to be extremely sensitive to the suggestion that he is, first and foremost, a religious propagandist, or that the syllabus which he teaches is taught in the interests of a religious denomination. But if he is a believer, of however tenuous a kind, how may he avoid the charge? If he holds that his belief is capable of rational criticism, and that he persists in holding it despite rational objections of many kinds, then what he teaches and what he believes to be true cannot be rigorously kept separate.

None the less, the argument for a thorough study of the doctrinal substance of Christian faith remains a cultural one. The doctrines to be studied are those to which we, at this particular time and place, are heirs, and their study may legitimately be dominated by that form which, even regionally, conveys the contemporary impact of Christianity as a factor of cultural significance. However, if he is an heir to the tradition of *Aufklärung*, which is the inheritance of Kant and Schleiermacher, the theologian will insist on the presence of at least two further conditions for the contemporary study of theology. First, he will desire the presence of a critical philosophy, developing independently of the activities of the Christian Churches, but prepared to respond when Christian theologians employ arguments of philosophical kinds (as they are bound to do) in exposition of their doctrines. Kant's willingness to pull out the theologian's plumage when his arguments strayed beyond their proper sphere, is a continuous reminder of the disciplinary function of philosophical criticism. Secondly, the study of the Christian needs the further ascesis of the 'borrowed propositions' to which Schleiermacher referred. The danger of the ecclesiastical isolation of theology, an unintended consequence of Schleiermacher's own insistence on praxis as its outcome, can be minimized by careful attention to those studies by which the concept of 'religion' is, today, clarified. Though Schleiermacher was himself innocent of any prescience of the future impact of Marxism upon the understanding of religion, the idea of correlating the non-theological with the theological interpretation of the identity of Christianity clearly lends itself to the development of a searching Christian–Marxist dialogue. A fully theological study of the substance of Christian doctrine prefaced by an exposure to the Marxist critique of religion would be in little danger of relapsing in the contrasting, but not dissimilar comforts of an ecclesiastical establishment or a religious ghetto.

III

The development of this essay has been, admittedly, systematic. It has sought to construct a plan or order for theological study, in which what is spoken of as 'systematic theology' plays a larger role than is customary in England. No student of Donald MacKinnon, however, could fail to add that he himself has devoted a substantial part of his intellectual energies to the destruction of that systematic, metaphysical idealism which has offered an illusory *sturmfreies Gebiet* to the post-Kantian theologian, and in which the concepts of 'system', 'dialectic' and 'totality' have played so seductive a role. MacKinnon's argument has been, and is, that what the Christian learns from his faith is that the study of the particular and actual takes precedence over the ideal or merely possible. My gloss on that argument is that its force assumes the impact on the student of the doctrinal substance of the Christian faith itself, for the unified study of which this essay has pleaded.

Notes

1 D. M. MacKinnon, 'Theology as a Discipline of a Modern University', in T. Shanin (ed.), *The Rules of the Game* (London, 1972), p. 164.
2 Ibid., pp. 169f.
3 Ibid., p. 172.
4 Ibid., p. 173.
5 Ibid., p. 174.
6 Ibid., pp. 172f.
7 Ibid., p. 170.
8 Ibid., p. 169.
9 Ibid., p. 166.
10 Ibid.
11 Ibid., p. 167.
12 Ibid., p. 172.
13 See D. F. S. Scott's Inaugural Lecture at Durham, *Wilhelm von Humboldt and the Idea of a University* (Durham, 1960), p. 15.
14 Kant's essay 'Beantwortung der Frage: Was ist Aufklärung' is repro-

duced, together with other contributions from the *Berlinische Monatsschrift*, in an exceptionally useful edition edited by Norbert Hinske, *Was ist Aufklärung?* (Darmstadt, 1973), cited here as *WiA*. An English rendering of Kant's essay is to be found in G. Rabel, *Kant* (Oxford, 1963), pp. 140–2.

15 *Kant's Gesammelte Schriften* (Berlin edition), volume VII (Berlin, 1917), pp. 1–116, cited here as *SF*. A very few pages of this are translated into English in Rabel's *Kant*, pp. 328–37.

16 *WiA*, p. 463.

17 *WiA*, pp. 455–9.

18 *WiA*, p. 458.

19 *WiA*, p. 455.

20 *WiA*, p. 461.

21 *Kant's Gesammelte Schriften* (Berlin edition), volume VI (Berlin, 1907), ET by T. M. Greene and H. H. Hudson, *Religion Within the Limits of Reason Alone* (New York, 1960); preface to the first edition, ET, pp. 8f.

22 *SF*, p. 23.

23 *SF*, p. 28.

24 *SF*, p. 31.

25 *SF*, p. 33.

26 *WiA*, p. 462.

27 *SF*, p. 35.

28 *SF*, pp. 59f.

29 J. E. Biester, in 'Vorschlag, die Geistlichen nicht mehr bei Vollziehung der Ehen zu bemühen', a contribution from 1783, *WiA*, p. 102.

30 J. F. Zöllner, in 'Ist es rathsam, das Ehebündniss nicht ferner durch die Religion zu sanciren?' (1783), *WiA*, p. 115. Both discussions use the question of civil and church marriage as a pretext for a discussion of the role of religion in contemporary society.

31 M. Mendelssohn, in 'Über die Frage: Was heisst aufklären?', *WiA*, p. 450.

32 *SF*, p. 23.

33 *Friedrich Schleiermacher's Sämmtliche Werke*, part III, volume I (Berlin, 1846), pp. 535–644; usefully reprinted with essays by Schelling, Fichte, Steffens and von Humboldt in *Die Idee der deutschen Universität* (Darmstadt, 1956). Page numbers refer to the Berlin edition, cited here as *GG*.

34 Critical edition by Heinrich Scholz, based on the second edition of 1830, *Kurze Darstellung des theologischen Studiums* (Darmstadt, 1969). ET *Brief Outline on the Study of Theology* by T. N. Tice (Richmond, Virginia, 1966). The paragraphs of this work are cited (in German and English) as *KD*.

35 G. Ebeling in *The Study of Theology* (London, 1979), p. 8.

36 F. W. J. Schelling, 'Vorlesungen über die Methode des akademischen Studiums', and J. G. Fichte, 'Deduzierte Plan einer in Berlin zu errichtenden höheren Lehranstalt', both reprinted in *Universität*.

37 *GG*, p. 539.

38 *GG*, p. 572.

39 *GG*, p. 584.

40 *GG*, p. 586.
41 *GG*, p. 550.
42 *GG*, p. 558.
43 *GG*, p. 558.
44 *GG*, p. 559.
45 *GG*, p. 561.
46 *GG*, p. 559.
47 *KD*, §§ 54–62.
48 F. Schleiermacher, *Der Christliche Glaube*, new edition, edited by M. Redeker, based on the second German edition (Berlin, 1960), ET of second edition, *The Christian Faith*, ed. H. R. Mackintosh and J. S. Stewart (Edinburgh, 1928). The paragraphs and subsections of this work are cited (in German and English) as *CG*. In this case the reference is to *CG* § 2, 3.
49 *KD*, § 29.
50 *KD*, § 22.
51 *CG*, § 2, 1.
52 *CG*, §§ 7–10.
53 *KD*, § 23.
54 *CG*, § 11.
55 *KD*, § 38.
56 *CG*, § 2, 3.
57 *CG*, § 2, 2.
58 *KD*, § 67.
59 Two points are made; first, the pervasiveness of the concept of 'system' in philosophical idealism and secondly, the sheer ambiguity of the term. See, for example, D. M. MacKinnon, 'Idealism and Realism: an Old Controversy Renewed', reprinted in *Explorations in Theology* 5 (London, 1979), pp. 138–50.
60 *KD*, § 1.
61 *GG*, p. 581.
62 *KD*, § 5.
63 *KD*, § 1.
64 This is the argument of Speech 5 in Schleiermacher's Speeches *On Religion*; ET by John Oman (New York, 1958), pp. 210–65.
65 E. Troeltsch, 'The Dogmatics of the "Religionsgeschichtliche Schule"', *American Journal of Theology*, vol. XVII (Jan. 1913), 7.
66 ET, London, 1976.
67 This incoherence is said by Pannenberg to consist in the fact that whereas Schleiermacher *claims* that the unity of the theological is a function of its relation to praxis, in fact the implications of the act of defining the essence of Christianity unify the disciplines quite adequately. I beg to disagree with this argument. That the concept of the 'essence of Christianity' is central in Schleiermacher's theology is not to be doubted; but it is the Christian theologian who develops the idea on the basis of his interest in Christianity's present and future. Pannenberg also seems to overlook Schleiermacher's distinction between 'philosophy of religion' and 'philosophical theology', pp. 252ff, referring to *KD* §§ 21, 22 and 24.

68 H. Hale Bellot, *University College London, 1826–1926* (London, 1929), p. 23.

69 Ibid., p. 56.

70 This condition must be emphasized in view of the objection that the study of the supposed 'perennial problems' of Christian theology, abstracted from their social, political and philosophical milieu would be highly abstract. It should be noted that the relation between the study of philosophical problems and the study of the history of philosophy poses a similar problem. Therefore it must be underlined that what is proposed is *both* the study of the central doctrinal substance of Christianity *and* particular studies of periods of the history of Christianity.

PART THREE

Metaphysics and morality

7

Optimism, Finitude and the Meaning of Life

R. W. HEPBURN

The notes to this essay will be found on pages 142–4

One way of understanding the fluid language of 'meaning' in relation to a human life is to see meaning as something to be won – often through struggle and precariously – from the sub-personal, the contingent and brute-factual. Human freedom is crucially involved; and with it the contrasts between what just happens to a person and what a person makes of what happens to him: between what is given, in nature or in human psychology, and what of value is achieved with the given: between what is merely suffered, undergone, and what a person achieves with and through his sufferings, the active stance he assumes: between what can be accounted for simply in terms of cause and effect; and what is explicable in purposive terms, having been adopted into the teleological world and made the bearer of some human project with value, intrinsic or instrumental.[1]

There is an obvious analogy with the artist who annexes features of his environment, natural substances, together with their textures, knots, idiosyncrasies and recalcitrances, 'persuading' and shaping them as they could not shape themselves. Sometimes his persuasion succeeds; sometimes it fails.

My relation to my own body, itself a material object, is the most familiar case of taking up the impersonal into the life of personhood to become the vehicle of freedom and purposiveness. At the same time it gives the sharpest reminders of the partial and temporary nature of all these meanings, these personalizings, of the material and given. Disorder in bodily functioning quickly shows me the limits of my power to adopt or annex. Recall Proust: 'It is in moments of illness that we are compelled to recognise that we live not alone but chained to a creature of a different kingdom, whole worlds apart, who has no knowledge of us and by whom it is impossible to make ourselves understood: our body.'[2] This situation easily prompts a resentment, if an unreasonable one, that my body's fate has to be *my* fate. The body is both that through which our purposings and discoveries of meaning are achieved and expressed, and that whose failures can not only frustrate particular purposings and searchings for meaning, but also bring down the organism as a whole.

Analogies to the above are to be found, more intimately still, in the complex of relationships within the life of experience itself, between the central, active, organizing ego, and our varied mental contents. With some of these contents we identify ourselves: it is through these that we articulate to ourselves the aims and hopes that constitute meaningfulness in our individual lives. Other contents are recalcitrant in varying degrees, sometimes obsessive, liable to impede or to swamp our efforts towards constructing intelligible life-plans and life-ideals. They are experienced as 'unadopted' drives, impulses or desires. One kind of meaninglessness arises when the self is 'driven' by some ill-understood, rogue desire or aversion, rather than actively exercising its autonomy. The achieving or restoring of meaningfulness here is a matter of attaining a better integrated or better orchestrated system of desires – a task primarily requiring a deepened self-understanding.

If meaning can be sought in such ways, without the denial of human finitude, and without the support of Christian or other religious hopes, what would count as excessive optimism and as excessive pessimism in relation to that search? Nothing guarantees that an individual will always have the perceptiveness and imaginative resources to discover meaning in every situation. A sense of meaningfulness has to be striven after and maintained. An excessively optimistic attitude would be one that played down the struggle and the uncertainty. On the other side, excessive pessimism would gratuitously take temporal finitude and precariousness as depriving the quest for meaningfulness of all point and value. It would stress, and put in an unfavourable light, the way in which the exercise of freedom, what we take as self-transcendence, remains absurdly tethered to our existence as members of a particular biological species. Even what we aspire after is determined by our embodied nature – our physical form. We are taken no distance at all from these particular attachments and arbitrarinesses by our search for meaning: so says the pessimist. Hence a sense of the absurd and grotesque is in place *vis à vis* our illusions of self-transcendence.

Is this pessimism 'excessive'? Certainly the scope for the exercise of freedom is modest and circumscribed. Certainly too it has often been exaggerated, in fantasies of self-making and even self-divinizing.

But it is far from nugatory. The shift from an egocentric to a moral viewpoint, for instance, is a free and momentous commitment to the universalizable, the inter-subjective, the disciplining and subordinating of arbitrary and immediate individual impulsions and appetites. This, furthermore, is only one, though the most important, of several shifts from the particular and idiosyncratic to the inter-subjective – manifest also in language, in science, in art:[3] all testifying to the reality of freedom and spontaneity of consciousness. Grant the biological specificity and 'arbitrariness' of human life: not the least distinctive feature of that life is its power to diminish that arbitrariness itself, and in some measure to overcome it. At a very basic level it remains a ground for wonderment that, in a universe unthinking and unfeeling over vast tracts of space and time, creatures like ourselves should mirror and in their freedom 'annex' aspects of nature, play upon it in their subjectivity, orchestrate their own complex natures and weave their chosen patterns of living.

In this, human life is all of a piece. There is – once again – more than a fanciful analogy between a painter who bravely incorporates, rather than omits, a recalcitrant, jarring object in his landscape – engulfing it in his total pattern – and the person seeking meaning in his life who struggles to incorporate or make sense of some personal tragedy or some moral defeat, perhaps through an extension of his sympathies and compassion, perhaps in action of a restoring or self-regenerating kind, through which he ceases to see himself simply as the person who has suffered or undergone such and such, or the person who failed to make or maintain the shift to the moral-centred viewpoint.

These reflections do not constitute a complete philosophical theory of freedom, and it is important to avoid suggesting that they do. The psychologist Victor Frankl wrote: 'Man's freedom is no freedom from conditions but rather freedom to take a stand on whatever conditions might confront him':[4] 'he always retains the freedom to choose his attitudes toward' the conditions.[5] What I have been saying comes close to that; but for a full theory a great deal of supplementation would be needed. Is the 'taking of a stand' itself 'free of conditions', or is it conditioned? The question of how to relate human action to *causality* has not been circumvented. Both 'incompatibilist' determinists and libertarians would deny that there is any freedom if the taking of a stand is itself a matter of causally explicable events, if the agent would have no power to prevent himself taking his stand. Such an agent 'chooses' to act, but could not have chosen not to...

Once more, neither optimism nor pessimism of a thorough-going kind is warranted by the data. No single attitude or evaluation is uniquely appropriate. We could defend a response of awe, or Kantian reverence, at the possibility of freedom and self-transcendence, at the scope for responsible creativity; at the malleability of our aims and forms of relationship; and at the fact that thought, with its spontaneity, can modify forms of feeling and desire. But no less justifiable would be anxiety and foreboding at the consequences of the misuse of freedom. Or a poignant sadness, through our uniquely lucid awareness of our limits and mortality. Other attitudes still are defensible; and I cannot see any single ultimately rational attitude to which they can be argued to give place.

I shall return to the general evaluation of the quest for meaning in the context of finitude, after opening up the topic of unity of being and integration.

Integration: unity of being

The task of discovering and creating meaning in one's life is deeply concerned with unity, with a struggle to unify. The well-integrated person shows consistency of character and personal resources. He does not find himself pulling down what he has just been building up; he is not taken aback by seemingly alien urges and aversions, or taken by surprise by crises of identity. Failures in unifying a life-pattern may, familiarly, be seen as failures to overcome a sense of meaninglessness: fragmentation, dispersedness are common complaints of those who feel their lives lacking in point or significance.

At the extreme end of the spectrum, dis-integration is a form of mental disorder, whether in the quietly desperate form of a pervasive sense of futility and unreality, or in the grim and violent form described by Plato as the final stage of the soul's degeneration.[6]

The ideal of integration, however, is not one that can reasonably be taken *à l'outrance*. The most meaningful life is not necessarily ruled by a single aim or inspired by a single all-unifying ideal. Again, like a work of art in one recurring account of it, a meaningful life must have its diversity as well as its unity; and the more diversity, the more challenging is the task of unifying and preventing mere fragmentariness. The pathological is touched when unity, of a kind, is reached only by a person's withdrawal from diversified aims and projects. He feels that personal unity is all too easily threatened by any but the simplest life-plan. He tries to make his life-pattern secure and invulnerable by not venturing more than he absolutely must. There are to be no hostages to fortune, no self-giving in relationships, for fear of being let down or involved in the unforeseen. A felt risk of breakdown in personal integration may be staved off also by retreat to irrationalisms – dogmatism, fanaticism, bigotry. Each of these treats a set of beliefs, attitudes, practical policies as above criticism, precisely because the overthrowing of them would entail loss of unity and hence the loss of a sense of identity and meaningfulness.

Some writers have opposed the whole project of seeking meaning in life, on the ground that the language of 'meaning' gives an arbitrary priority to activities of a sustainable and long-term kind. The project involves an intellectualization of life, which implicitly discredits the values of sense-experience with their relative immediacy, the enjoyment of colours and textures, momentary sensuous pleasures unplanned in any life-scheme. This does seem a serious point: experience can surely have value without having meaning in a sense that involves linking before with after or the subordinating of present experiences to some over-all pattern. An intolerable consequence of such intellectualization would lie in the evaluation it could suggest for the lives of the mentally handicapped, the brain-damaged and the senile, whose conceptualizing powers are diminished, and for whom the whole dimension of the 'meaningful' has little or no application. Even if such lives cannot be called 'meaningful' nor (in the sinister term) 'useful', they are not for these reasons incapable of realizing those simpler forms of value, and such persons of course merit no whit less moral respect and consideration than the livers of more meaningful lives.

An out-and-out identification of *worthwhile human life* with *meaningful human life*, and meaningful with thoroughly integrated, unified, could be taken to imply that values are ultimately *one*. Whether or not there is some point of view or some level from which this can be seen to be so, it is not true of our ordinary experience. Notoriously, the demands (for instance) of justice and of love and benevolence may conflict; and attempts to unify them conceal the unresolved diversity of values in their formulas. 'Justice is love distributed', writes Joseph Fletcher – but less wisely than Nicolai Hartmann, who wrote, 'Love and justice make fundamentally different demands'.[7]

Unity, in a word, is a regulative idea, pulling a life away from the fragmentation that can threaten to destroy its identity. It can reasonably be pursued, however, only to the point at which the costs, oversimplifications and retreats from venturesome openness to new experience, begin to over-top the gains.

Attainable and unattainable: 'invulnerable' sources of meaning

Kant's 'Moral Argument' drew its energies from his belief that only if the fundamental goals of the moral life can be thought of as attainable, is that life saved from ultimate absurdity or hollowness. And it is sometimes argued that the hazards and limits of human life, on a non-theistic view, render similarly absurd the search after the goals that would securely give meaning to a life; or that there is a grotesque gap between our meaning-conferring projects and aspirations, and the scale and the finitude of human life. This generalizing pessimism, however, presents as an all-or-nothing matter what can admit of degrees. An unattainable objective is not worth working for and imparts no meaning, if all the value of the enterprise lies solely in the final outcome, which is never to be. Other projects can be incompletable, yet yield experiences of value, or worth-while products, on the way; so that with them unattainability does not entail futility. Examples would be: coming to a fuller but never complete knowledge of another person; also cultural pursuits such as history, philosophy, natural science. Finitude, that is, does not sabotage projects which we cannot complete, so long as the *approach* has value of its own. (For another sort of counter-case, imagine a would-be virtuoso who, over a long period, cannot master elementary technique on his instrument. Here we do speak of futility.) Other meaning-conferring activities like loving a person do not derive their value from having any 'external point' (loving has none), nor require the fulfilling of some end.[8]

Love, however, is a complex and many-sided topic in the context of meaning and finitude. It is arguable how far meaningfulness could be said to be conferred on a life by (say) a protracted, impassioned pursuit of an inaccessible or unreciprocating object of romantic love. More generally, where romantic love is the organizing principle and focus of a life, a peculiar poignancy is present, since its object is irremediably vulnerable to all the hazards of human finitude, harm from without and alteration from within. The threat, that is to say, is not from incompletability or unattainability-in-principle, but from the essentially fragile nature of the object.

It is of the nature of *agape*, in contrast, never to lack an object, never to admit defeat, and to demand no reciprocity. It is thus less vulnerable as a source of meaningfulness. And invulnerability (even if relative) does seem a very frequently expressed *desideratum* for whatever is to serve as an object or focus for meaning. Even within the field of *moral* action, one can distinguish between action whose value is realized only if the course of events in the future runs as the agent hopes; action, therefore, vulnerable to disruption and loss of the goal: and (on the other hand) moral action which does not 'depend upon future outcome', where 'the demands of justice or integrity or truth' are met whatever subsequently happens, action whose significance is thus assured. I am quoting from Stewart Sutherland's paper 'God, Time and Eternity'.[9] Sutherland's examples are the death of Socrates and the death of Jesus. These display an ethical 'independence of time' – or, in relation to our present discussion, invulnerability. The main ethical point here seems sound and highly important.

In *Purity of Heart* Kierkegaard makes certain claims that are relevant to the theme of 'invulnerability', and also connect equally directly with the topics of integration and independence of time. 'To will one thing...can only mean to will the Good, because every other object is not a unity...For as the coveted object is, so becomes the coveter.' Would an evil aim equally well unify a life? No, claims Kierkegaard, 'Is not this evil, like evil persons, in disagreement with itself, divided against itself?' A life centred upon the passions certainly will not achieve this end: passion changes a person's 'life into nothing but instants and as passion cunningly serves its deluded master, it gradually gains the ascendancy until the master serves it like a blind serf!' 'Shall a man in truth will one thing, then [that thing must remain] unaltered in all changes, so that by willing it he can win immutability. If it changes continually, then he himself becomes changeable, double-minded, and unstable.'[10]

Has Kierkegaard really ruled out the possibility that commitment to an evil objective might equally well serve to unify and to furnish an 'invulnerable' source of meaning for a life? Not all moral evil consists in the fragmenting brought about by the domination of passions. In partial answer: moralists point out the essentially conflictful nature of a life committed to policies against the interests of others and in denial of others' rights. Duplicity and hypocrisy, inevitable to such a way of life, must isolate to the extent of even threatening loss of personal integration, and show the way of life to have a far from invulnerable set of objectives. (Compare Erich Fromm: 'To feel completely alone and isolated leads to mental disintegration.')[11]

This is an impressive argument against thoroughgoing, out-and-out immoral policies, where a person is hostile to the rights of everyone else. It is not, however, so obviously effective against a person who is on terms of friendship with even a few people, to the extent of removing the threat of isolation, but (with their connivance or cooperation) is hostile and unscrupulous towards others. That people do live precisely in this way is not, of course, in question: our question is whether they could achieve the unification and possession of an invulnerability with respect to their goals, like that claimed for the person who is oriented towards the Good. There is clearly a failure of unification in an arbitrary, irrational restriction of respect for persons to a group of friends (respect without which friendship and trust are impossible)[12] in contrast to the non-respecting, exploitative attitudes held towards everyone else. Such a person is very much at the mercy of his friends – has he correctly identified them; and can he trust that the boundary between friend and non-friend will remain static? The threat of isolation is not permanently disposed of. There can be no certainty that the friends, who know the immoralist's policies for what they are, will remain confident of their exclusion from the class of potential *victims*.

I do not want to claim, however, that the issue of invulnerability by itself provides a test for the meaningfulness or meaninglessness of a life-plan. Were it to happen, against the empirical, psychological odds, that a person combined a high degree of integration and resilience with a high degree of malevolence or ruthlessness, the former features would do nothing to improve the moral quality of the latter. In so far, therefore, as a judgement on a life, as meaningful, incorporates a moral evaluation, such a life would fail the test of meaningfulness, though its policies were well-unified and resistant to change from outside pressures.

Meaning and the moral life

It has become abundantly clear that the relations between the search for meaning in life and the demands and ideals of morality are complex, fluid and not always coincident. They invite further illustration.

It is possible, for instance, for an intense concern with personal meaning to become a form of egocentricity or even a state of self-obsession. Again, an individual's search for meaning can lure him into an exaggeratedly *aesthetic* view of his life – once more in tension with the moral viewpoint, and giving a higher priority to the satisfactory shaping of his life's pattern than to moral requirements that would sometimes break through the pattern and intrude upon its unified projects. Indeed, from the moral point of view, self-criticism is essential to the project of discovering personal meaning. It is needed to guard against adopting a style of life, a mode of unifying one's life-plan, which implicitly denies full moral respect for the persons of others, and casts others in subordinate roles in the agent's organically unified personal drama. Supposing a person says: 'To respect the autonomy of others is not compatible with, not harmonious with, my individuality and chosen style of life, on which my sense of life's meaning depends.' I claimed above that if that is not an acceptable line of self-justification, it is because we recognize that the point of view of morality has power of veto over certain means of giving pattern or unification to a life. Failure of the agent's own moral self-criticism does not prevent the informed spectator passing a moral judgement that rejects the agent's attempts at self-justification.

The vocabulary of meaning is without doubt very often used in closest conjunction with the moral vocabulary. It can indeed function as an important part of that vocabulary. Finding meaning can be equivalent to finding some moral initiative, even if sometimes it is no more than the taking up of an attitude such as patience or hope.

D. Z. Phillips describes how in his final illness Tolstoy's Ivan Ilych comes to see his former life as meaningless: the transition to understanding 'comes to Ivan... when he is able to care for others, when he ceases to be the centre of his world, when he is freed from his egocentricity and need for compensation'. And again: moral judgements of 'meaninglessness are unconditional judgments: they do not wait on what the unjust man wants or happens to think worthwhile'. We can judge the latter as meaningless despite what the agent himself believes. Moral judgements 'constitute a veto on purposes however magnificent'.[13]

The concern with personal unity and integration is certainly of moral relevance. It is reasonable to expect better-coordinated, better-sustained and more consistently motivated behaviour from someone with a sense of meaning and 'point' or purposiveness, than from one who feels his life as 'dispersed' and is burdened with a sense of futility. But we have not been able altogether to rule out the patterning and organizing of a life in a morally objectionable sense; and thus the two enterprises, moral and meaning-discovering, can on occasion fall apart. What we call the search after meaning contains a *many-stranded* set of objectives: from this come the difficulties.

Temporal finitude

The conception of a meaning in life that cannot be snatched away is a problematic one in the context of human finitude generally: but it is felt as most acutely problematic when brought into relation with *time* – with the constraints of human temporality. How can a person sustain a sense of the meaningfulness of his life, the sense that it 'adds up' to something, while being well aware that his life is never in any literal sense a simultaneously achieved whole, like a durable and surveyable object, actualized and present?

Some models and metaphors would make it altogether impossible to think of life as significant if it is subject to temporal passage. Suppose that the only genuinely 'real' or actual phase of one's life is the present: the rest of the would-be meaningful structure is lost in the past – no longer exists, or else has the non-existence of the future. Once that line of thought gets under way, the present too suffers erosion towards an extensionless instant – all we really have. There is no room at all for 'significance'. How could the vanishing edge of an instant-present have or fail to have meaning?

Again, suppose, on a different model, that the past is allowed a reality; awareness of it does not guarantee *meaning*. In some cases a person may not so much possess his past, as be possessed by it. He may be enslaved to remembered actions, be haunted by them with shame or remorse or a sense of failure. What is realized is not a sense of worthwhileness, of value retained or built up, but of imprisonment or of paralysis: a sense of futility also, because the troubling events are indeed past; and the weight of that too-well-remembered past impedes any constructive attempts in the present. For example: he sees himself as, in his essence, 'the person who harms everyone he loves'. His life does not lack pattern, but it is a pattern that destroys or denies meaning in the sense that includes worthwhileness.

So we have sampled two extremes. In the first, one feels too remote from one's past; and in the second too close to it. Against these very different threats, various consolatory reflections have been offered, reflections of varying reasonableness and soundness. Let us try to appraise a sample of them.

What can be said, first of all, against the claim that life attenuates to the vanishing instant of the present? Whitehead once wrote: 'There is no Nature at an instant.'[14] The processes and dynamic patterns, the sub-atomic events that make up physical matter, take time to constitute themselves. Still more obviously, one can argue, there is no life and *a fortiori* no rational life at an instant. Our very ability to raise the question, and to be anxious about meaning, presupposes that rational reflection works in a remarkably extended present (alternatively, in a still effectual and existentially relevant *past* as well as in the present). Rational reflection necessarily involves the using of language, learned and retained over time, and the holding together of arguments that take time to articulate and appraise. If, as I am suggesting, the idea of living in the 'strict' present, and of attenuating a person's sense of his own being towards that dimensionless limit, is an incoherent idea, it cannot logically be incumbent on us to realize it, or to see our lives in terms of it as unable to bear meaning. *Human* reality is not life-on-that-limit. Human reality sprawls and spreads over its past and extrapolates its projects – necessarily, in order to think of them *as* projects – into the anticipated future. To make these points is not, of course, to deny the undeniable – that there is ample room in every human life for regret at the passage of time and the losses it brings, and at the limited power of memory to make its synopses: but they check the deeper and ungrounded pessimism that sees temporality as incompatible with meaningfulness. On the contrary, the past can be drawn upon in the constructing of the sense of one's life's meaning. The human past is not altogether lost or unavailable.

On the one side, again, was the nightmare of the unavailability of anything but the present instant (and 'availability' consorts uneasily with the idea of a vanishing, instantaneous present as much as with the pessimist's idea of the past!). On the other side was the problem of a past that domineers and paralyses. Achieving release from the obsessive past is in great part a task of individual psychology rather than philosophy, though it can be made unnecessarily difficult by misleading philosophical models of the mind. This happens, for instance, with the person who interprets the pattern 'harming everyone he loves' as revealing what he takes to be his individual, unchangeable essence. To remind oneself of the 'recessiveness' of the self – of its freedom – is to realize that the very discerning of trends and patterns in one's past can be an occasion for effective resolution to modify them, to take account of them, and thereby not to remain their victim or prisoner.

Our past is not adequately represented as simply a set of contingent occurrences correlated with states of clocks and calendars, together with their alluvial deposit in memory-traces. Such a representation would offer little hope to anyone who asks: 'Where in all this is meaning to be located?' Rather, an important part of the operating of freedom is the active ranging of the mind over its memory-store, the resolute revival of memories we have been shunning, and the selective ordering and re-ordering of memories – not merely in order of occurrence, but in groupings that show us the dominant concerns that define our character, show where our fundamental satisfactions lie, and so provide direction and meaning. Reverting again to the theme of freedom and self-transcendence, we can say that the interpretation, the *placing* in our developing conception of our own life, of any particular event or phase is always revisable, in the light of new exercises of our freedom. In Max Scheler's words: 'the whole of the past...never ceases to present us with the problem of *what we are going to make of it*'. The active revival of memories 'so far from being a factor in the "stream of psychic causality"...interrupts this stream...liberates us from the determining power of' our past as sheer succession of events, subject only to contingent cause–effect relationships.[15]

The measure of transcendence of the present moment which we have been discussing, and the possibility of a sense of meaning being linked to a sense of continuity and transformation of patterns and themes, does not do anything to mitigate the depression of those who say: 'When my life is over, whatever meanings and values it realized will also be gone from the world.' In *The Will to Meaning*, V. Frankl, whose approach to questions about the meaning of life is confessedly 'optimistic', offers consolation on the following lines. 'In the past', he writes, 'nothing is irrevocably lost.' Rather, all is 'preserved and saved'. 'Once [a person] has fulfilled a meaning, he has fulfilled it once and forever.' The therapist can assure a dying patient that 'in the past nothing is lost, but everything is stored as though it were safely deposited in a store-house'. Similarly, in *Psychotherapy and Existentialism*: 'As soon as we have succeeded in actualizing a potentiality, we have transmuted it into an actuality, and thus rescued it into the past.'[16]

One hesitates to criticize any line of thought which actually brings solace to the troubled. But solace will not be reliably effective if it is not soundly based. Some of these reflections are, of course, irrefutable. The hazards and uncertainties of what is potential and future are indeed replaced by achievements, now past – achievements that are unchangeable *because* past. As 'achievement' rules out 'futility', so being past does not entail being futile. What can be challenged is the metaphor of the 'repository' or 'store-house', the metaphors that see all meaningful acts and events as 'rescued' and 'safely stored' in the past, even after the person's death. The unwarranted implication of these metaphors is that the past meaningful contents have their own independent mode of being (not simply that of memories active or ingredient in the living subject's present thought and action – as discussed above), such that it is almost logically conceivable that they might be revisited and recovered. For why else do we deposit objects for safe storing, or take comfort from the assurance that they are 'safely stored' or 'rescued'? The metaphors build an exaggeratedly optimistic interpretation upon those necessary truths about the past.

The pathology of problems about meaning

'The moment a man questions the meaning and value of life, he is sick.' That is Freud's most memorable comment on the problems of the meaning of life.[17] It is false, but a useful exaggeration. Psychological and philosophical interpenetrate here. Concern about questions of meaning and futility can of course be genuinely philosophical and moral, but underlying it in particular cases, as we have already noted, there may also be an important measure of psychological malaise: the proportions and interminglings are indefinitely variable. Discerning the extent to which a person's anxieties about meaninglessness and futility are pathological is a necessary condition of understanding how they can be tackled and possibly mitigated. It is not only on moral grounds that discriminations have to be made between ways of imparting meaning to life. Some ways, some attempts, can be seriously faulted for concealing or exacerbating psychological disorders rather than relieving them.

A striking and persuasive psychological contribution to this topic can be found in the work of Fairbairn and Guntrip on schizoid personality. Summarizing certain aspects of this will not be a digression. A deep sense of futility stands out as a recurrent symptom of the schizoid personality, whether manifested in intense psychological illness, or in a set of much less intense, long-term tendencies and dispositions. Crucial in its formation are factors dating from very early life, especially the failure of a mother to convince her child of her love. The child feels equally convinced that 'his own love for his mother is not really valued'. Disturbance occurs at the early 'oral' phase, with the consequence that 'not only does [the child] feel empty himself, but he also interprets the situation' as his having 'emptied his mother'. He has a sense of powerful 'anxiety over destroying his libidinal object'. Not surprisingly, such a person has great difficulty in emotionally giving. He has constant need for solitary replenishing of his emotional store. His failure to relate himself satisfactorily to outer objects promotes a 'tendency for the outer world to derive its meaning too exclusively from the inner world' – an inner world that seems to promise some security but cannot provide it reliably. The same failures prompt him to construct a 'false self' and to play roles, roles that at the same time he secretly disowns. Since the schizoid person fails in his relations with other persons as objects of his love, he sees his very love as destructive: consequently his internal objects, thoughts etc. become libidinized. But his overmastering feeling remains one of futility and emptiness. 'All interest in the world around fades, and everything becomes meaningless.' 'The very existence of the ego may be compromised.'[18]

Philosophers concerned about the topic of the meaning of life would be ill-advised to ignore this account. Philosophical analysis may have steered too far from the psychological; for it is clear that some strategies for finding meaning are pathological, in that they unwittingly accept or even reinforce some features of schizoid personality, and may make it harder rather than easier for a person to recognize it for what it is. They may, on the contrary, prompt him to intellectualize still further what is basically a condition not of intellectual origin. Any encouragement, for instance, towards the intense development of the inner life in terms of private symbolism or 'meaningful' personal mythology would also intensify the failure with object-relations, and could well serve as a mere palliative over the sense of meaninglessness and futility – a superficial and no doubt temporary palliative. This would furnish no more than a screen behind which to retreat to the confirmed 'false self'; and withdrawal would become the more deeply established. This is not at all to condemn any and every tendence of the inner life or concern with meaning, for that in a healthy context, morally and psychologically, is very much concerned with relations with others, and is not in its nature necessarily narcissistic. All that is being said is that it could very easily become so, in a person with a schizoid personality structure; and that where this structure is more than mildly present in a predominantly healthy person, the philosophical approach will not be sufficient to cope with whatever sense of futility is present. Pessimism here can be not simply a function of realizing vividly the fact of common human finitude, but it may have deeper roots. The therapeutic work of tracing the very early origins of a schizoid sense of futility, so that for the first time more satisfactory object-relations can be established, would be in fact (for such a person) a necessary condition of making a start on a psychologically healthy and morally mature concern with meaning and value. Only then, for instance, can the taking of moral initiatives *vis à vis* other persons be seen as imparting meaning to the agent's own life. Only then is the connection broken between the act of giving and the suffering of an intolerable loss of resources, and even a threat to his own personal being. Only the psychological–therapeutic and the philosophical *in combination* can effect the rescue so much needed by a person in this predicament.

It is one of the most poignant testimonies to human finitude – 'absurdity' if one prefers the word – that the earliest and brief phases of life can so powerfully determine the structure of the decades that follow them, and that great toil, perplexity and distress should be necessary to unravel them and to rebuild a life, so far as that is possible, with a rational and creative rather than a destructive and irrational – or plain false – meaning or pattern.[19]

Meaning and the cosmic setting of human life

The topics I have so far chosen to discuss have centred on the individual's attempts to win a sense of meaningfulness in applying his freedom to order and integrate the constituents of his personal life. Men and women also look outwards, however, and attempt to relate themselves and their projects to a much wider context. Human rationality and the religious imagination persistently prompt us to reckon with, or take account of, the cosmic setting of human life.

If now this wider sphere is brought imaginatively alive (I am thinking once again, in non-theistic terms), the earth seen as only a temporary home of life in an expanding universe, what must be the impact on questions about the meaning of life? Must it not be overwhelmingly pessimistic?

Some philosophers claim that there is something gratuitously self-tormenting and self-depreciating about taking this cosmic or 'absolute' perspective as authoritative – a perspective from which our activities and powers can easily seem to attenuate to vanishing point, to total futility. This perspective, they argue, is in no way authoritative: on the contrary, to take it up is irrelevant and pointless. Vilification from this perspective has no claim to be taken seriously. To say: 'Ultimately human existence in its cosmic setting is meaningless' is to utter only a veiled truth of logic. All meaning is created or 'projected'; and although nothing prevents us projecting it on to all sorts of human-scaled tasks and their achievement, it naturally cannot find positive work to do in relation to the remote regions of space and time, in which no human activity can make any difference.

In reply, it could be said that words like 'gratuitous' and 'pointless' are too strong. There *is* something diminishing to man in cutting out altogether such ventures of imagination and evading their unflattering implications. The capacity of imagination to extend our view and to extrapolate from our activities and enjoyments here-and-now to future times and remote spaces constitutes part of our distinctiveness and dignity as persons. It means, on the other hand, that we are vulnerable to a sense of tragic constraints, limited intelligibility and the unalterable contingency of value.[20] The outcome, nevertheless, does not have to be a thoroughgoing pessimism. A tragic sense of life is very different from a blank depression. It combines a recognition of the chanciness of life, the ultimate and uncompensatable waste of value and a resolution to live the best life available within these limits.

Let us sample a few more particularized arguments on these themes.

Grant that from the 'absolute perspective', or *sub specie aeternitatis*, all value attenuates to zero, *nothing* matters: then this fact (the fact that *sub specie aeternitatis* nothing at all matters) does not matter either.[21] How are we to interpret this argument? We can distinguish an optimistic and a pessimistic reading of it. First the optimistic: we take the conclusion to mean, 'The fact that from that perspective all value goes out of the world does not constitute any impediment to giving one's attention and effort to what (seen doubtless from some other viewpoint) *does* matter'. In other words, we can afford to say 'Forget the view *sub specie aeternitatis*'. On the pessimistic reading, we are left with nothing mattering at all. That is, the view *sub specie aeternitatis* does uniquely reveal how things stand; and from that point of view all 'mattering' (having of value, being of importance) is annihilated. Certainly then if nothing is of any consequence or value, neither is this value-annihilating viewpoint of importance. But that fact does nothing to restore value to anything. So there is no shrugging off the appeal to the view *sub specie aeternitatis*. Things are not as they seemed before the appeal.

All depends, then, on whether or not the view *sub specie aeternitatis* is in fact uniquely revealing. If it is not, then we could grant that it does not matter that values vanish when they are seen from that viewpoint. I want to claim that the movement of mind which leads towards it (by way of questions about the 'cosmic place of man') is not arbitrary and pointless, but neither is it finally revealing or authoritative. It is certainly not authoritative when carried to its logical (maybe it should be 'illogical') conclusions. Illogical in that it may well be true of any value realized by any person, other than an omnipotent and eternal deity, that there are shifts of viewpoint which cause that value to attenuate and finally to vanish altogether. This may not, however, amount to any demonstration of the 'ultimate valuelessness' of the subject-matter. For a suggestive, though limited analogy: a painting has a 'best viewing distance' and it can be made to seem valueless if viewed from a remote viewpoint. Value cannot be restored to it through a synthesis of viewpoints (an incoherent notion), nor by a viewpoint-less appraisal – which is no more coherent.

In *The Meaning of Meaninglessness* G. Blocker considered the question, 'What will it matter 5,000 years from now?'. From the 'absolutist standpoint' things do indeed seem senseless and absurd. But 'the objection to the supposed meaninglessness of things *sub specie aeternitatis* is simply that we live here and now, not elsewhere or nowhere 5,000 years hence'. The absolutist view 'has no greater claim to truth than the engaged point of view...' 'If we were constantly engaged in some immediate point of view, meaninglessness would never enter our experience.'[22]

This is worth saying, though as it stands it is a little facile and incomplete. It lurches overmuch towards the optimistic pole. True: meaningfulness of a kind can very often be assured by reducing the span or scope of our awareness; but beyond a certain point (not constant) trivializing is entailed by this meaning-protective reduction. Think of someone who knits individual stitches with care and satisfaction, but ignores the shapelessness of the 'garment'. Again, it is not arbitrary or gratuitously self-destructive that we seek to take a longer view, to take account of the wider context. We are not moles or slugs. But as with the painting, so with the human drama: there is a best distance or distances, and beyond these – necessarily diminishing importance and point. One such distance, obviously, is the participant's 'meaningful' standpoint itself, human making, working, thinking, person relating with person. Secondly, there is the view from the standpoint of terrestrial evolution: life annexing mere brute matter, mentality and purpose annexing mere biological existence; the extraordinary series of levels of complexity and the emergence of qualitatively different modes of being, that culminate in our self-placing in the process, in the light of which we can hold the whole process to be 'meaningful'. But we cannot, I think, equate the evolution of terrestrial life with some more grandiose conception of a *cosmic* evolution, despite the temptation to do so, to which philosophers sometimes succumb.

Some writers speak predominantly of *giving* a meaning to.... Others speak of *finding* meaning in, or finding the meaning of.... I think it best to say that there is both creating or projecting and discovering of meaning.[23] Some of our attempts to see meaning in given sets of events are successful, others not. I cannot accept the optimism of Blocker: 'the tragic sense of meaninglessness depends entirely on an ideal we have ourselves erected'.[24] If the metaphor of 'projecting' meaning were uniquely apt, we should not be able to understand how it could be a *task* to search for or discover meaning, or where the resistances and recalcitrances could lie.

Spatio-temporal immensity and its bearing on questions about the meaning of life

It is quite unsurprising if a twentieth-century non-theist, after immersing himself, so far as he is able, in contemporary cosmological theory, should feel strongly that the scale of the universe in space and in time threatens completely to obliterate any sense of human significance. Theism itself has always had its remedies for such threats: it is not on a scale of spatial and temporal magnitude that human existence is to be appraised, but by the revealed divine assessment of humanity testified supremely by the Incarnation, *multum in parvo*, the paradox of infinite deity become little child.

> His mother's arms Him bore, He was so weak
> That with one hand the vaults of Heaven could shake;
> See how small room my infant Lord doth take
> Whom all the world is not enough to hold![25]

Among Christian poets whose imagination has responded to the theme of the *multum in parvo* of the divine child, William Blake is specially notable. He quite explicitly celebrated minuteness. 'As against the Newtonian universe, overwhelming man's sense of his own value by awe-inspiring vistas of space and time, Blake affirmed the holiness of life, omnipresent, no less in the tiny than in the vast.'[26]

If, on the other hand, infinity and eternity are seen as symbols of the infinities of God's nature, then since God is source and guarantor of values, spatial and temporal magnitudes will not overwhelm in any way that robs human life of its meaning or value. So when Pascal ponders the recurrent image of an infinite sphere whose centre is everywhere and whose circumference is nowhere, in this, he concludes, we have the greatest sensory presentation of God's omnipotence; and 'our imagination loses itself in the thought'.[27]

If, now the theistic consolations are called in question, a sense of desolation and lostness may well be prompted by attempts to 'place' humanity amongst nature's immensities. In a poem called 'At a Lunar Eclipse', Thomas Hardy described the curve of the earth's shadow over the moon:

> And can immense Mortality but throw
> So small a shade, and Heaven's high human scheme
> Be hemmed within the coasts yon arc implies?...
> Is such the stellar gauge of earthly show?[28]

Physical minuteness implicitly challenges here the theistic logic of *multum in parvo*. If our planet is as small as the eclipse shows it to be, can the events upon it have any great significance? In more recent years, the image of earth as a spaceship without base or objective to its journeying has expressed a still more intense desolation. Yet there remain other remedies to check an out-and-out pessimism – some of them common to theism and agnosticism, some more appropriate to the latter.

Against the intimidating vision of nature's vastness can be set the visions of minuteness: as well as the macroscopic, there exists also the microscopic. Any comparison of size that dwarfs us can be matched by a comparison that makes us enormous. As a yardstick of significance, therefore, neither comparison carries any more authority than the other. 'What is man in nature?' Pascal asks: 'a nothing in comparison with the infinite, an all in comparison with the nothing, a mean between nothing and everything'.[29]

Various recent discussions of the issue of size and significance converge in the judgement that although certainly no inference about the high importance of human affairs can be drawn from the scale and cosmic setting of human life, equally certainly no trivializing of it can be inferred either. Much relied on as a restorative is the simple insistence that size and human value are incommensurables; that no degree of the former can annihilate the latter.

More adventurous responses, however, are possible, for some

temperaments and for some types of imagination. The thought of immensity can be interiorized or imaginatively appropriated, attached to a sense of 'expansion of being'. 'Away with boundaries...!' 'All these constellations are yours, they exist in you...'[30] For many poets, to span the great magnitudes in perception and imagination is to possess them, to assimilate them, to be in one way *equal* to them and aesthetically to enjoy them rather than be crushed by them. Compare also, for a nineteenth-century Idealist example, Schopenhauer on the sublime:

> ...if the heavens at night actually bring innumerable worlds before our eyes, and so impress on our consciousness the immensity of the universe, we feel ourselves reduced to nothing ...But...there arises the immediate consciousness that all these worlds exist only in our representation...The vastness of the world...now rests within us. [We are] not oppressed but exalted by its immensity.[31]

In another no less lyrical movement of the mind, the novelist John Cowper Powys expressed a different way of responding to the spatial immensities. They are taken this time as a mysterious and thrilling background to the human scene. He thinks of a townscape – bricks and mortar, smoke, tree-branches: but also, and astounded, he points to the 'tiny patch of clear sky over there, between that tree-top and that chimney, which, small as it is, goes on and on and on and on, without end, for ever and ever'. It is part of a 'spectacle...[a] vision that is beyond the power of our brain...to understand...': 'simply infinity...an enigma that thrusts itself out of our universe altogether and into a region of mystery'. It is the 'everlasting background of the chances and changes of our whole life...' No religious 'dogmatic explanation' can be found for 'this undying wonder'. 'The mere fact that the infinite sky surrounds the smallest detail of our life makes the mystery of that life *even if we are annihilated at the end of it*, as satisfying as it is insoluble.'[32]

What is obvious from this sample of responses is their great variety: no simple, decisive pessimistic depreciation of human life is entailed by the thought of cosmic immensity and the scale of human life. Rather, there remains scope for creative imagination to fashion its self-affirming response.

Consider, finally that powerful image mentioned a little earlier, human life likened to a spaceship, irretrievably pointed away from its home planet toward alien regions. It is a desolate image: but is the sense of desolation justified? It is – to the extent that the image makes vivid the inhospitability of the regions beyond our immediate life-supporting environment, and the inevitability of our end. But the image also suggests, misleadingly and with inappropriate poignancy, that just as a lost spaceship has (or once had) a home, earth, from which it is now cut off, so earth itself and we human beings upon it are, in an equally grim way, forever distancing ourselves from...from what? – presumably from some home that is really or permanently ours. Nothing however fills the gap in the analogy. Earth *is* home to us, in a way the spacecraft is not for the astronauts. The analogy therefore misleads as a picture of the human predicament and thrusts an excessive pessimism upon us.[33]

Death – a critique of some metaphors

Few things are harder than to contemplate the thought of death, including one's own death, without a choice of language that expresses either excessive optimism or excessive pessimism. Some examples, first from optimism. Since my death is not an event I can experience, the world to me is always a world I occupy: so in the sense that matters most to me I can think of myself as immortal. Alternatively, the thought of death should be no more dreadful than the thought of a cadence in music: death rounds off my life rather than devastates it. In contrast, from the viewpoint of pessimism, death has been seen as annihilating in advance the point of any present human action. Whatever is done in its shadow is as good as undone again. The years of my life are nothing in number to the endless centuries before and after. Non-existence furnishes, as it were, a vast frame for the picture of my life – a life that, in that setting, shrinks to vanishing-point.

All of these characterizations seem to me to mislead and over-simplify. Death is so unique and fundamental a feature of the human predicament, that we are unlikely to find a single image or formula that will sum up its significance for us. Metaphors and images we certainly need, but a plurality of them, correcting their individual one-sidedness.

First, some points can be made against the excessively pessimistic interpretations. The thought or illusion of immortality does not accompany every human action and project, or therefore enter necessarily into our sense of their value. If the thought of finitude and death does cast sadness over our activities, it can be only because we value these activities in themselves, and regret the thought of the limits that death imposes on our engagement in them and our enjoyment of them. If they did not have value, we would not regret those limits. But there is no valid inference from recognizing the limits imposed by death to the thoroughgoing devaluation of the activities. Undeniably a powerful sense of regret that the limits are there and are irremovable can pervade a person's experience and even swamp his enjoyment of the value his activities intrinsically possess. But the task of coping with anxiety, foreboding or sense of insecurity is again a matter of individual psychology rather than of the philosophy of value. This task can be hard, but the obstacles are not logical or metaphysical.

Thought about one's own death seems peculiarly liable to cast up inappropriate implications. Attempts to think of the world continuing after my death, and of others continuing to experience it after I cease to have a place among them – these can take on an excessively forlorn or desolate tone, through my implicitly seeing myself as still the spectator of the continuing terrestrial scene, though unable to rejoin it – even in the act of telling myself that I shall no longer exist to spectate anything or to feel excluded from anything. In a parallel fashion, excessive sadness is often imparted to the thought of the final disappearance of mankind as a whole. Again it is imparted through the vague suggestion of a ghostly mind regretfully spectating the absence of humanity and the loss of its achievements, its treasures and store of memory. But no one will spectate that loss or experience it as loss.

To correct the image is at once, however, to be in danger of lurching to the opposite pole, to a brash optimism. The loss will be a real loss, a tragic waste of value; and the absence from the world of even an individual is the loss of something irreplaceable and unique, whether his potentialities were realized or thwarted.

Consider then, those excessively optimistic images of death. If mortality and finitude are accepted, it seems to be more sensible to deny oneself the vocabulary of 'immortality' or 'eternal life', even though these expressions can be given senses compatible with the recognition of mortality. It is true that death itself cannot be experienced; but ageing and dying can be experienced, and a person's regrets about stages in the lives of younger friends and family which he will not see can be perfectly well-grounded regrets. One may use the expression, 'the immortality of the soul' to indicate no more than an acceptance of death freed from selfish obsessions, that is, a mode of life and experience here and now. But it is also true that the contexts which established the webs of implications and associations for the expression were contexts in which this life was by no means thought to be all, nor death the final horizon of the individual's experience. Misleadingness can hardly be avoided in trying to cut the phrase free from these connections.

Michael Frayn in his *Constructions* (1974) develops the metaphor of death as cadence. 'The dynamic of tonal music comes from its progression towards a cadence... ' Even the 'simplest and most direct pleasures of life – conversation, making love, going for a walk – all depend upon [the] elaboration of structure towards a cadence'. 'Death is the cadence to life. The structure of life is polarized and given meaning by its culmination in death.' (Here is precisely the opposite claim from the pessimist's lament that death destroys all meaning.) We do not say 'that a play is futile because eventually it ends. That a play ends, and that life ends, is, on the contrary *of the essence*.' Nothing 'enriches life as much as the certainty of death'. (That does not, however, prevent Frayn from writing that, though 'our mortality is the condition of life's painful sweetness', the cruelty of that condition is more than we can bear.[34] I shall comment here only on the arresting metaphor of cadence.)

Without doubt there are human lives well-fulfilled and ample enough to allow the developing of their 'thematic material', so that 'cadence' and 'death' are in their cases nearly interchangeables. The metaphor is inept, however, for a great many pain-racked and premature deaths, where death is not a completion, but much more like a forceable breaking off of the music. More generally, in music a cadence takes account of what has gone before, is mindful of it. It is not simply a stopping, a petering out, the terminus of a decline; least of all is it an abrupt cessation imposed by forces external to the music itself. In these various respects the metaphor of death as cadence is euphemistic as a description, though suggestive and valuable as an ideal, a *focus imaginarius*.

Through the balancing and mutual correcting of images we can come nearer to focusing on death, accepting the irremediable insecurity and provisionality of human existence, with their sadness, but without dramatizing them into life-destroying fantasies and nightmares. We may see in that very human fragility an occasion for wonderment: exchanging, if we can, fear and resentment at the certainty of death for wonder at the life which it will close.

Exaggerated pessimism over human finitude often takes its origin from an equally exaggerated set of oppositions between distinctively human life, with its aspirations, on the one hand, and the provision of non-human nature, on the other. The pessimist may see himself as in essentially alien hands, believing that he can conceive and long for a context for living – 'elsewhere', in which properly human values would be realizable. Our actual condition, however, is very different from the pessimist's caricature. The imagination, impatient as it is with limits, nevertheless (as we noted at the start) draws its own resources, and draws them successfully, from nature perceived. Our images of paradise are selective renderings of the nature we know here and now – the same nature that checks and frustrates us. Even Samuel Palmer's visions needed trees, apples and sheep. It is only as dwellers among the objects of the world that we come to have the value-experiences we do have, for those experiences are object-directed, and phenomenologically the values are apprehended as *in* the objects of nature. Yet the values we find in the objects are no less dependent on the beings we are ourselves, on our sense of scale, our necessary interest in all analogues to human life and the human form, wherever found, our sense of ourselves as moving objects in a terrestrial landscape. The values brought into being thereby, the experiences realized – are essentially the result of a cooperation of man and non-human nature: the universe would not contain them, were it not for our perceptual–creative efforts, and were it not equally for the contribution of the non-human world that both sustains and sets limits to our lives. To realize that there is this cooperative interdependence of man and his natural environment checks the extreme of pessimism by showing our earth-rootedness even in our aspirations. There is no wholly other paradise from which we are excluded; the only transcendence that can be real to us is an 'immanent' one.[35]

Notes

1 To avoid making this chapter excessively long, I have not included any recapitulation of recent writings on its themes. I attempt to follow a suggestion of the editors that I 'build upon' my earlier papers, 'Vision and Choice in Morality' (first published in *Proceedings of the Aristotelian Society*, Supplementary volume xxx, 1956), and 'Questions about the Meaning of Life', *Religious Studies* 1 (1966).

2 M. Proust, *The Guermantes Way*, I; ET by C. K. Scott-Moncrieff (London, 1967), p. 408.

3 Cf. J. N. Findlay, *Values and Intentions* (London, 1961).

4 V. Frankl, *The Will to Meaning* (New York, 1969; London, 1971), p. 16.
5 V. Frankl, *Psychotherapy and Existentialism* (New York, 1967; London, 1970), p. 3.
6 Plato, *Republic* VIII and IX.
7 J. Fletcher, *Situation Ethics* (London, 1966), p. 99; N. Hartmann, *Ethics* (Berlin, 1926; ET S. Coit, London, 1932), vol. II, p. 272.
8 Cf. F. C. White, 'The Meaning of Life', *Australasian Journal of Philosophy*, 53 (1975), 148–50.
9 S. Sutherland, *Proc. Arist. Soc.*, LXXIX (1978–9), 119f.
10 S. Kierkegaard, *Purity of Heart* (Copenhagen, 1847; ET D. Steers, London and Glasgow, 1961), pp. 58, 45, 53.
11 E. Fromm, *The Fear of Freedom* (London, 1950), p. 15; quoted Anthony Storr, *The Integrity of the Personality* (Harmondsworth, 1963), p. 36.
12 Cf. Charles Fried, *The Anatomy of Values* (Cambridge, Mass., 1970), ch. 5.
13 D. Z. Phillips, *Sense and Delusion* (London, 1971), pp. 56, 60.
14 A. N. Whitehead, *Nature and Life* (Cambridge, 1934), p. 48; cf. R. G. Collingwood, *The Idea of Nature* (Oxford, 1945), p. 146.
15 M. Scheler, *On the Eternal in Man* (Leipzig, 1921; ET B. Noble, London, 1960), pp. 40f.
16 Frankl, *Will to Meaning*, pp. 74, 120; *Psychotherapy*, p. 39.
17 S. Freud, *Letters*, ed. E. L. Freud (London, 1961), p. 432.
18 W. R. D. Fairbairn, *Psycho-Analytic Studies of the Personality* (London, 1952), pp. 10–19, 50f.
19 Harry Guntrip's *Psychoanalytic Theory, Therapy and the Self* (London, 1971) offers further material on the same themes. The schizoid tendency, in whatever degree it manifests itself, involves lack of assurance about one's 'viability as a person'. A patient typically says, 'I haven't got a real self'. 'We are faced with a human being who has lost psychic unity' (*Psychoanalytic Theory*, pp. 185, 170).
20 On the 'contingency of value', see A. M. Quinton, 'Tragedy', *Proc. Arist. Soc.*, Suppl. vol. XXXIV (1960), 162–4.
21 Cf. T. Nagel, 'The Absurd', *Journal of Philosophy*, LXVIII (1971), and in *Moral Questions* (Cambridge, 1979).
22 G. Blocker, *The Meaning of Meaninglessness* (The Hague, 1974), p. 75.
23 Particularly illuminating here is David Wiggins, 'Truth, Invention and the Meaning of Life', *Proceedings of the British Academy*, LXII (1976).
24 Blocker, *Meaninglessness*, p. 113.
25 Giles Fletcher the Younger, *Christ's Victory and Triumph* (Cambridge, 1610).
26 Kathleen Raine, *William Blake* (London, 1970), pp. 50f.
27 B. Pascal, *Pensées* (Garnier edn., Paris, 1948), p. 87.
28 T. Hardy, *Works*, vol. XIX (London and New York, 1903), p. 81.
29 Pascal, *Pensées*, p. 88.
30 G. Bachelard, *The Poetics of Space* (ET M. Jolas, Boston, 1969), pp. 183–90. Bachelard quotes O. Milosz, *L'Amoureuse Initiation* (Paris, 1910), pp. 155 and 64.
31 A. Schopenhauer, *The World as Will and Representation*, I, § 39; (ET E. F. J. Payne, New York, 1958, I, p. 205).

32 J. C. Powys, *In Spite of* (London, 1953), pp. 240, 236ff; italics in original.

33 For a different discussion of the image, see W. Barrett, *The Illusion of Technique* (London, 1979), p. 134.

34 M. Frayn, *Constructions* (London, 1974), §§ 109–15. In the same book, Frayn also makes the point that human life is not lived on the razor edge of the present.

35 On treating psychological states and their objects as equal and reciprocal partners, see Wiggins, 'Truth, Invention and the Meaning of Life', especially section 5. On 'immanent transcendence', see Karl Jaspers, *Philosophy*, vol. 3 (Berlin, 1932; ET E. B. Ashton, Chicago and London, 1971), especially pp. 113ff, 116f, 119ff.

8

Practical Necessity

BERNARD WILLIAMS

The notes to this essay will be found on page 152

I remember a Joint Session of the Aristotelian Society and the Mind Association, held at the University of Hull in 1972, when I took the chair for a symposium entitled *The Euthyphro Dilemma*, in which Donald MacKinnon was the first speaker. He opened his remarks by reading a translation of the closing lines of Sophocles' *Trachiniae*, ending:

> ...Maiden, come from the house with us.
> You have seen a terrible death
> and agonies, many and strange; and there is
> nothing here which is not Zeus.

These strange words, delivered with deep intensity in Donald's great black voice, drove out almost everything else, and anything I may have said, or the other symposiasts, and indeed a great deal of what Donald himself went on to say, have been obliterated by them. Joint Sessions are not normally occasions for pity and terror; the one occasion I have known on which such a note was struck, it was struck by Donald MacKinnon. He has always had respect, and yet no fear, for the less domesticated areas of moral experience, and indeed, for those areas of experience – as that paper, and its opening quotation, illustrated – which can make the concept of morality itself seem domesticated.

I am not going to take up any large, threatening or reconciling, Sophoclean theme. I want to pick out some threads which do indeed eventually lead to those themes: they are threads in a complex web of ideas which may be labelled 'moral necessity' or, more broadly and significantly, 'practical necessity'. Both the Sophoclean hero and the Kantian moral agent are controlled by conceptions of what they must do, conceptions which are closer to one another than is usually supposed. This paper offers some preliminary considerations which may help in bringing out their nature.

It will be best, in fact, to start from *ought*. Whatever other *oughts* there may be,[1] we can recognize the use of the expression in the conclusion of deliberation: 'This is what I ought to do' expresses the agent's recognition of the course of action appropriate, all things considered, to the reasons, motives, and constraints that he sees as bearing on the situation. The sense of that conclusion is what gives the sense to the question it answers, 'What ought I to do?'

Of that conclusive *ought*, it is clear that it is *practical*, in the sense that not only is it concerned with action (as opposed, for instance, to being concerned merely with desirable states of affairs), but the action in question has to be one possible for the agent: here, at any rate, 'ought' does imply 'can'. Such an *ought*, moreover, is *exclusive*, in the sense that if I cannot do both A and B then it cannot be the case both that I ought to do A and that I ought to do B.[2]

It will be very obvious that this *ought* has nothing specially to do with moral obligation. The question: 'What ought I to do?' can be asked and answered where no question of moral obligation comes into the situation at all; and when moral obligation does come into the question, what I am under an obligation to do may not be what, all things considered, I ought to do – if only (though this is not the only case) because I can also be under a moral obligation to do some other and conflicting thing.

It is worth mentioning that there are important second – and third – person uses of what is, in effect, this *ought*, in contexts of advice or of discussion about what it is reasonable for an agent to do. So used, this *ought* also reveals itself to be *relative*, in a broad sense, to the projects, motives, and so on of the agent in question. If A tells B that he ought to do a certain thing, but A is under a misapprehension about what B basically wants or is aiming at, then A's statement, if it is intended in this sense, must be withdrawn.

Ought is related to *must* as *best* is related to *only*. This seems to be a general feature of these terms, even in contexts which are quite removed from either practical deliberation or morality (such as those in which inferences are expressed). In this connection, Prichard was mistaken when he claimed[3] that the *ought* which was 'hypothetical' on an agent's intentions expressed a necessary means to the agent's reaching his objective. What is characteristically expressed by telling someone that he ought to do X if he wants Y is that X is the best or favoured means to Y; if it is the only means to Y, then he *must* do it if he wants Y.

I shall not try to say anything here about the supposed distinction between categorical and hypothetical imperatives, a topic which has generated an exceptional degree of confusion. All that is needed here is the obvious point that if A wants X, and if it is true that if he wants X he must do Y, it does not follow that he must do Y; that will follow only if, further, X is the thing that he must pursue. So in the first person: if I conclude that I must do Y, rather than merely that I ought to do Y, then it is because I have come to see not just that it is the only means to some end I have, but that it is the only thing I can do.

However, this raises a difficulty. It is very rarely the case that there is only one thing that I *can* do, and that all the alternative courses of action are – in a phrase which invitingly begs all the questions – *literally* impossible. Usually, the alternatives are vastly more costly, or are excluded by some moral constraint (which is itself identified in terms of what one cannot do, rather than in terms merely of what one ought not to do). Various considerations that come into deliberation uniquely single out the preferred course of action; the others being ruled out, one is left, and that is what I must do. The difficulty is that this seems a correct description of any deliberation which uniquely selects a course of action – and that is any deliberation which issues in a unique conclusion, that is to say, any deliberation which is successful. So it is obscure why any conclusive practical decision should not be of this form, and so every deliberative *ought* be a *must*. But it is not true that every *ought* is a *must*. Why not?

That question might have had only a rather boring answer: for instance, that *must* is selected when the preferred course of action is very markedly favoured over others, or the weight of reasons overwhelmingly comes down on one side. But the boring answer is wrong. Necessity is not the same as decisiveness. Nor, any more than in any other field, is it the same as certainty. It may only be after a long and anxious consideration of appealing alternatives that an agent concludes that a certain course is what he has to take, and he can have that belief while remaining uncertain about it, and still very clearly seeing the powerful merits of alternative courses.[4]

The language of rhetoric and deceit makes the same point. Those who are bargaining, blackmailing or threatening, often say that some inadequate response from the other party 'leaves them with no alternative' to taking unpleasant action. These are simply words, but something is to be learned from what the words are meant to suggest. These people would certainly not make the same point if they merely said that this action was, by a long way, the one that they most favoured. Some notion of impossibility of the alternatives, or of the agent's incapacity, is at work. What he is pretending to is what we are trying to locate, and that is something other than the mere decisive weight of one set of reasons.

Any notion of necessity must carry with it a corresponding notion of impossibility, and any statement in terms of one can no doubt be recast in terms of the other, but it can make a difference which of them presents itself first and most naturally. In the case of deliberation, there is a significant distinction between two ways in which necessity may enter the structure of my thought. It may be the case that I conclude that I have to do X, for instance because it is the one item to which I attach overwhelming importance, or because, unless I do it, everything will be ruined. Then, as a consequence of this, Y and Z, alternatives to X, are no longer alternatives – they are things I cannot do. Alternatively, it may be the impossibility that bears the priority. Y and Z, the only alternatives to X, are things which I cannot conceivably do, and are excluded; then consequently, X is what I must, or have to, do.

One point which is implicit in this way of expressing these structures of thought is that there is nothing special about *moral* necessity, in any of the narrower senses of that expression which relate specially to such things as obligation; though there may be a broader sense – an ultimately broad sense, relating to character and action – in which all such necessities are moral necessities. Among the constraints, requirements, and impossibilities which an agent recognizes are those that obtain for distinctively moral reasons. In particular, the class of things that he cannot do, come (more or less) what may, includes those things he cannot do to other people, courses which are excluded from his range of alternatives, in virtue of what he sees as those people's rights.

In face of 'I must', the other alternatives are no longer alternatives: they become things one cannot do, as, in the other structure, an alternative was something one could not anyway do, and that consideration *led* to 'I must'. But how can an alternative be, or become, something I cannot do? Here someone will reach for the weapon of distinguishing senses, and will speak of there being two or more senses of 'cannot', that which signifies whatever rejection is embodied in the agent's deliberation, and that which expresses what one 'literally' cannot do. But why should we resort to such a distinction of sense? Why should this kind of *cannot* be anything other than *cannot*? It has, for instance, the central feature that if the agent is right in thinking or concluding that he cannot do a certain thing, then – subject to an important qualification which I shall come back to – he will not do it.

It may be said that this is because the situation involves practical acceptance, not because it involves necessity. Thus if an agent accepts that, in the practical sense, he ought to do X, he will – in general, and leaving aside problems of *akrasia* – do X. But this is because people generally (at least) do what they see most reason to do, and not because of the mere implications of *ought*. Thus an adviser may say that A ought to do X and, at least if the adviser speaks in the mode of relative practical advice, he surely says the same thing as A would say if A said 'I ought to do X', and something that would be contrary to A's saying 'I ought not to do X'. But clearly 'A ought to do X', even in this relative practical sense, has no predictive implications about what A will do; and if A does something else, the adviser can stick by his original judgement in the form of saying 'A ought to have done X'.

But this precisely brings out a contrast with *must*. There are indeed some significant ambiguities in this area, and some things that an English speaker may mean by 'you cannot' have nothing to do with prediction at all: thus it may mean 'you are not permitted to'. If the agent does what, in this sense, the observer thinks that the agent 'cannot' do, the observer can retain his original opinion. But the situation is different with the necessity of relative practical advice. The most distinctive English formula for that is perhaps 'You will have to', or, indeed, 'You have no alternative'. These formulae, unlike *must*, have a past tense, but it is an impressive fact that their use in the past tense indeed implies that the agent did do the act in question. Nothing stands to the practical *must* as *ought to have* stands to *ought*. The language of other persons, advisers and observers, itself has features that should encourage us to take seriously the idea that the language of practical necessity is not related by a mere pun to the 'literal' uses of *cannot*; the *cannot* of practical necessity itself introduces a certain kind of incapacity.

What I recognize, when I conclude in deliberation that I cannot do a certain thing, is a certain incapacity of mine. I may be able to think of that course of action, but I cannot entertain it as a serious option. Or I can consider it as an option, but not in the end choose it or do it. These incapacities can be recognized also by the observer. The observer can, moreover, recognize a dimension of this sort of incapacity which the agent himself necessarily cannot register in his deliberation: that the agent could not think of this course of action at all, that it could not occur to him. The agent can, so to speak, edge up to that condition in his deliberation, in dismissing something as 'unthinkable' – but thinking that something is unthinkable is not as direct a witness to its being unthinkable as is being incapable of thinking of it.

I said that there was a qualification to be made to the claim that if an agent has this kind of incapacity to do X, then he will not do X. What should rather be said is that he will not do it intentionally. The agent who sincerely says that he cannot do a certain thing, or that he must do something else which excludes that thing, cannot mean without qualification, and no more can an observer, that the world will not contain his doing that thing, for it is certainly compatible with the beliefs of both agent and observer that the agent might do the act unintentionally, for instance in ignorance.

It may be this point, if anything, that is meant by contrasting this incapacity with what an agent 'literally' cannot do. What an agent *simply* cannot do, he cannot do even unintentionally, and that presumably extends to everything that he physically cannot do, so long as the physical, as in our present modes of speech, remains contrasted with the psychological. The incapacities we are concerned with here might broadly be labelled 'incapacities of character', though this needs considerable extension and refinement to cover all the cases introduced by the model of deliberation. These incapacities do not extend to the unintentional, and in many of these cases it is possible that the agent should do the act unintentionally, and his so doing will not falsify the claim that he was incapable of it. Of course, if the act seems only superficially to be unintentional, and we believe that it is not an accident relative to the description of the action under which we thought him incapable of it, that he did it, then what we believe is that he is really capable of it, though he may not believe that himself.

It might be suggested that a more radical asymmetry can be found between these kinds of incapacities and standard 'physical' incapacities, with respect to the notion of trying; on the ground that if A cannot physically do X, then it follows that if A tried he would fail, whereas this is evidently not true of the cases under consideration, or at least of all of them. But it is simply not correct that this follows from 'A cannot physically do X', since in many cases there is not anything that counts as trying; while if the world were different enough for something to count as A's trying to do X, then perhaps it would also be a world in which he could do X. The most that follows from 'A cannot do X' is that either it is true that if he were to try to do X he would fail, or it is impossible that he should try to do X; and that disjunction follows equally in the case of the incapacities which are under discussion here.

We are subject to the model that what one can do sets the limits to deliberation, and that character is revealed by what one chooses within those limits, among the things that one can do. But character (of a person in the first instance; but related points apply to a group, or to a tradition) is equally revealed in the location of those limits, and in the very fact that one can determine, sometimes through deliberation itself, that one cannot do certain things, and must do others. Incapacities can not only set limits to character and provide conditions of it, but can also partly constitute its substance.

To arrive at the conclusion that one must do a certain thing is, typically, to make a discovery – a discovery which is, always minimally and sometimes substantially, a discovery about oneself. The context, nevertheless, is one of practical reasoning, and that fact, together with the consideration that the incapacities in question are, in a broad sense, incapacities of character, will help to explain the important fact that this kind of incapacity cannot turn away blame. I mentioned before the dishonest use of 'I have no alternative'; part of its deceitfulness may lie in this, that it carries an implication that the speaker cannot be to blame for what he will now do, since there is only one thing for him to do. But the fact that an agent has come to that point, if he has, is certainly not enough to turn away blame. The incapacities we are considering here are ones that help to constitute character, and if one acknowledges responsibility for anything, one must acknowledge responsibility for decisions and actions which are expressions of character: to be an expression of character is perhaps the most substantial way in which an action can be one's own.

Conclusions of practical necessity seriously arrived at in serious matters are indeed the paradigm of what one takes responsibility for. That is connected with the fact that they constitute, to a greater or lesser degree, discoveries about oneself. The thought that leads to them, however, is not for the most part thought about oneself, but thought about the world and one's circumstances. That, though it still needs to be understood in philosophy, is not a paradox: it must be true, not only of practical reasoning but more generally, that one finds out about oneself by thinking about the world that exists independently of oneself. The recognition of practical necessity must involve an understanding at once of one's own powers and incapacities, and of what the world permits, and the recognition of a limit which is neither simply external to the self, nor yet a product of the will, is what can lend a special authority or dignity to such decisions – something that can be heard in Luther's famous saying, for instance, but also, from a world far removed from what Luther, Kant, or we, might call 'duty', in the words of Ajax before his suicide: 'now I am going where my way must go'.[5]

Notes

1 I have tried to say something about one other, at least, in '*Ought* and Moral Obligation'; in *Moral Luck* (Cambridge, 1981).

2 Its being exclusive does not follow immediately from its being practical, in the sense of implying possibility. The simplest connection between the two properties requires also what I have elsewhere called the 'Agglomeration Principle', to the effect that if A ought to do each of two things, he ought to do both of them. See 'Ethical Consistency', in *Problems of the Self* (Cambridge, 1973).

3 *Moral Obligation* (Oxford, 1949), p. 91. Prichard says that 'the thought which we wish to convey' is that if the agent does not do the act in question, his purpose will not be realized; indeed, 'this is what we really mean by our statement'.

4 It is important that an agent's conviction in serious matters that some course of action is what he must take, may carry all the more authority if he arrives at it not only after deliberation but reluctantly, as in the case of Sir Thomas More.

5 Sophocles, *Ajax* 690, translated by John Moore. The Greek exactly catches the nature of the practical necessity, which is in this case utterly personal, by expressing it impersonally: literally 'for now I am going where it must be gone'.

9

Religion, Ethics and Action

STEWART SUTHERLAND

The notes to this essay will be found on pages 166–7

I

The thesis of the essay has arisen through a dissatisfaction with the general adequacy, rather than the detailed competence of much that has been written about the relationship between religion and ethics. In fact if the central thesis of the essay is acceptable it will have application in a number of areas of the philosophical discussion of ethics, and in the elucidation of a variety of different patterns of ethical beliefs other than those which are associated with religious beliefs (e.g. Marxist or humanist ethics). This essay, however, will be limited in scope to the relation between ethics and religion. By way of introducing the issue which is the concern of this discussion, I shall sketch in broad outline a position which I wish to reject.

According to some it is a reasonable expectation that within the context of ethics at least, the secular lamb may learn to lie down with the theological lion. That when it comes to what is good and right, what is wrong and malevolent, believer and unbeliever may well agree with one another. Stealing is bad, and promise-keeping is good, respect for persons is fine, and *agape* might be marginally finer! If it is a matter of doing, rather than believing, there is much 'common-ground' between the sacred and the secular. Indeed, so great is the overlap in present enlightened times, that believer and unbeliever may in some instances be said to 'share an ethic', although disagreeing in ideology. If this assumption is correct, then it would also be true that the ethic, or ethical content of, say Christianity, is detachable from the theology without essential loss. (*Mutatis mutandis*, of course, the same might be said to hold for Marxism, and so on.)

The popularized version of this is to be seen in claims like 'I don't believe in the God in the New Testament, but I do accept the ethical teaching of the Sermon on the Mount', or 'Jesus may not be the Son of God, but he has given us an admirable picture of the moral life'. Alternatively, as exemplified in occasional appeals to us by Church leaders to mend our ways in the national interest, there is at times a desire on the part of a number of Christians to suggest a shared ethic between themselves and non-Christians. That there is such confusion in ecclesiastical or anti-ecclesiastical utterance, is not perhaps remarkable: what is less than desirable however, is that philosophers should either endorse it or at least create the conditions in which it flourishes.

One of the most widely discussed endorsements of this view is to be found in R. B. Braithwaite's 'Empiricist's View of the Nature of Religious Belief'. He writes of the need to:

> Discriminate between assertions belonging to one religious system and those belonging to another system in the case *in which the behaviour policies, both of inner life and of outward conduct inculcated by the two systems are identical.* For instance, I have said that I take the fundamental moral teaching of Christianity to be the preaching of an agapeistic way of life. But a Jew or a Buddhist may, with considerable plausibility, maintain that *the fundamental moral teaching of his religion is to recommend exactly the same way of life.*[1] [My italics]

The same, of course, presumably applies to the humanist, although it might have been instructive for Braithwaite to consider this. For, of course, there is as yet, no developed humanist mythology of stories attached to humanist ethics as the stories of creation and incarnation are attached to Christian ethics. Is humanism then simply religion *minus* something or other? Braithwaite's account of the differences between various religions is that they reside in the different 'stories' which are attached by a 'psychological and causal' relation to the way of life shared between religions. Whatever faults or merits belong to Braithwaite's view, he does at points adopt the position which I wish to contest. This thesis I shall refer to as 'the transferability of ethical beliefs'. It is also to be found clearly stated in the following extracts from R. L. Cunningham and R. M. Hare respectively.

> Most analysts believe that with the possible exception of knowledge of duties to worship God, there is no reason to believe that a theist has any advantage over an atheist. Put more concretely: if Brown is today a theist, and tomorrow

> becomes an atheist, his knowledge of what is right or good will not have changed, except possibly with regard to duties of worshipping God; and if Jones is today an atheist, and tomorrow becomes a theist, his knowledge of what is right or good will not have changed, except possibly with regard to duties of worshipping God.[2]
>
> This notion that Christianity has got to be *different* is a very difficult one to overcome. But I ask, suppose that someone produced an interpretation of Christianity that could be accepted by the best humanists, would this necessarily be a bad thing? We have, at present, in our civilization, a very absurd state of affairs. I constantly meet people who evidently share my outlook on life quite as much as my fellow-Christians do, and who yet call themselves humanists. It is a source of scandal to me that I am supposed to make myself different from these people, some of whom I very much admire.[3]

II

Apart from specific endorsement by Braithwaite and others the plausibility, and for some the desirability, of the view that an ethic can be shared between people adopting different theological or metaphysical positions, has been strengthened by its compatibility with a variety of alternative beliefs, philosophical and otherwise. These are, or may be, variously called upon to support the general thesis of the 'transferability' of ethical beliefs. Since they may contribute by confused amalgamation to the support of this view, it would be valuable to distinguish between them, and to show that in most cases they offer no formal support at all, and indeed are compatible with the 'non-transferability of ethical beliefs'.

(1) Much contemporary discussion of religion and morality focuses upon the question of whether they are independent, and one most popular version of this view is to insist that morality is autonomous. If by this is meant that one may have a systematic and coherent set of moral beliefs which are not derived from a logically prior set of religious or theological beliefs, then that is quite compatible with the 'non-transferability of ethical beliefs'. If, however, acceptance of the autonomy of morality precludes the possibility of anyone appealing to religious premisses as part at least of the justification for a

particular moral decision, then that view *is* incompatible with the 'non-transferability' thesis.

(2) The views of Hare and Braithwaite gain plausibility from the fact that there is an undoubted prima facie plausibility in assuming that Christians and non-Christians can share some responses to certain ethical situations. 'Of course', it might be insisted, 'both atheists and believers are concerned in the work of Oxfam or Amnesty International.' ('Christian Aid' I should think is always a troublesome one for the strict humanist conscience.) 'Certainly both believers and unbelievers observe the duties of citizens and show concern for the well-being of friends.' It is easy to see how this prima facie identity of responses loses its prima facie quality when set in the context of Hare's initial claims in *The Language of Morals* that a man's moral principles are most reliably ascertained by seeing what he does.[4] The risk is that this can lead to confusing what a man does with what he is seen to do. My point here is not related to the distinctions either between hypocrisy and sincerity, or between public and anonymous well-doing. It relates rather to the acceptability of equating what a man does with what is public and observable. This assumption I regard as central to most 'transferability of ethical beliefs' views, and I shall return to it later.

(3) One traditional way of distinguishing between Christian and non-Christian ethics has been to insist that there are specific and distinctive religious duties. On this view, most ethical beliefs may be shared between believers and non-believers, but Christianity also enjoins a number of additional duties, what Hume called 'the whole train of monkish virtues'. My version of the 'non-transferability' thesis neither requires nor prohibits 'additional' virtues.

(4) A further long-standing view of the matter is to concede what would actually take quite some establishing, that certain distinctive virtues or ethical beliefs historically took root in Christianity, but now belong, in full flower, equally to secular world-views. The 'non-transferability' thesis would question whether, even if the historical hypothesis were true, these ethical beliefs could be absorbed without mutation into a non-religious pattern of beliefs.

(5) A fifth way of determining the relation between religion and morality which accepts the 'transferability' thesis, and which is favoured by a number of believers including some philosophers is expressed in the following remarks from William James: 'The chief of all the reasons why concrete ethics cannot be final is that they have to wait on metaphysical and theological beliefs.'[5] The lack which metaphysical and theological beliefs finally help us avoid is

described rather graphically as follows: '...in a merely human world without a God, the appeal to our moral energy falls short of its maximal stimulating power'.[6] James refers in this context to a distinction between 'the easy-going' and 'the strenuous mood', but I do not think it would be true to say that he saw the mood of secular ethics to be easy-going whereas the mood of religious ethics was strenuous; rather that in the end he endorsed St Paul's characterization of moral effort: 'I do not do the good I want, but the evil I do not want is what I do.' The 'non-transferability' thesis is not content to distinguish between religious and secular ethics purely in terms of either motivation or additional stimulation of some sort.

These various possible views which can be combined with the 'transferability' thesis each have the apparent advantage of providing none the less a possible clear basis for an account of the relationship between religion and morality. They help clear the apologetic air and let us see the issue of a distinctive Christian ethic as one of whether Christianity adds anything to an already agreed and shared set of moral beliefs. It may add something either in terms of content – additional 'religious' virtues or duties – or in terms of the formal justification for such a set of beliefs. In either case, at least the argument is clearcut, and one knows how to proceed. However, with one exception each of these points can, if so desired, be interpreted in a manner compatible with the '*non*-transferability' thesis, and as such does not necessarily provide support for the 'transferability' thesis. The one possible exception is Hare's insistence that we look at what a man does in order to determine his moral beliefs. If this is extended to become the much stronger assertion that what makes an action the action that it is, is a matter of what may be seen by others, then that is not compatible with the 'non-transferability' thesis. Also, in so far as each of the views outlined can be interpreted to support the 'transferability' thesis, I do wish to contest such interpretations.

III

One basis for rejection of the 'transferability' thesis, is to question the view that if Christian ethics is distinctive, it is so by being secular ethics +X and that if one doesn't like X, then one still may be said to share a great deal if not almost all of what constitutes an ethic, with a believer. But the real source of the trouble is that many philosophers and theologians seem not to have asked a series of questions, starting with: 'What is it to share an ethic?'

One of the features of morality which the discussion of universalizability has underlined is that if two people are said to share a moral view, or more broadly, an ethic, then we should expect of them that in relevantly similarly situations they will perform the same (≡ similar) actions. This raises an issue to which despite the considerable volume of writing on the subject of actions, comparatively little attention has been given: when are two actions the same (≡ similar)? There are here far-reaching questions about the description, identification and individuation of actions, which seem to me to be unduly neglected. If sharing an ethic involves doing the same actions in similar situations, what guidelines can we give as to when the same actions have been performed? Clearly by 'the same actions' here, we do not simply mean bringing about the same states of affairs. Either pressing a button in one's car, or stopping the car, getting out, walking to the garage and pulling on the handle, may result in the garage door being opened, but during a thunderstorm there is the world of a difference between the two actions.

Elizabeth Anscombe, amongst others, has pointed out that even where we may take ourselves to be talking of the same, in the sense of 'identical' action, that action may fall under a number of different descriptions.[7] These descriptions may all be compatible with one another. For example, 'talking', 'giving a lecture', 'discussing Locke on Primary qualities', may all be accepted by Bruce as descriptions of what he is doing. All may be included in an account of his intentions, each compatible with the others and arranged in some sort of scale so that one might correctly say 'the intention *with* which Bruce is doing X is to give a lecture on Locke on Primary Qualities'. To say this is to express the view that Bruce is aware of his action falling under this implied description and also of it falling under other descriptions upon which this depends for its fulfilment, for example, 'talking', or 'giving a lecture'. There are two possible grounds here for rejecting the view that Bruce is engaged in three different activities. On the one hand one could argue that the three descriptions are related to a single slice of the spatio-temporal continuum, and that this is what constitutes the numerical identity of this particular action. On the other hand one could argue that the individuation of one single action falling under three different descriptions is possible only if these descriptions do each generate a possible statement of intention and that one can relate these intentions to one another in something like the manner specified above.

I do find difficulties with the first of these two means of giving an account of why we are dealing here with one action rather than three. The problem has its source in the temptation to regard actions as being rather like physical objects. If we do this, of course, then as in the case of physical objects, so in the case of actions, we may draw a sharp distinction between, on the one hand, the individuation of actions, and on the other, the description or characterization of actions. If I may adapt Shakespeare, 'This rose by any other word is still this rose'. One can give a comparatively uncontentious account of this, for when we are talking about *this*, we are talking about what can be individuated and re-identified by locating it on the spatio-temporal continuum of which we are a part: to characterize *this* as a rose, or to describe it by any other word is to describe what can be individuated quite independently. This is undoubtedly one of the most important features of our concept of a physical object.

If it turned out to be possible to regard actions as being rather the same sort of things as physical objects, then there would not be substantial difficulties in correlating rather different descriptions of actions with one segment of the spatio-temporal continuum. Thus we could all agree that *this* is what Johnny did although we may disagree about the characterization of what he did. Now certainly the situation is sometimes like this, but as Camus makes strikingly clear in *The Outsider*, this is not always the case.[8] The problem which Meursault poses for the judge and the public prosecutor, is not simply the problem of giving a *moral* characterization of 'what he did'. As becomes apparent in the course of the trial, the real difficulty is that of identifying or individuating precisely the action in question. Sometimes, and very often in the cases which we find most difficult to handle in moral terms, the disagreement about how to characterize an action is a disagreement about what the action in question is, that is, a disagreement about how to individuate or identify an action which is not simply an empirical disagreement about, say, whether he was standing on this rock or that, or whether he fired two shots or three.

There are many different sorts of case where the individuation of actions is not obviously a task which can precede their characterization. For example, it is true to say 'Richard Nixon deceived the American people', or that 'Freddy Flanders deceived Esmeralda Earnshaw about his intentions'. Now in each case the truth of the claim will be dependent upon how one individuates the deed or deception in question, and it is not at all clear that the deed can be individuated in the same way as physical objects can, namely through a set of spatio-temporal co-ordinates. In fact it may well be that there is a case to be made for abandoning the notion of the individuation of an action, but I do not see a clear way of establishing such a radical conclusion. None the less I believe that it is quite evident that there are severe difficulties in the way of any attempt to draw close analogies in this respect, between actions and physical objects.

A second possible way of reconciling different descriptions of one action is through the comparison of intentions, and this can provide us with an alternative approach to the question of what constitutes sameness, in the sense of 'similarity', of actions. Initially I wish to take two general points from this. First, the fact that a number of different descriptions can correctly be given of *one* action may help loosen any inclination which we may have to argue that actions are such that there is for each action a basic or fundamental description which is *the* correct description. Second, the description or classification of Bruce's action as of type X, say, 'giving a lecture', may often depend upon what Bruce's intentions were. (Not always, of course, for one may do more than one intends; for example, people who play games with loaded guns may kill someone without intending to, or people who sign dotted lines without reading what is above them may enter into contracts to buy books on the Second World War at the rate of one per month for the next twelve years. But since my concern here is with actions which are done with specific intentions, I do not think that this will affect the points which I wish to derive from the connection in some cases between Bruce's intentions, and the classification of his action as being of type X or Y.)

Restricting ourselves then to numerically separate intentional actions, when may we say that they are similar, exactly similar, or different? In so far as similar descriptions are offered of X and Y, then we may say that X and Y are the same in the sense of similar actions. If, even in the case where a variety of descriptions is given, there is complete overlap in descriptions we may say that they are exactly similar actions. If there is little or no overlap in descriptions we are talking about rather different actions. The real difficulties, however, and the ones most germane to the 'transferability-thesis' are those where there is only a partial overlap of descriptions.

Consider the following example. Barry and Brendan are both engaged upon what prima facie seem to be the same (≡ similar) actions, say initially described as 'driving lorryloads of food to the refugee camp'. Upon questioning, the following descriptions of what they are doing are offered, respectively, by Barry and Brendan.

Barry (1*a*) Driving lorryloads of food to the refugee camp.
(2*a*) Meeting the needs of the politically oppressed masses.
(3*a*) Preparing the peasants physically for the coming revolutionary struggle.
(4*a*) Heeding the teaching of Chairman Mao.

Brendan (1*b*) Driving the lorryloads of food to the refugee camp.
(2*b*) Meeting the needs of one's fellow creatures.
(3*b*) Partially realizing the Kingdom of God on earth.
(4*b*) Obeying God's will.

Let us assume that Barry and Brendan have discussed the matter and do not see (3*a*) as in any sense a translation of (3*b*) and so on. Then it would seem both confused and misleading to suggest that Barry and Brendan were engaged upon or carrying out the same (≡ similar) actions. There are some similarities, marked by the partial overlap in descriptions, but their intentions are also expressed in divergent ways incorporating radically divergent descriptions of what they are doing. It would not be sufficient to argue that the overlap in this case in the description 'driving lorryloads of food to the refugee camp', is in itself adequate to give us sameness of action, unless this were somehow or other identifiable as 'the', or 'the basic' description of the action. But what grounds could be given to support that assertion? It would be a peculiarly laconic reply by either Barry or Brendan to the question 'What are you doing?' to offer *only* this description. Nor is it at all plausible to suggest that this description would hold the primary or pivotal position in any ordering of descriptions designed to establish compatibility of descriptions. Clearly this could not be offered in either case as an account of the intention with which they were doing what they were doing. Of course there are differences and differences. For example, Boris may give as an account of what he is doing:

(1*c*) Driving a pick-up truck full of food to the refugee camp,

and when questioned expand in exactly the same way as Barry (2*a*) to (4*a*), except that he substitutes 'pick-up truck full', for 'lorryload'. We can, however, rule this out as a non-relevant difference if it is clear that in Barry's shoes, or rather 'driving-seat', Boris would have used the lorry which was the one and only vehicle available to him, and vice versa were Barry in Boris's driving-seat. The means of transport, that is to say, is irrelevant if it does not affect the realization of the intention with which the action was undertaken.

If, however, we are confronted by Bertrand who tells us that he is:

(1*d*) Driving lorryloads of contaminated food to the refugee camp,

then we do have a relevant difference. This could be either because Bertrand is a latter-day Harry Lime who in fact does not share either Barry's, or Brendan's intentions, or because he is a black comedy Frank Spencer, who shares Barry's intentions but not the wit necessary to carry them out without creating disaster. In each case, rejection of the action as 'not the same' as that of Barry, rests upon its compatibility with the further description generated by Barry's intentions.

The point here is that some differences in description are not relevant to the question of whether, from the point of view of ethical similarity, two men are engaged upon the same action. Such 'irrelevant' differences can, I believe, be resolved into two main types:

(*a*) Differences of a factual nature about physical features of the world which could be dropped from the descriptions without altering the ethical significance of the action in question, for example, the difference between 'driving through rocky landscape' and 'driving through tropical rain forest'.

(*b*) Differences which arise in cases where a shared intention can be carried out equally well in the circumstances, by different means, for example, the difference between driving a truck and driving a van.

The former category is trivial, but the latter illustrates a general point. In attempting to decide whether the difference between descriptions at one level is significant, one should appeal to a higher-level description which makes clear whether the intentions which in part constitute these actions, are shared.

Hence I wish to suggest as an initial criterion of sameness/similarity of action, restricting oneself still to intentional actions, sameness of *range* of descriptions. Thus,

C1. Whether or not two men are 'doing the same thing' depends upon whether or not the same range of descriptions can be applied to the intentional actions in question.

Where it applies this would be a sufficient condition, but as we have seen some descriptions are not interchangeable, for example, 'Driving a van-load of food...' and 'Driving a pick-up truck load of food...'; yet as we have also noted we might not want to count this difference as significant. To rule out some divergences of this sort, I suggest a second criterion:

C2. Whether or not two men are 'doing the same thing' depends upon whether or not after reflection and discussion there is agreement between them to apply a completely overlapping range of descriptions to what they are respectively doing.

The reflection and discussion are to rule out one sort of irrelevant disagreement: this arises where the disagreement is because they have not seen that the form of words used by one is completely translatable into the form of words used by the other; for example, where by 'fellow creatures', Brendan might in fact simply mean 'fellow human beings', which then becomes acceptable to Barry. Where it applies this would be a sufficient condition.

On the other hand there are important cases not covered by either C1 or C2 for which we require:

C3. Whether or not two men are 'doing the same thing' depends upon their discovering that differences of description at *one* level are not significant because they do not conflict with agreed descriptions at a higher level.

This criterion covers the points (*a*) and (*b*) raised above, and is a sufficient condition of deciding that two men are engaged upon the same action.

A consequence of accepting these criteria is that the description and classification of actions is not a matter for observers alone: the *agent's* viewpoint is also crucial for the correct classification of actions. The sameness of range of descriptions in the actions in question implies sameness of expressions of intention, and beyond that, of course, sameness of intention. This point should make clear why an extended or more radical version of Hare's recommendation to look at what a man does in order to ascertain what his moral beliefs are, is unacceptable. I want to claim that identification of what a man does, that is, of his actions, cannot always be carried out wholly independently of identification of what he intended to do, and to state what he intended to do may not always be possible without reference to what his moral beliefs are. This does not preclude using Hare's test as a means of distinguishing hypocrisy from integrity.

The significance of this for the 'transferability-thesis', is that sameness of ethic can only be established where we have sameness of expression of intention and resultant sameness of range of descriptions of action in one of the senses C1, C2, or C3 above, from the agent's viewpoint. The 'transferability-thesis' assumes sameness of ethic, but denies the need for sameness of descriptions of actions or expressions of intention. It assumes that two men may agree about what ought to be done without necessarily agreeing about the way the world is. The 'non-transferability-thesis' insists that such a view is superficial and misleading. It is superficial because it assumes that there will be one description of an action which is, not surprisingly, always the most theologically or metaphysically neutral, and the one apparent to the most casual of observers. In so far as theology or metaphysics involve views about the way the world is this is inadequate, and that for the following reason.

Some expressions of intention have, to borrow a phrase from Nowell-Smith, a 'Janus-like' character. Expressions of intention of types (2*a*), (2*b*), (3*a*), (3*b*), (4*a*), (4*b*) have at least two aspects to them: on the one hand they betray or declare a man's preferences, interests and values; on the other hand they offer descriptions or characterizations of one's actions which entail beliefs about the way the world is – that relationships between human beings are structured on class membership, or that we are creatures of a God whose will is knowable. It is this feature of the expressions of intention of Barry and Brendan which precludes the transferability of their ethical beliefs from one to the other without loss. They cannot be said to share an ethic because in the end they would disagree radically on how to characterize their actions, and indeed in what their intentions and *ipso facto* their actions were. This does not preclude partial overlap in descriptions, but the overlap, as we have seen may turn out to be very limited indeed both in extent and significance. Nor, of course, does anything I have said preclude the possibility of co-operation between those of different theological or metaphysical persuasion: it is rather a plea not to *over*-estimate the significance of such eminently worthwhile co-operation.

Perhaps it will help clarify the general direction of the arguments which I have been offering if I indicate that they may be seen as one way of elaborating the following assertion by Stuart Hampshire: 'In this way the habits and rules of my thinking limit the possibilities of action for me. We cannot represent human conduct as detachable from the thought that directs it, as if actions were a universal system of natural signs, always intelligible on mere inspection.'[9] My difficulty with Braithwaite, Hare, Cunningham and other advocates of the transferability-thesis is that they do represent human conduct as detachable from the thought that directs it, thus providing themselves with a superficial and confused account of 'sameness of action', and 'sameness of ethic'. A rose may well be a rose by any other word, but an action is not.

If there is then a distinctiveness in Christian ethics, it is to be found initially at least in the range of descriptions of action generated by the expressions of intention to act within the 'habits and rules of thinking' of Christian belief. On this view, it is not necessary to insist upon separate Christian virtues, nor perhaps always upon the availability of moral situations in which there is no overlap of descriptions at all, although I am inclined to think that such differences will also be apparent from time to time. The hope of a pluralistic society is that there is considerable overlap of description of actions between the various groups, theological and ideological, who make up that plurality: the delusion of a pluralistic society is that there can, in ethical matters, be complete overlap or agreement.

One of the more common objections to the view which I have defended is to argue that in the case of Barry and Brendan, there is overlap if not in all descriptions of action, at least in all morally relevant factors; i.e. both bring about the same good, or pleasure, or happiness: both relieve the suffering of others. This objection makes three assumptions each of which is highly questionable: (1) only the results of actions are morally significant: a view vulnerable to many of the standard objections to utilitarianism; (2) an action is what it achieves, a view which I have contested earlier in this paper; and (3), the converse of (1), an agent's intentions are irrelevant to the ethical value of what he does, an assumption which seems to me to be plainly incredible as soon as it is made explicit.

By way of a concluding note I should like to reiterate the point that although the argument of the essay focuses upon the relationship between religion and ethics, the conclusions reached in that context have rather wider implications, the nature of which would certainly bear fuller discussion. Clearly, for example, the analysis of 'an ethic' offered above is not compatible with any attempt to draw rigid and mutually excluding divisions between judgements of fact and judgements of value. The converse of this, of course, is that the suggestion that value judgements can be derived, inductively or deductively, from factual premisses, may be equally misconceived in the assumptions upon which it depends. A further corollary of the discussion is that the conception of 'an ethic' would benefit from additional examination, for although the thesis of this essay does not commit one to the view that there are as many 'ethics' as there are thinking human beings, an elucidation of the reasons for this would be instructive. An even more general philosophical issue arising is that of the criteria for the identification and individuation of actions. In order to discuss sameness (≡ similarity) of actions one must have an account of what it is that constitutes an action. Minimally, the conclusions offered here imply that the logic of the concept of an action is rather different from the logic of the concept of a physical object. One crucial difference is that whereas one can individuate physical objects by giving their spatio-temporal location, there is no equivalent and unambiguous procedure for actions. Settling what one is talking about in referring to *this action* is a much more context-dependent business than settling what one is talking about in referring to this house, and the context may relate both to the point of view of a spectator, and to the point of view of the agent. Or again, for some purposes it may be perfectly adequate to talk of 'driving food to the refugees' whereas for others it may be necessary to talk of 'feeding one's fellow creatures'. In so far as what one is doing may be characterized correctly in a number of different ways, then there are grounds for suggesting that one may be correctly described from varying points of view as doing a number of different things. There seems to be no compelling reason why one should only be doing one thing at a time, and this essay attempts to characterize a context (the discussion of what it means to share an ethic) in which it is important to insist that, say, in driving a lorry down an unmade road one may be *doing*, not simply bringing about as consequences, a number of different things.[10]

Notes

1 R. B. Braithwaite, Eddington Lecture, Cambridge, 1955, repr. in I. T. Ramsey (ed.), *Christian Ethics and Contemporary Philosophy* (London, 1966), p. 65.

2 R. L. Cunningham (ed.), *Situationism and the New Morality* (New York, 1970), introduction, p. 31.

3 R. M. Hare, 'The Simple Believer', in G. Outka and J. P. Reeder (eds.), *Religion and Morality* (New York, 1973). See pp. 416–17.

4 R. M. Hare, *The Language of Morals* (Oxford, 1952).

5 William James, 'Moral Philosophy and the Moral Life', repr. in W. James, *The Will to Believe* (New York, 1956). See p. 210.

6 Ibid., p. 212.

7 G. E. M. Anscombe, *Intention* (Oxford, 1957).

8 I have discussed this example in some detail in 'Imagination in Literature and Philosophy: A Viewpoint on Camus' *L'Etranger*', *British Journal of Aesthetics*, 10, 3 (July 1970).

9 S. Hampshire, *Thought and Action* (New York, 1967), p. 206.

10 I should like to acknowledge the help which I derived from the critical discussion of an earlier version of this paper with R. A. Duff and A. M. MacBeath.

PART FOUR

Truth and falsehood in theology

10

Theological Realism

T. F. TORRANCE

The notes to this essay will be found on pages 193–6

The root of the traditional contrast between idealism and realism would appear to be found in our ability to distinguish between image or idea and reality, and to let one thing stand as a sign for another thing. That is a basic and natural operation of the human mind, for it belongs to the very essence of rational behaviour that we can distinguish ourselves as knowing subjects from the objects of our knowledge and distinguish our knowing from the content of our knowing. If we are unable to do that, something has gone wrong: our minds have somehow been 'alienated' from reality. In normal behaviour, however, we are not aware of ourselves in this way, for our attention is concentrated upon the objects we are handling or the objective we are pursuing. Thus in all our basic acts of perception and knowledge, meaning, as Polanyi has expressed it, is displaced away from ourselves, so that when we adopt something, sensible or intelligible, as a sign for something else our attention does not rest upon the sign but on what it indicates or points to: it is, so to speak, a transparent medium through which we operate. That is to say, the natural orientation of the human mind is, in this sense at least, quite 'realist'.

We use the distinctions, then, between subject and object, image or idea and reality, or sign and thing signified naturally and unreflectingly, although we rely upon an implicit awareness of them in all explicit rational acts, and only turn a critical eye upon them when something arises to obscure signification. Much now depends on where we focus our attention: upon idea or reality, upon sign or thing signified, and upon what we consider as a sign, something sensible or intelligible, to stand for something else. In this state of affairs the contrast between idealism and realism arises out of an oscillation in emphasis from one pole of the semantic relation to the other. The distinction sharpens into a conflict, however, when the two poles are extended to a breaking point or when the relation between them is disrupted through some dichotomy of thought. However, since the relation between idea and reality or sign and thing signified is never completely severed, there would seem to be an almost inevitable tendency in correcting one extreme position in respect of the other, for each to pass over into the other, so that sometimes idealism passes over into a form of realism and realism passes over into a form of idealism. Thus in natural science, for example, one thinks of the dialectical relation that arises out of a split between the theoretical and empirical factors in knowledge, when an emphasis upon mathematics separated from experience ends up in a mechanical and materialist understanding of the world, and when an emphasis upon sense experience ends up in a rationalist empiricism or even a conventionalism. The same problems arise in theology, as is particularly evident, in the dialectic between radically divergent approaches to the understanding of Christ traditionally characterized as 'ebionite' and 'docetic', for in modern as in ancient Christologies each tends to turn into a form of the other, or simply to appear under the guise of the other.

Let us turn back for a moment to the distinction between signs and things signified, or symbols and realities symbolized, and consider our elaboration of that distinction in the invention of formal or symbolic systems as conceptual instruments enabling us to cope with the world of our experience. We make a restricted set of more manageable things, such as words, concepts, or numbers, to represent through their various combinations an unrestricted set of less manageable things, a host of people, objects, events, relations, structures and so on, and thereby achieve a measure of rational control in our apprehension of them which enables us to reflect upon them, accumulate information, engage in public communication, and reason consistently. Moreover through this process of symbolic representation and controlled manipulation of symbolic systems we are able to extend the power and range of our thought far beyond what it would have been capable of without them and to add quite new dimensions to our knowledge.

Everything depends on the actual bearing of the signs or symbols upon the realities they stand for or refer to. If, for example, as Plato once argued, a sign images the reality it represents so closely as to be indistinguishable from it, the sign will be mistaken for the reality and fail in its function as a sign. Hence if a sign is to do its job properly it must have some measure of detachment or incompleteness or even discrepancy to allow it to point away from itself to the reality intended, in the light of which the truth or falsity of the sign will be judged. On the other hand, if the sign is merely an artificial convention or is so completely detached that it has no natural bearing on the reality for which it is said to stand, then it is empty of import or semantically useless, and all grounds for raising questions of truth and falsity are removed. In view of this argument we may make an initial generalization. An ultra-realist position, in which sign and thing signified perfectly coincide or a statement is absolutely adequate to its object (e.g. in the identification of a statement about the truth with the truth itself, or the identification of the truth of a statement with the truth of being), tumbles over into its opposite extreme, some form of nominalism or conventionalism. A truly realist position will be one in which the sign differentiates itself as sign from the reality on which it actually bears, and therein reveals a measure of disparateness or discrepancy which is an essential ingredient in its successful functioning as a sign. For true statements to serve the truth of being, they must fall short of it and not be mistaken for it, for they do not possess their truth in themselves but in the reality they serve: a dash of inadequacy therefore is necessary to their precision.

A relation of outright identity or of utter separation between sign and thing signified is not so infrequent as it might at first appear – after all, fundamentalism and conventionalism in different areas of thought are not so uncommon. More often the referential relation between sign and thing signified suffers from a process of refraction, so that the sign relates to the reality intended only indirectly. This has happened regularly in the history of thought whenever sign and reality have been construed within a dualist framework of thought, cosmological or epistemological, such as that which arises with the *chorismos* between the *kosmos aisthetos* and the *kosmos noetos* or the separation between the *mundus sensibilis* and the *mundus intelligibilis*.[1] With the inevitable change in the nature and function of the sign which such a disjunction brings, different possibilities, not unrelated to each other, emerge. Two of these are of particular relevance to theology.

When the signitive relation is damaged, the sign tends to break loose from the objective control of reality so that it bears upon it only in a free tangential manner. As such it becomes vague and ambiguous and is subject to the forces of constant change in the cultural framework in which it is employed. Since a detached, changeable symbolic representation of this kind, that is, a myth (to give it its technical name), has no more than an oblique, indirect or metaphorical relation to reality beyond itself, it inevitably becomes the carrier of our fantasies, anxieties, self-references and projections.[2] We are familiar with mythological thinking of this kind, poised upon man's own self-understanding and shaped through his own devising, not only in the pre-Christian culture of the Graeco-Roman world, but in its resurgence in the Gnostic and Arian challenges to the realist theology of the Christian Church. Mythological thinking of this kind, however, is always a by-product of an underlying dualist framework of thought involving a radical dichotomy between a realm of events and a realm of ideas, a realm of phenomena and a realm of noumena.

On the other hand, the impact of dualism has often had a divisive effect upon the sign itself, splitting it into an outer sensible aspect and an inner intelligible aspect, that is, into form and content. This is very evident, for example, in one strand of the Stoic tradition in philosophy in which a two-tier semantic structure of sign and thing signified was replaced by a three-tier structure of sign, significate, and thing, but is even more evident in the Neoplatonic and Augustinian tradition in theology. The significate (*semeinomenon, significatum*) is the conceptual content of the sign by means of which or through which as an ideal form or sign reference is made to the object or thing conceived. This form of indirect reference to reality almost always gives rise to a substitute ontology (or phenomenology). Since the significate is what is immediately signified by the sign, it tends to stand for or replace the objective reality in our thought, and thus takes on an objectified status itself. It is frequently in this objectification of ideal forms that idealism arises. But here the dialectic, which we noted earlier, comes into play. In so far as this idealism leans toward objective reality it can become a form of realism, but in so far as it leans toward the conceptual content as what is signified, it can be a form of conceptualism or even tumble into nominalism. It is within the context of this problematic state of affairs in semantics and on the ground of the epistemological dualism which underlies it, that coherence and correspondence theories of truth have continually been thrown up in the history of thought, dating back to the philosophical positions of Plato and Aristotle. What has always been at stake is a damage in the semantic reference of sign and concept to objective reality, a distorting break in the ontological substructure of knowledge.[3] The lesson that is constantly being taught is that there can be no satisfactory theory of truth within the brackets of a dualist frame of thought, for it can only yield the oscillating dialectic between coherence and correspondence. Certainly the pragmatic theory of truth may be regarded as an attempt to break out of that impasse, but all it does is to make some form of operationalism a substitute for truth. There would seem to be no way forward except through a rejecting of dualist modes of thought in an integration of empirical and theoretical factors in knowledge and of form and being in our understanding of reality, for that would import the recovery of a whole or undamaged semantic reference of sign and concept to reality, in which reality would have ontological priority over all our conceiving and speaking of it. Strictly speaking, the contrast, let alone the conflict, between idealism and realism would not then arise, nor would the distinction between a coherence and correspondence view of truth which depends on a disjunction between form and being.

However, with the above qualification in mind, and for lack of a better term, we shall use the expression 'realist' to describe the orientation in thought that obtains in science, philosophy or theology on the basis of a non-dualist or unitary relation between the empirical and theoretical ingredients in the structure of the real world and in our knowledge of it. It may be noted at this point that it was a realist orientation of this kind which Greek patristic theology, especially from the third to the sixth century, struggled so hard to acquire and which it built into the foundations of classical theology.[4] Moreover, it is a realist orientation of basically the same kind that we now find restored in the foundations of modern science (e.g. in the concept of physical law), as there have been drawn out the profound epistemological implications of general relativity for the indivisible unity of the space–time field in respect of structure and matter or form and being at all levels throughout the contingent universe.

The general position adopted, however, by large tracts of European thought in medieval and modern times has been thoroughly dualist, owing to the immense impact of Augustinian culture and of a return to Platonic and Aristotelian modes of thought. On the one hand, there predominated for many centuries an Augustinian–Aristotelian tradition in science, philosophy and theology, not least in its Thomist form, which has left a permanent mark on Roman Catholic thought. On the other hand, there has predominated in modern times an Augustinian–Newtonian tradition in science, philosophy, and theology, not least in its Kantian form, which lies behind the neo-Protestant outlook with its strong slant toward a secular culture, but which through phenomenology has now spilled over forcefully into

Roman Catholic philosophy and theology. Both these dualist traditions may be properly characterized as phenomenalist.[5] In Western medieval thought an Aristotelian epistemology, governed by the principle that there is nothing in the mind but what was first in the senses and grafted on to an Augustinian basis with its disjunction between the sensible and the intelligible, the temporal and the eternal, resulted, for the most part, in ways of thinking through the medium of images and ideas that intervened between the mind and reality, the so-called *objecta mentis*, which rendered the relation between the mind and reality or between sign and thing signified *oblique*.[6] This bit so deeply even into would-be realist epistemology that a master idea such as *adaequatio intellectus et rei* became quite ambiguous, for it could be interpreted either as the conformity of the mind to its object or the conformity of the object to the mind.[7] With the Renaissance and the Reformation the great switch from medieval to modern thought with its emphasis upon force, motion and event, took place once again on a broad Augustinian basis. Into this there flowed the dualist approaches of Galileo and Descartes with their separation yet external co-ordination of experience and mathematics which gave a mechanical slant to man's outlook upon the universe. It was Newton, however, who gave paradigmatic formalization to this development imposing upon it the massive dualism of absolute mathematical time and space and relative apparent time and space which constituted the framework within which all cultural and scientific advance took place. Within the deistic outlook upon the created order which this implied, a phenomenalist and empiricist epistemology now increasingly projected itself everywhere into European culture. Typical was the claim of John Locke that sense impressions alone provide an acceptable basis for rational knowledge, while his influential doctrine of 'representative perception' revived the old medieval notion of 'images in the middle' in the form of 'sense data' (which now look rather like idealist fictions in a would-be realist theory of knowledge). Here the notion of *data*, applied to phenomena or appearances abstracted from an objective, intelligible base, involved a confusion or conflation between what is subjectively and what is objectively given, so that the ambiguity of the 'significate' came back even more forcefully. Since it is impossible from within appearances to determine their relation to any alleged reality beyond them, Hume's scepticism was well-nigh unavoidable. Hence by way of rescuing rational and scientific knowledge from that kind of impasse Kant produced his mighty conception of the synthetic *a priori*, the strange but paradigmatic amalgam of objectivism and constructivism,[8] and so there developed the dogma, which has had such disastrous effects on many aspects of modern life and thought and not least on theology, that we cannot know things in themselves or in their internal relations, but only as they appear to us. That is to say, we arrive at the position in which it is held that the meaning of things may be found by reference back to the knowing or observing subject, construed in terms of what they mean *for him*; or, otherwise expressed, that our thought may be related to reality not through any act of direct cognition but only in an indirect or oblique way.[9] This idea that rational knowledge may be gained only by deducing ideas from our observations bit so deeply into natural science and the philosophy of science that it was claimed by positivists, such as Ernst Mach and the 'Vienna Circle' that stemmed from him, that scientific theories cannot be claimed to have any bearing upon being, or upon objective reality independent of our knowing of it, for they are no more than convenient economic conventions which we employ in organizing our 'observational data'.

So far as pure science is concerned, of course, the situation is now radically changed. One need only recall what happened to Mach's claim, in his argument with Max Planck, that since we cannot know things in themselves or their internal relations 'atoms' must be regarded as no more than convenient 'scientific fictions' (i.e. as operational 'as ifs').[10] It was completely shattered by empirical and theoretical scientific penetration into the internal relations of the atom and the grounding of atomic physics irreversibly upon knowledge of its inherent rational structure. Although the idea that we cannot know things in themselves but only in their appearances to us was quickly and vigorously rejected by the great scientists of our time (for example by Planck and Einstein who insisted that in science we are concerned to *grasp reality in its depth*), it has taken a long time to die for it has received a strange anachronistic extension to its life in linguistic and existentialist philosophy and not least in corresponding types of theology which have their roots in Kantian dualism between phenomena and noumena, or in Lessing's 'ugly ditch' between accidental truths of history and the necessary truths of reason. It is this hang-over of a phenomenalist and empiricist dualism, operating within the brackets of a deistic disjunction between God and the creation and of a mechanistic conception of the universe as a closed determinist continuum of cause and effect, stemming from eighteenth- and nineteenth-century Newtonianism, that continues to provide modern theology with its recurring problems. This applies no less today to Roman Catholic theology than to Protestant theology, for Roman Catholic theology elides the difficulties of medieval and modern dualism, as one can see very clearly in the history of thought from Blondel and Maréchale to Rahner and Schillebeeckx, and not least in the subtle blending of Thomist and Kantian ideas. Let us take the theological position of Edward Schillebeeckx as our test case, for it is particularly illuminating.

We shall confine discussion to two connected issues which affect the very basis of Schillebeeckx's theology: a *non-evidential* and a *non-conceptual* relation to God and the reality of our salvation in Christ. In classical Christian theology, such as we find in the teaching of Athanasius and Cyril of Alexandria, it was held that God is open to knowledge in himself on the ground of his own self-evidencing and self-manifesting reality. Through his Word and Spirit God brings us face to face with himself so that through faith we may know him in the light of his own self-evidence and under the immediate compulsion of his own being. That kind of immediate evidential knowledge, however, was undermined by the Augustinian–Aristotelian basis of medieval scholastic theology, in which Schillebeeckx's own thought is rooted, and was reckoned not to be possible except for the *beati*. Evident knowledge is grounded in immediate experience, for evident knowledge of something is directly caused by it and not by something else; but if it is held that there is nothing in the mind except what was first in the senses, evident knowledge would seem to be limited to sense-experience. Thus according to St Thomas the mind does not derive knowledge from hidden principles but only through the senses of the body so that the proper objects of the mind are known only as they are embodied. The intellect may rise above sense-experience but only as it actively gives the *species* it passively receives from the senses an intelligible form. Moreover, St Thomas taught that that to which the mind gives assent does not move the mind by its own power but by the influence of the will; that is, the intellect assents to something not through being sufficiently moved to this assent by its proper object but through an act of choice.[11] So far as knowledge of God is concerned, this had the effect of detaching the understanding, even in the assent of faith, from the self-evidence of God in his own being and truth, so that in the last resort faith has to rest on moral grounds and operate only with an indirect relation to God. That was the theory of knowledge which Schillebeeckx took over from his Thomist sources, but the indirect relation between the understanding and the immediate compulsive evidence of its object was reinforced by the Kantian dualism which he took over in his somewhat phenomenological approach, so that he admittedly operates with what he calls an 'inward non-evidence' in our knowledge of God and the reality of salvation.[12] Hence, like St Thomas Schillebeeckx requires something *additional* to give our knowledge of God what it lacks by way of direct evidential grounds, which he speaks of as infused grace or infused light of faith, so that it may be made in spite of non-evidence to terminate after all upon the intelligibility of God and the reality of salvation. And like Kant in his appeal to the practical reason Schillebeeckx is forced to appeal to 'moral guarantees', that is, to an experience of faith which rests on the appreciation of the knowledge of God as a value for human life, or an experience in faith which rests on the relevance of the truths of salvation to our human life.[13] Before we pass on to discuss the other issue connected with the problem, it may be noted that according to Schillebeeckx it is the tension between the inward non-evidence of the reality of salvation and the dissatisfaction of the human intellect which is essentially attuned to the inward evidence of reality, that gives rise to the reflective activity of theology as faith seeking understanding. As he understands this Anselmian principle, however, theology is a second-order activity concerned not immediately with God but with faith and its intelligible subject-matter, which takes him very close to the *Glaubenslehre* notion of neo-Protestantism and differentiates him rather sharply from the view of Karl Barth.

Fully in line with this non-evidential relation to God Schillebeeckx also operates with a non-conceptual relation to him. This is a position that Protestants can understand, especially in the post-Kantian tradition, with its cultivated contrast between the noumenal and the phenomenal and its severe refraction of cognitive relations with God. That is precisely, of course, what has been vigorously challenged by the realist theology of Karl Barth which he reinforced by an appeal to the teaching of St Anselm who, while holding that God is infinitely greater than we can conceive, insisted at the same time that we cannot have any knowledge of God or even faith without a conceptual relation to him – *fides esse nequit sine conceptione*. There is no non-conceptual gap between God's revealing of himself and our knowing of him, for God reveals himself to us on the ground of his own inner intelligibility which is the creative ground of all rationality in the universe and as such enables us to conceive and speak of him truly in ways that are ultimately grounded in God's supreme Being. Hence theology, interpreted as faith seeking understanding, is a humble enquiry into the intrinsic reason of things in God, and takes place as we allow the truth of God's own Being to impress itself on our understanding in its own inherent intelligibility, so that our judgements and statements about it are formed under its authority, that is, the authority of the *solida veritas* of God himself.[14] For a modern Thomist like Schillebeeckx operating with a basic dualism of a phenomenalist kind, it would be understandable if this position were rejected as 'rationalist' or 'conceptualist' (not least in view of the hard cataphatic conceptualism evident in some of the pronouncements emanating from the Roman Curia),[15] but that could be a justifiable reaction to St Anselm only if he split form from being and yet identified the truth of concept and truth of statement with the truth of being, which is exactly what St Anselm did not do.

What does Schillebeeckx mean, then, by a non-conceptual relation to God? To interpret him *in meliorem partem*, it might be said that Schillebeeckx wants to safeguard an empirical relation to the divine Being, in recognition of the fact that true relation to being cannot be reduced without remainder to a conceptual, let alone a linguistic or logical, relation. And that would be right, for what is at stake here is an ontological relation which cannot without error be converted into anything else. We would have to add, of course, that the empirical and the theoretical must never be divorced for they are not separable in reality or in our knowing of it. This is just where Schillebeeckx's problem lies, for he is setting a noetic and an empirical or dynamic relation of the human spirit to God in contrast. By 'non-conceptual' knowing of God Schillebeeckx means that we are quite unable to grasp divine reality in concepts and that there are 'no real concepts of God'. We do operate with concepts, to be sure, but they are creaturely constructs and have only a creaturely content. What we actually do with them, he claims, is to use them in a projective act of knowing grounded in the dynamism of the knowing subject in order to intend God beyond them altogether. The Being of God is not open to our conceptual grasp, for God does not communicate himself to us in his own internal intelligible relations nor does he lift us up to share knowledge of himself in those internal relations, except in some indirect way through the Church. That is to say, God in his own intelligible reality and existence is not directly present to us as the object of our knowledge, so that the non-conceptual and non-evidential relations have to be combined in any account of our human knowing of God.[16]

There is an important element of truth here that must be readily granted. This has to do with the fact that, as St Augustine pointed out long ago, knowledge depends on the knowing subject and on the object known.[17] That is to say, in all knowledge, not least in knowledge of God, we have to reckon with what is subjectively given as well as what is objectively given. What Schillebeeckx is emphasizing is the objective bearing of the subjectively given element: it intends the objectively given element that transcends it. In a realist theory of knowledge, however, we have to do with the apprehension of some object in its inner structure which is the source of our conceptions of it, and thus regard the conceptuality which arises in this way as having a bipolar character. It is grounded in the objective intelligibility of reality, but it incorporates also a subjective counterpart, since it is we the knowing subjects who conceive and express our knowledge of it. In this case what is subjectively given is revisable in the light of the objectively given for it is grounded in it and controlled by it. Thus as MacKinnon has said: 'The transcendent...is manifested by its intrusive presence as something continually demanding that we transform our understanding of its content more and more rigorously, as if every articulation of that content were precarious and necessarily incomplete, in order that we may *begin* to grasp what we seek to refer to.'[18] How can that take place, however, if the relation between the two conceptual poles is snapped, and indeed if the objective pole cannot be grasped conceptually at all?

In Schillebeeckx's own view such a constant transformation of the conceptual content of our knowledge of God must take place if we are not to subject God to the control of our conceptions and representations of him. And indeed it can and does take place but, as far as I can see, only indirectly through the spiritual transformation of our lives in their relationship with God in love and within the fellowship of the Church. Nor must this be discounted in any way for theology cannot be uprooted from the Christian life, although a good deal depends on how we are to regard this transformation of the conceptual content of our knowledge of God as taking place. According to Schillebeeckx (and St Thomas), as we have already seen, we require some kind of infused grace or faith, in fact an inward *lumen fidei*, in view of the evidential deficiency in our knowledge of God, which can operate within us enabling us from below, as it were, to assent to the truth in spite of its non-evidence, and motivating us to consent to the statements of the faith proposed to us by the Church for belief. In this way the infused light of faith makes up not only for the inner non-evidence of the reality of our salvation but also for our inability to grasp it in its own intrinsic reasons, that is, to grasp it conceptually. If we ask what this inner light of faith or inner illumination is, Schillebeeckx speaks of it as an inner instinct, an inner address (wordless and non-conceptual), an inward adaptation or determination of our humanity which we experience under the supernatural impact of divine grace, but it is emphatically differentiated from any direct intuition of God's testimony of himself or from any experience of God's speaking to us in itself, since that is God himself.[19]

How are we to react to this?

In the first place, it must be said that this detachment of the understanding even in the act of faith from the self-evidencing reality of God in his own self-communication, means that in the last resort faith is made to rest on moral grounds and to operate only with an indirect relation, mediated through the will, to what the great Alexandrian theologians called the *autousia* and *autexousia*, the self-being and self-authority, of God. In the nature of the case this opens up a dangerous gap between faith and its divine object which is inevitably occupied by an authority other than the compulsive truth of God's own being. If the assent and consent of the faithful to the truth are indirectly induced through some special infusion of grace or light, independent of the truth, then the way is opened up in the Church which mediates that infusion of grace or light for an authoritarian exercise of its *magisterium*, that is, one bearing upon the will of the faithful not requiring certainty based on evidence but requiring firmness in consenting to non-evident truth. However, if the assent and consent of the faithful rest directly upon the truth of God in his own self-light and self-evidence as he is proclaimed and worshipped, experienced and known within the common fellowship of the Church, then the way is open in the Church for an authoritative exercise of the *magisterium* in serving the inherent and ultimate authority of the truth itself in God. If the truth of being is given its rightful priority and prerogative over all truth of statement, that need not mean any rejection or depreciation of the *magisterium* but an enhancing of it through appropriate exercise of it in the service of Christ the supreme Truth.

In the second place, it must be said that the positing of a non-conceptual relation between our understanding and God means that, instead of terminating upon God himself as their rational ground and being controlled by his divine intelligibility, our concepts can only bend back and terminate upon our own inward experience and spirituality, so that in the last analysis it is our own self-understanding which becomes the criterion of their value for us. They never get beyond being what the medievals called the *objecta mentis*, so that there is no independent rational ground for determining their truth or falsity, or therefore for their constant revision in the light of the objective realities they are claimed to stand for or intend. This state of affairs would again open the door for an authoritarian exercise of the *magisterium* in imposing upon the mind of the Church a formalized unity of belief in order to prevent disruption from the subjective fancies, idiosyncracies or deviations of its members. However, if there is no such break in our conceptual relations with God, then we have to reckon with the bipolar nature of conceptuality in a relation between the creative intelligibility of God's own self-revelation and the obedient response of the faithful in their understanding and expression of it. This means that the conceptuality of the Church's faith can be sustained only through a relation of obligation or indebtedness to the intrinsic conceptuality of God's self-revelation, but that the truth of the latter is in no way indebted to the former, for the truth is not made but discovered. Thus a distinction must be drawn between the unchanging substance of the faith and the Church's formulations of it which may be maintained in their truth as they are grounded beyond themselves in the God-given substance of the faith, 'the solid reality in Christ', as St Paul called it. It is only when the Church yields to the temptation to invert that relation of indebtedness between on-going formulation and permanent substance, clamping its own man-made formulations prescriptively and restrictively down upon the substance of the faith, that it becomes entangled in a perverted authoritarianism. Thus the dogmatic formulations of the Church's traditional and developing understanding of God's self-revelation in Jesus Christ must be regarded not as closed but as open conceptual structures which it is incumbent upon the Church, in fidelity to the substance of faith entrusted to it from the apostolic foundation of the Church, constantly to revise and refine in the light of the objective intelligibility of divine revelation in Christ and through his Spirit which they are meant to serve.[20]

There can be little doubt that the serious difficulties within which Schillebeeckx is trapped and troubled are due to the dualist substructure of his theology, in which medieval and modern discontinuities combine to disrupt from below all-important connections in knowledge of God. The situation in which he and not a few other modern theologians, Roman and Protestant, are placed today, is not unlike that which we find at the end of the Middle Ages when the ambiguous realism of Thomist thought began to fall apart. The detachment of the understanding in the basic assent of faith from its evidential and intelligible ground in God's own being and truth, due to the Augustinian–Aristotelian dualism underlying it, inevitably made difficulties as soon as a more direct relation between the understanding and its object opened up with the emergence of empirical science and its more realist way of interrogating and handling evidence.[21] It degenerated into a damaging hiatus between faith and reason, especially evident in late Occamistic circles and in Renaissance thought, to which the Roman Catholic Church reacted in a strangely nominalistic authoritarianism with a view to tightening its formalizations and closing its ranks, which had the unfortunate effect of postponing *aggiornamento* for four hundred years. It would be an enormous tragedy if the Roman Catholic Church after the marvellous advances of the Second Vatican Council were to react in a similar way to the heretical deviations of Schillebeeckx, Küng and others, for the blame cannot be laid simply at their door. Their error is rooted in the Augustinian–Aristotelian dualism underlying the Roman conception of truth and authority which can no longer be glossed over by formal pronouncements from the Papacy.

Before we go on to offer a realist christological answer to the problem of non-evidential and non-conceptual relations posited by Schillebeeckx in our knowledge of God, let us glance at the answer given by present day science, *mutatis mutandis*, to basically the same problem which it has inherited from Newtonian and Kantian dualism. Instead of trying to deal with its difficulties within that dualist structure of thought it has steadily abolished dualism from its epistemological foundations, and set natural science upon a radically new, unitary basis. As we have had occasion already to remark, it was only when the epistemological implications of general relativity were worked out that, as Einstein himself soon admitted, against his earlier views, this new state of affairs first became clear.[22] It was not that a decision was taken to abolish dualism and start on another basis. On the contrary, the actual progress of empirico-theoretical science in grasping the rational structure of the space–time universe in its reality in such a way that experience and geometry were brought indivisibly together (i.e. as what James Clerk Maxwell had earlier called 'embodied mathematics'),[23] forced physics off a dualist on to a unitary basis.[24] Thus it began to turn away from the empiricist and positivist process of abstracting appearances from reality or deducing abstract ideas from observations and then erecting them into a nomistic structure only to impose it prescriptively upon experience, for that involved the bifurcation of form and being which had been obstructing progress. However, since this new realist science operated with the indivisible unity or integration of being and form in the continuous dynamic field of space–time reality, it found itself committed to the conviction that reality may and must be grasped conceptually in its own depth, but that the objective intelligibility of reality always transcends and far outruns our conceptual formulation of it. Hence the subjective pole of scientific conceptuality must be continuously revised and adjusted in the light of the objective pole to which it is correlated. Thus while, on the one hand, science refined a heuristic mode of inquiry in which it penetrated into the inherent relations within nature in such a way as to let them unfold themselves in their own intelligible structure and come to appropriate expression in a rigorously obedient interpretation of them; on the other hand, it learned to operate with a corresponding mode of verification, prescribed by the nature of the reality into which enquiry was being made, in accordance with which reality itself in its inherent unity of form and being was allowed to be the ultimate judge of the truth or falsity of our conceptions and statements about it. Just as experiments were set up to allow nature to disclose itself in its own rationality, so experiments were devised to allow nature to say 'yes' or 'no' to theoretical formalizations of that rationality. That is to say, in the last resort scientific theories are justified by the grace of reality alone.

In order to illustrate how this realist science regards and operates the bipolar conceptuality to which the unity of being and form gives rise, we may point to the place of *invariance* in relativity theory. On the one hand, invariance refers to an invariant relatedness inherent in nature irrespective of our observations and independent of our conceiving of it. But on the other hand, invariance refers to the mathematical instrument devised and refined under pressure from the relatedness inherent in nature as the conceptual lens through which we apprehend the rationality in nature or through which the rationality in nature discloses itself to us. By their very nature scientific theories or conceptual instruments of this kind are compound questions put to nature and have to be revised progressively in the light of the answers that come back from nature so that they may become more and more transparent media through which nature discloses its mysteries to us and imprints its truth on our understanding with its own self-explicative and evidential power. We may express this in another way by saying two things. First, the bipolarity of invariance reflects the fact that nature is found to be inherently and antecedently in itself what it manifests itself to be in our scientific enquiries. As such it has ontological priority and authority over our understanding of it – a relationship which may not be inverted without the grave error of claiming that the truth is made, not discovered. Second, the bipolarity of invariance also reflects the fact that our conceptual formalization of invariance serves the invariance inherent in nature, and is therefore relativized by it and is always revisable in the light of its fuller or deeper disclosure. This revisability of conceptual or mathematical invariance is an essential mark of its objective reference, for it means that it is in actual contact with reality and falls under its controlling power.[25]

As far as I can see, again *mutatis mutandis*, it was a realist revolution of this kind in the very foundations of knowledge that took place in the classical theology of the early conciliar period of the Christian Church. There was no initial decision to set aside the dualist modes of thought rampant in contemporary culture, but that nevertheless is what the Church found it had to do in sheer fidelity to its subject-matter: the self-communication of God to man in the incarnation of his Son, through whom the universe was made, within the created realities and conditions of that same universe. The oneness of God, the Father, the Son and the Holy Spirit, the undivided reality of Jesus Christ who embodied the fullness of God's self-giving to mankind, the inseparability of incarnation and creation implied in the Gospel of salvation of the world: all called for a basic reconstruction not only in modes of life and thought but in the understanding of the structure of the universe and its relation to God who created it out of nothing, continually sustains it in being, and who has made himself personally present in a staggeringly new way in Jesus Christ in order to make all things new. It was as that biblical and evangelical content of the Christian faith, deriving from the apostolic foundation of the Church, came into sharp conflict with the inveterate dualisms of the ancient world which kept on disrupting the essential pattern of faith and life in Christ, severing it from its ground in God, that the Church came to realize what was at stake.

But it was not until the Council of Nicaea in A.D. 325 that the minds of the faithful coming to conjoint expression converged on the crucial issue: whether God the Father is inherently, antecedently and eternally in his own being what he is in his self-manifestation toward us in Jesus Christ, or not; whether the understanding of Jesus Christ by the Church as indivisibly God and man is grounded in the eternal reality of God, or whether it is but a detachable and changeable myth with no objective validity. When the fathers and theologians of the Nicene Council found that they were forced by the inherent intelligibility and consistency of the faith to reject the dualist basis upon which pagan religion rested, they affirmed their faith in the unity of God's self-revelation in Christ which depended upon a unity in being and act between Christ and God. They looked for a decisive expression which could carry their distillation of the sense of Holy Scripture and convey the indivisible oneness between Christ the incarnate Son and God the Father, and they chose the phrase *homoousios tō(i) patri*, that is, of one and the same being with the Father. The effect of this was epoch-making. Not only did it give expression to what they had always believed but greatly confirmed and assisted the faith of the Church. And what is more, its enunciation and lodging in the heart of the Creed as its kingpin holding together faith in God, in Christ and in his Spirit, understanding of what God is in his own eternal being and what he is toward us in his saving acts in our world, into a coherent structure, proved to be one of the great irreversible acts of history. Once the *homoousion* was formulated it was found to provide the essential clue to the coherent understanding of Holy Scripture and the Gospel it enshrines, upon which, once grasped, the Christian Church can no more go back or forget, than any of us who after having solved a jigsaw puzzle can go back to the scattered pieces in forgetfulness of the picture which they make when fitted coherently together.[26] The *homoousion*, however, expresses not just a conceptual coherence with which we operate in organizing our own notions, but an objective coherence in the ontic relatedness of divine and human reality in Jesus Christ and indeed in the intelligible communion of the Triune God in himself as well as in his relations toward us through Christ and in his Spirit.[27]

Here, then, in the *homoousion* we have an intensely compressed and far-reaching act of scientific theological activity within the community of the faithful empirically correlated to Christ and his Gospel. In the *homoousion* the understanding of the Church is firmly set on a unitary basis which is both epistemological and ontological, for it entails a unity in being and a unity in intelligibility in God's *self*-giving and *self*-revealing in Jesus Christ, and correspondingly in our knowing of him in so far as it is allowed to fall under the compelling power of that *self*-giving and *self*-revealing in Jesus Christ.[28] As such the *homoousion* both clarifies and expresses the fact that in the Nicene theology the worshipping and enquiring Church was enabled to grasp God, in some real measure, in the depth of his own reality in such a way as to affect the whole structure of the Church's understanding of him, and yet in such a way that there is no suggestion that the transcendent mystery of God can be captured and comprehended within the bounds of our creaturely conceptualities,[29] for God in the beauty and majesty and light of his being infinitely exceeds all the Church's theological or dogmatic formulations. As we move from Ecumenical Council to Ecumenical Council in the history of the Church we find that its developing theology can be traced back from all decisive points to this central affirmation and its essentially doxological character in the Nicene Creed.

In the context of this realist theology in the Nicene Creed, on which all Christendom rests, we may offer a twofold answer to the problem of the non-evidential and non-conceptual relations posited by Schillebeeckx in knowledge of God: in terms of *the homoousion of the Spirit*, and *the homoousion of the Word*.

(1) The *homoousion* of the Spirit. If God is present to us in his Spirit and if we are given access to God in his Spirit, it makes an enormous difference if the *homoousion* applies not only to Christ as the Son of God but also to his Spirit as the Spirit of God. And that is precisely what the Church had to do, especially after it was shown so decisively by Athanasius in his *Letters to Serapion* that the *homoousion* of the Spirit is implied in the *homoousion* of the Son and indeed that the latter could not stand without the former. If the Holy Spirit is of one and the same being with God, then in giving us his Spirit God makes himself immediately present to us in his own divine being and reality which constitute the evidential ground for our knowledge of him. Moreover it was shown that the activity of the Spirit inheres in the very being God as *enousios energeia*, which not only means that God's activity toward us is grounded in his own being, but that God's being is present to us as Spirit in a dynamic and creative way. That is to say, God does not make himself present to us in his own being in a merely passive way but in such an active way that he grounds our knowing evidentially on the present reality of his divine being. Thus to posit a non-evidential relation between our minds and God is

tantamount to substituting for the Holy Spirit a human and creaturely 'spirit', the dynamism of the human spirit, which in actual effect is what Schillebeeckx does, for the break in evidential relation with God throws his understanding back upon himself and some inner experience in the activity of the human spirit. The whole situation is very different, however, if we take our stand on the non-dualist, unitary basis of the Nicene theology. Then we do not need to resort to the device of bringing in some intermediary element of 'created grace' which cannot be finally distinguished from human nature.[30] The problem, then, does not lie where Schillebeeckx thinks it does, but in his own damaging dualist mode of thought.

(2) The *homoousion* of the Word. The Creed speaks of the *homoousion* of the Son but it is quite clear that this applies to Christ as the *Word* made flesh. The question to be raised here is whether the Word who became incarnate in Jesus Christ and in him is addressed by God to us inheres as *Word* in the being of God himself, or (otherwise expressed) whether God is inherently, antecedently and eternally in himself the same Word who became incarnate in Jesus Christ and through whom he makes himself known to us. The answer given by the Church, of course, was an emphatic affirmative. To cite St Athanasius again, the *Logos* is *enousios* in God, for the Word belongs to and inheres in the very being of God as God. His being is not wordless but divinely eloquent. In that case, when God makes himself known to us in and through Christ we are given to know God in his own inner being and intelligibility or *Logos*. It is because God has incarnated his own eternal Word and Rationality within the realities and intelligibilities of our creaturely existence in Jesus Christ that we, creatures though we are, may grasp God conceptually in his own divine reality. To apprehend God in this way, of course, is not to say that we can comprehend him within the limits of our creaturely conceptualities, as we have seen. Thus while we must say with St Anselm on the one hand that there can be no faith without conceptual knowing, we must also say with him on the other hand that God infinitely exceeds our conceptions of him. The difficulty of Schillebeeckx goes back to the notion of a *wordless* relation between God and us which is found deep in his Augustinian and Thomist roots, and therefore to a non-conceptual relation between us and God. St Thomas followed the tradition set by Peter Lombard in teaching that God and the blessed or the angels communicate wordlessly through the light of the intelligence alone, and he consciously differentiated himself from St Anselm at such points,

attacking him for distinguishing *dicere* and *intellegere* in God, as though word belongs to God as word and not simply as intellectual light.[31] The root of the problem there as here with Schillebeeckx is the underlying dualism which snapped the subjective pole of conceptuality from its objective pole deep in the being and intelligibility of God. Already in the Middle Ages the question had been raised, even by Thomists, as we must raise it now, whether this is not in fact to reject the application of the Nicene *homoousion* to the incarnate *Word* of God which implies that what God is as Word to us he is as *Word* inherently and eternally in himself, and whether this does not introduce an irresolvable contradiction into the very substance of the faith.[32] Certainly such a rejection could only lead to serious problems in Christology, as indeed Schillebeeckx has demonstrated in his own case.

Classical theology has always regarded the self-mediation of God to us in Word and in Spirit as inseparably one. That goes back to the teaching of St Paul that through the Son and in the Spirit we are given access to God, for in the incarnation of his Son in Jesus Christ and the presence of his Spirit mediated through Jesus Christ, God has established such a relationship between himself and man that has made access to himself a reality for man. This is the twofold communion in Word and Spirit between God and man and man and God stressed by St John. But this Word, as patristic theology reminds us, is not some 'word' detached from God, but *enousios logos*, Word who eternally inheres in the being of God even when incarnate and addressed to us on earth and in time; and this Spirit is not some 'spiritual activity' detached from God, but *enousios energeia*, Spirit who inheres eternally in the being of God even when he comes to us and acts upon us within our creaturely existence. That is to say, in the incarnation of his Word and in the coming of his Spirit God has actualized for us the openness of his own being and intelligibility within the conditions, realities and intelligibilities of our contingent being in such a way that neither his revealing of himself to us nor our apprehending of him may be halted or negated by the conditions, realities and intelligibilities of our contingent being. In fact the real presence of God to us in the immediacy of his own divine Being as Holy Spirit is bound up with and mediated through his sheer unreserved self-humiliation and self-commitment to us in the incarnation of his Son, the Word made flesh. It is therefore in proportion to the realism with which we appreciate the *kenosis* that we can appreciate the realism of the *homoousion* of the Son, for they are the obverse of one another, and on that ground also appreciate the realism of the *homoousion* of the Spirit. Thus the question whether there is ground for holding an evidential and conceptual relation to God in our knowing of him is an ontological question, or more precisely, a christological question. It stands or falls with the question whether the incarnate Son or Word is of one and the same being with God, that is, with the very heart and substance, with the innermost sanctum, of the Christian faith.

In order to throw into relief the pivotal significance of this epistemological/ontological question let us return to an analogy taken from natural science mentioned earlier: the great hinge upon which modern science has swung away from phenomenalism to realism. This is the decisive point of Einstein's critique of the empiricist and positivist approach to knowledge, which cut short the basis of knowledge at the phenomenal surface of nature and what we can deduce from our observations or the appearances of things to us. If nature is not in itself what it is in its relations toward us, if we are not able to grasp nature in the depth of its own reality, then we are not really concerned with science but only with useful arrangements of our own observations and experiments. However, as Einstein insisted, 'God does not wear his heart on his sleeve' – the truth of things cannot be read off their phenomenal surface. Rather must we penetrate through appearances and apprehend the structures of reality in their ontological depth, in the conviction that nature does not deceive or play tricks with us, for it is inherently in itself what it is toward us in our enquiries and is everywhere trustworthy and reliable. Since it was at that point that physics was switched from resting on a dualist to resting on a unitary basis represented by the ontological integration of structure and matter or form and being, it might be understandable if we were to think of this as 'the *homoousion* of physics'! At any rate, that is the kind of cardinal issue in the foundations of knowledge with which we have to do here in Christian theology.

In closing this discussion it may be useful to take this analogy one step further. The Einsteinian revolution found it had to reject the idea that scientific enquiry proceeds by way of logical deductions from observations, or by moving from appearances to reality, and demonstrated through relativity theory that in actual fact it proceeds the other way: by coming at appearances from behind in such a way as to explain through the refraction of space and time the distorted appearances of things relatively to the observer, and to show how all observable realities are controlled by the invisible dynamic structure of the space–time metrical field.[33] It is by coming at appearances from behind in this way, from their objective ground, that we can discern what not to read back from appearances of things to what they are in themselves, while nevertheless correlating what we may know of things as they are disclosed to us in our enquiries with what they are in their internal relations. Thus, for example, scientific devices are invented enabling us to refer the images in our observations imagelessly back to the intelligible ground on which they arise, so that we may not project our image-thinking back into reality which would only end in a distorting anthropomorphism, that is, the very kind of thing against which D. M. MacKinnon has so often warned philosophers and theologians alike.

Properly understood that is how the *homoousion* must be allowed to operate in theology – with a keen critical edge in a constructive discrimination of the material handed down to us. We do not proceed in an empiricist and positivist way by trying to deduce who Jesus Christ was from 'observational data'; nor do we seek to determine his 'reality for us' by interpreting his 'appearances' in terms of what we think they must have 'meant for people' thereby reading back our own cultural assumptions into their understanding – all of which would only lead back into the all too familiar impasse of phenomenalist dualism and its fictional 'significates' in the middle.[34] Rather do we come at the material from behind, from a very different unitary position in which theoretical and empirical elements or form and being are never separated in what is objectively given and in our conceptual interpretation of it, that is from a position in which we penetrate into the ontological structure informing and organizing the material in the light of which it is integrated in our understanding and grasped in an objectively coherent way. That is the kind of bipolar conceptuality that arises with the irreversible insight expressed by the *homoousion*. When we proceed in this way we do not read back distorting appearances into reality or cut them short by accepting a non-evidential and non-conceptual reference and retiring into the prison of our own self-understanding. Nor do we project uncritically the eidetic images or iconic signs that arise in our creaturely conceiving as we encounter God's self-revelation in Christ into the being of God himself, for since these figurative and conceptual patterns of thought are employed in the light of the objective intelligibility to which they refer they are subjected to its critical and discriminating control. That is to say, the *homoousion* does not allow us to read back all that we know of Jesus Christ in the flesh indiscriminately into God, for that would entail some form of mythological projection of what is human and creaturely into God.

Here we return to an extremely important point made by Schillebeeckx, which weighs very heavily in his argumentation, and to which we must give heed: that all our conceptual thought of God includes creaturely representations which we may not project into God.[35] We cannot do without these figurative and conceptual patterns of thought, such as we employ for example in the notions of 'fatherhood' or 'providence', for then our thought of God would be quite empty, but they are not as such grounded and rooted in the being of God, so that they may be used only in such a way that they point entirely beyond themselves. But, as we have seen, on the dualist basis with which Schillebeeckx works, this has the effect in the final analysis of throwing his thought back on himself in order to give it meaning, so that he frankly admits that the objective and real value of our knowledge of God is explained by the dynamism, not of the content of our awareness of being, but of the knowing subject. That is to say, he retreats into an existential self-understanding and into what he calls a metaphysics renewed on an anthropological basis.[36] Nevertheless, we must accept the point Schillebeeckx has made, which, with due allowances for a very different standpoint, was the same as that constantly made by Athanasius against the Arians that we must be aware of confounding *theologia* with *mythologia*, that is objective theological thinking which is controlled from a centre in God and his inner Triune relations as Father, Son and Holy Spirit, with a subjective way of thinking in terms of our own creaturely devising and projecting from a centre in which we are engrossed with ourselves and our own fancies.

How, then, is the *homoousion* to be handled in such a way that we do not simply read back the human and creaturely features embedded in God's incarnate self-revelation to us into the being of God himself? Here we find the enormous importance of yoking together in our thought the *homoousion* of the Son and the *homoousion* of the Spirit which are just as inseparable and coinherent as the Son and the Spirit are in the coinherence of Father, Son and Holy Spirit in one God. Just as in 'the *homoousion* of physics' we operate with a cohesion of experience and mathematics, and therefore with an epistemic co-ordination of empirical and theoretical factors in the structure of scientific knowledge whereby the natural images we use are made to refer imagelessly to their invisible, intelligible ground in reality from which they are controlled, so here we learn how to co-ordinate the *homoousial anaphora*, or reference back, of what God is toward us in Christ and in his Spirit to what he is inherently in himself, in such a way that we do not project into him, or subordinate him in our thought to, the creaturely representations in our conceiving of him. If we operate only with the *homoousion* of the Son, or Word made flesh, detached from the *homoousion* of the Spirit, we would have great difficulty, to say the least, in referring from what God is toward us in Jesus Christ to what he is inherently in himself, without projecting the creaturely content of our knowing into him. If, however, we operate only with the *homoousion* of the Spirit, detached from the *homoousion* of the Son, we would have no conceptual content in our reference back to God apart from what we might derive from our own subjective states, and no objective ground of intelligibility in God to control and relativize our creaturely representations and conceptions. It is through the co-ordination of both of these, the *homoousion* of the Son and the *homoousion* of the Spirit that we are enabled to discriminate between what we may and what we may not read back into God, and to discern the essentially spiritual, imageless nature of that reading back under the control of God's own self-interpreting and self-evidencing reality mediated through Christ and in his Spirit. Just as the infinite God whose being is Spirit discloses himself to us within the concrete conditions and contingencies of our finite existence without destroying them, in the staggering humiliation of God in Jesus Christ, so he enables us from within those concrete conditions and contingencies of our finite existence, where he has given *himself* to us, to apprehend him who infinitely transcends them, without engaging in deifying objectifications of our creaturely representations and conceptions.

We are not concerned here with logical inferences or abstractive operations of thought but with a movement of thought which cannot be described in explicit terms, for while it does entail explicit elements it relies on implicit elements which can only be learned in what Polanyi has so often called *apprenticeship* but which in the Christian Church we know as *discipleship*, through which we acquire within the evangelical and doxological fellowship of the faithful what St Paul called a *spiritual discernment* or *discrimination*. Thus at the very basic level of faith and worship there becomes engendered within us a heuristic vision, to borrow another expression from Polanyi,[37] or what Clement of Alexandria called long ago, a proleptic grasp,[38] enabling us to engage in an intuitive leap of the understanding in apprehending and appreciating the significance of basic aspects of reality pressing for realization in our minds, that is, objective patterns in terms of which other relevant clues become integrated into a comprehensive whole constituting a conceptual instrument through which reality progressively discloses itself to us and constantly presses upon our understanding as the judge of the truth or falsity of our conceptions of it.

What I have called the *homoousial anaphora* through Christ and in the Spirit made on the ground of God's own self-giving to us through Christ and in the Spirit, is the discriminating movement of theological thought which gives the figurative and creaturely representations in the Gospel their proper place and function as transparent media through which Christ confronts us with himself, clothed in the power of his own Spirit, as the creative ground of our faith and the one place where we may meet and know the Father. But because we deploy those figurative and creaturely representations in this way we are not trapped in a projective movement of thought grounded in the knowing subject in which they are read back through Jesus into God's own eternal being. The all-important semantic and ontological relation between Jesus Christ, the incarnate form of God's concrete self-revelation to us in space and time, and God the Father, is activated by the Word and Spirit of God in and through Jesus Christ, for thereby the self-interpreting and self-evidencing reality of God in his own immediate being bears upon us within the communion of the faithful in such a way that there arises among us the bipolar conceptuality of faith and understanding which informs the Church. It is as our communion with God the Father through Christ and in his Spirit is grounded in and shares in the inner Trinitarian consubstantial or *homoousial* communion of the Father, Son and Holy Spirit, that the subjectively-given pole of conceptuality is constantly purified and refined under the searching light and quickening power of the objectively-given pole in divine revelation. Within that polarity Christian theology becomes what it essentially is and ought always to be, *logike latreia*, rational worship of God.

Notes

1 D. M. MacKinnon is surely right in pointing out that so far as his cosmology is concerned Aristotle achieved his own variant of this Platonic dualism (*The Problem of Metaphysics*, Cambridge, 1974, pp. 100f). It might be added that if an epistemological dualism is not presumed by Aristotelian thought it is nevertheless imposed through abstractive reasoning in which form is prescinded from matter.

2 Cf. the illuminating analysis by E. H. Hutten, *The Origins of Science. An Inquiry into the Foundation of Western Thought* (London, 1962), pp. 113ff, 164ff.

3 Theologians may, with some justification, raise the question whether this apparently endemic tendency to split apart in our understanding

not only form and being but form and content, and image and idea, is not to be traced ultimately to original sin, i.e. the alienation of the human mind from the ground of rational order and truth in God. If so, what is needed, from a theological point of view, is healing or reconciliation in the ontological depth of man's relation to God.

4 There is more than a suspicion of dualism, however, in the christological formulation of Chalcedon, which was thrown into high relief by the critique of the post-Chalcedonian 'Cyrillians' who traced the problem back to the undeniable dualism in Leo's *Tome*. Western interpretation of Chalcedonian Christology is still affected, unfortunately, by this Leonine slant.

5 There are, of course, outstanding exceptions, for example, St Anselm in medieval times, and Karl Barth and Donald MacKinnon in our own day.

6 Perhaps the effect of this oblique mode of thinking was nowhere more unfortunate than in the allegorical and tropological exegesis of Holy Scripture which prevailed throughout the Middle Ages.

7 In Thomist thought this is tied up with an ambiguous notion of truth which kept swinging from a realist to an intellectualist position and vice versa, which, as St Thomas shows in his commentary on Aristotle's *Metaphysics*, has clearly an Aristotelian source.

8 That the element of genuine objectivity in Kant's thought is stronger than at first appears is convincingly shown by MacKinnon, 'Kant's Philosophy of Religion', *Philosophy*, 50 (1975), 131ff; *The Problem of Metaphysics*, pp. 2ff, 53ff; *Explorations in Theology* 5 (London, 1979), pp. 94ff, 140ff.

9 It is rather illuminating to trace the history of the distinction between *intentio recta* and *intentio obliqua* from Occam to Erasmus, from Erasmus to Dilthey, and from Dilthey to Bultmann.

10 Kant's own concept of 'as if', as MacKinnon points out, was more than an exercise in make-believe, *Philosophy*, 50 (1975), p. 141. Nevertheless it had a steadily deleterious effect in Ritschlian theology and in Machian science, not merely through Vaihingher!

11 In contrast to the 'willing assent' of Stoic thought, St Thomas' notion that the assent of the mind requires a movement of the will is reinforced by his notion of *intellectus agens*, which takes it very close to the Kantian notion of the 'active reason'.

12 E. Schillebeeckx, *Revelation and Theology* (London, 1967), pp. 67, 105f, 174; *The Concept of Truth and Theological Renewal* (London, 1968), pp. 45ff.

13 Schillebeeckx, *Revelation and Theology*, pp. 107, 169, 174, 277; *Concept of Truth*, pp. 44, 74, 83, 114.

14 Cf. here my discussions, 'The Place of Word and Truth in Theological Inquiry according to St Anselm', *Studia mediaevalia et mariologica P. Carolo Balié OFM septuagesimum explenti annum dicata* (Rome, 1971), pp. 133ff; and 'The Ethical Implications of Anselm's *De Veritate*', *Theologische Zeitschrift*, 24 (1968), 309ff.

15 Contrast, however, the fine paper by the late Gerard Philips (a prince of theological realists), 'Reflections on Purely Conceptual Theology and on "Real" Theology', *Louvain Studies*, II.1 (1969), 263ff.

16 See especially Schillebeeckx, *Concept of Truth*, pp. 9ff, 30ff, 157ff; cf. also *Revelation and Theology*, pp. 131ff.

17 Augustine, *De Trinitate* IX.12.18; and cf. St Thomas, *De veritate*, q. 19, a. 6.

18 MacKinnon, *Explorations in Theology* 5, p. 157.

19 Schillebeeckx, *Revelation and Theology*, pp. 81ff; *Concept of Truth*, pp. 65ff.

20 For a fuller discussion of this see my lecture 'Truth and Authority: Theses on Truth', given to L'Académie Internationale des Sciences Religieuses at its session in L'Institut Catholique de Paris, *The Irish Theological Quarterly*, 39, 3 (July 1972), 215ff.

21 Much the same problem opened up in Protestant thought, which soon became basically deist after the revived Augustinianism on which the Reformation was based became allied first with a new form of Aristotelian thought in the great Protestant Scholastics, and then with a masterful Newtonianism.

22 A. Einstein, *Ideas and Opinions* (British edn., London, 1973), 'On the Method of Theoretical Physics', pp. 270ff; see also pp. 290ff and 323ff.

23 James Clerk Maxwell also spoke in this connection of 'physical analogy' and 'physical idea', 'On Faraday's Lines of Force', *Scientific Papers*, vol. I, (Cambridge, 1890), pp. 155f. See here Richard Olson, *Scottish Philosophy and British Physics 1850–1880* (Princeton, 1975), pp. 299ff.

24 See especially A. Einstein, 'Geometry and Experience', his 1921 lecture before the Prussian Academy of Sciences, *Ideas and Opinions*, pp. 232f; and 'Physics and Reality', pp. 290ff.

25 It is rather astonishing to find Bernard Lonergan inverting the conceptual polarity of Einstein's notion of invariance, that is from objective structures in reality to subjective structures in man's rational self-consciousness – cf. *Collection* (London, 1967), pp. 121ff; *Insight* (New York, 1970), xxv ff, etc., and my discussion, 'The Function of Inner and Outer Word in Lonergan's Theological Method', in P. Corcoran, *Looking at Lonergan's Method* (Dublin, 1975), p. 120f.

26 The analogy has been taken from Piaget and Polanyi; see M. Polanyi, *Knowing and Being* (London, 1969), pp. 212f.

27 Hence I prefer not to think of the *homoousion* as a second-order christological proposition, *pace* D. M. MacKinnon, for the *homoousion* is the ontological obverse of the *kenosis*, and as such concerns Christ's relation to the Father and its ontological priority over our understanding of it. See D. M. MacKinnon's contribution '"Substance" in Christology: a cross-bench view', to the volume *Christ, Faith and History. Cambridge Studies in Christology*, ed. S. W. Sykes and J. P. Clayton (Cambridge, 1972), p. 297.

28 Cf. D. M. MacKinnon: 'What is realized in the mission of Jesus and perfected in the Father's raising him from the dead is the very unity of God, the consistency of God with himself in relation to his creation. We have to do with a prolonged human action that is grounded in God, that in fact provides the very rationale of creation itself.' In R. W. A. McKinney, *Creation, Christ and Culture. Studies in Honour of T. F. Torrance* (Edinburgh, 1976), p. 99. In going on to point out that

'the very being of God is put at risk' in the incarnation, MacKinnon reveals an almost unparalleled realism in his Christology. As I understand the *homoousion*, it puts the incarnation within the life of God himself, which is the other side of MacKinnon's point.

29 That might be the case, however, if the *kenosis* were not matched by the *anaphora* of the *auton huperupsosen* of Philippians 2: 8, which is the divine act in the *homoousion*.

30 The effect of the Aristotelian cosmological *chorismos* upon the Augustinian dualism between the sensible and suprasensible or intelligible realms, was to interpret God as an Unmoved Mover and thus to undermine the realist understanding of God's interaction with the world, thereby creating a hiatus which required an *inter-medium* if it was not to fall apart into sheer deism. That *inter-medium* was supplied by the realm of diffused grace. But all this had the effect of hardening the dualism between God and man and creating the state of affairs which led to the notions of non-evidential and non-conceptual relations.

31 On this difficult problem in St Thomas' thought, see my 'Scientific Hermeneutics according to St Thomas', *Journal of Theological Studies*, n.s. 13, 2 (Oct. 1962), 259–89.

32 The charge against this medieval trend was well argued by Johannes Reuchlin in his remarkable book *De Verbo Mirifico*, 1494.

33 Cf. Einstein's remark to W. Heisenberg, 'Whether you can observe a thing or not depends on the theory you use. It is the theory which decides what can be observed.' Cited by M. Polanyi, 'Genius in Science', *De La Méthode. Méthodologies Particulières et Méthodologie en Général*, ed. by S. Dockx (Brussels, 1972), p. 22.

34 An outstanding exception to this kind of approach is to be found in the work of Hans Frei, *The Identity of Jesus Christ. The Hermeneutical Bases of Dogmatic Theology* (Philadelphia, 1967) and 1975 (new edition), which operates with the unity of form and being, of identity and presence, in allowing Jesus Christ to interpret himself in his own uniqueness to our enquiry.

35 Schillebeeckx, *Revelation and Theology*, pp. 132ff; *Concept of Truth*, pp. 162–78.

36 Schillebeeckx, *Concept of Truth*, p. 120; cf. p. 66f, 113ff.

37 M. Polanyi, *Personal Knowledge* (London, 1958), pp. 199, 280, etc. For Polanyi 'heuristic vision' is an expression clearly associated with Christian worship of God.

38 Clement of Alexandria, *Stromateis* II.iv, 16.3, 17.1ff; xvi, 76.1ff, 77.1ff etc.

11

Notes on Analogical Predication and Speaking about God

ROGER WHITE

The notes to this essay will be found on pages 225–6

This essay is concerned with the appeal to the notion of analogical predication as an attempt to illuminate the question how finite and sinful men can use their ordinary language to talk of the infinite and holy God revealed to us in His Son, without on the one hand thereby talking and thinking of Him anthropomorphically and without on the other hand voiding our language of any sense that is intelligible to us, leaving our claims as only apparently making claims but ultimately doing no more than bear witness to our impotence to talk of Him at all. This topic is clearly an immense one, involving complex questions about when a word is used in the same or a different sense, how the different senses of a word are interrelated, and, inevitably at a different level, an attempt to grapple with questions of exegesis of Aquinas. As such, what follows can have the status of no more than a sketch with, at most, programmatic status, and also it isolates, from among the host of questions that crowd in upon one at this moment, a central thesis that is to be found in at least a qualified form in the *Summa Theologica*[1] and which finds its most explicit working out by Karl Barth in *Church Dogmatics*.[2] Both these references to Barth and to Aquinas, who for me represent in very different idioms the most sustained and profound exploration of the notion of analogical predication in the doctrine of divine names, already of themselves bring with them a range of problems – problems which are totally different in kind.

The problem raised by Barth's explicit discussion of analogical predication is relatively simple to specify. Barth is first and foremost a theologian and neither a philosopher of language nor a student of the ways that the logical and linguistic issues were discussed as such by Aquinas and his successors. This emerges with painful clarity in the long footnote on Quenstedt's doctrine of analogy,[3] where Barth argues for the view that the notion of analogy required for theology is an *analogia attributionis extrinsice*, with the accompanying claim that the analogy of attribution is a notion that is peculiar to theology. Some of Barth's Roman Catholic critics have referred to this footnote to show that Barth's train of thought commits him to a doctrine of religious language in which the difference between his account of the way a word is used both of God and a creature and an account which said that such words were used purely equivocally is virtually negligible. But reading that footnote in the context both of what immediately precedes it and of the second half of *Church Dogmatics* II/I shows rather that Barth has simply misunderstood some of the crucial vocabulary in which the debate was traditionally conducted. Specifically: the notion of the analogy of attribution (the varying uses of the word 'healthy' in 'healthy climate', 'healthy man' and 'healthy complexion') belongs most explicitly to what has been called the logical doctrine of analogy – a doctrine about the relation of the senses of words that are used neither univocally nor purely equivocally. But Barth, through misunderstanding the force of the phrase '*per dependentiam*' (healthy is said primarily of a man, but of the climate derivatively, '*per dependentiam*') has misconstrued what Quenstedt says in terms of a 'metaphysical' doctrine of analogy – a doctrine of the analogies between God and his creatures: namely that creatures only participate in the perfections fully realized in God in virtue of their dependence upon God. This means that a discussion of Barth inevitably involves one at several points correcting the letter of his discussion in the light of its spirit: a spirit that has little to do with the analogy of extrinsic attribution.

With Aquinas the difficulties are of a different kind: the discussions of analogical predication are scattered throughout his writings in such a way as to make it difficult to discern the precise lines of his thinking and even more difficult to construct a theory of language which is both fully worked out and which one can with certainty ascribe to Aquinas himself: in fact, although only someone who had dedicated his life to work on the Thomist writings could speak with certainty to this point, it may well be that we have a succession of profoundly suggestive insights which do not of themselves constitute such a theory, but present us with considerations which any such theory must weigh – that Aquinas was highly sensitive to the possibilities of a term's being used analogically and aware of the diversity of cases in which it was appropriate to allude to such possibilities, and that a danger which has befallen many of his disciples with their rival treatises containing differing 'divisions of analogy' is the danger of a premature attempt to introduce an over-schematic order into texts which wish to confront us with the multiplicity of cases in which it is appropriate to talk of analogical predication, and that he *appeals* to the phenomenon of analogical predication rather than presents us with a systematic theory of it: a theory that could falsify the diversity of linguistic phenomena that here are to be considered. With this, there goes a second difficulty: because of the absence of a systematic and succinct exposition of analogical predication, there has grown up around Aquinas' writings a body of secondary texts that attempt to present what Aquinas wisely shunned: a supposedly systematic and exhaustive treatise on 'the doctrine of analogy'; one thinks naturally, above all, of Cajetan's confused and confusing *De Nominum Analogia*.[4] These texts have so frequently been used by every reader of Aquinas as ways to orient oneself in his writings that it requires an immense effort to read what Aquinas himself said as opposed to what has been made of what he said by someone like Cajetan. One particular danger that threatens at this point is a confused presentation of the relation between a 'logical' and a 'metaphysical' doctrine of analogy. If I read Aquinas aright, it is almost always the logical doctrine that makes most immediate sense of his texts, but in the Thomist tradition this moves more and more into being just a starting point for a metaphysical doctrine of analogy: a doctrine of the analogy between God and His creatures, or between entities in different categories. This tendency is perhaps strongly evident already in Cajetan, who designates the example that Aquinas so frequently cites – the analogy of attribution – as only analogy 'improperly speaking' – partly because of Cajetan's continual appeal to the Greek etymology of Aquinas' language, but also because, being a species of analogical predication that implies no similarity whatsoever between the analogates, it is the one that is of no use for the exploration of a metaphysical doctrine. Despite the host of far more expert commentators speaking to the contrary, I am certain from my reading of Aquinas that what he has in mind is always in the first instance a logical doctrine: a doctrine about the interrelation between differing but closely-connected senses of a word. The relevance of such a doctrine to the metaphysical doctrine is clear: the possibility of the use of terms in these interrelated senses may depend upon there being similarities between the objects to which they are applied. But this very relevance may mislead one into short-circuiting the discussion so that one's discussion of the logical doctrine is no more than an introductory chapter to a treatise on the analogy between God and His creation: if one makes such a short circuit, one misses an enormous amount that is of great importance and interest in Aquinas himself. Perhaps the final difficulty in approaching the texts of Aquinas that I myself experience is a problem of translating what Aquinas is saying in a very different idiom into what is for me the far more familiar and manageable idiom of modern discussions of the senses of words: whether, for instance, the words *significatio* and 'sense' are as simply related as I suppose. And it could be, for example, that when I maintain that the distinction Aquinas draws in q. 13 of the *pars prima* between the mode of signification of a word and the thing signified by the word – a distinction introduced to explain conflicting tendencies in our attempt to answer the question whether a word used to predicate a perfection of God and of a creature is predicated primarily of God and derivatively of a creature, or vice versa – is misconceived, and that this is an ultimately untenable distinction in an account of the senses of words, I am misunderstanding him. This may not simply be, as I believe, an intelligible but unacceptable distinction to try to make in an account of the senses of words, but may reflect a distinction that would be defensible against the background of Aquinas' idiom for talking about language: a distinction that becomes lost when one tries to maintain it simply in terms of a discussion of the senses of words. But the importance of Aquinas for the topic in hand is such that I must simply run the risk of misinterpretation caused by my attempt to render what he is saying in an idiom that I am familiar with.

There are two issues in Aquinas that require explicit mention before I examine the central theme of this essay. First, Aquinas talks about analogical predication as lying between univocal predication and pure or chance equivocal predication. This can be taken in two different ways. Either we may construe analogical predication as a species of equivocation – we say that a word is used on two occasions analogically where, although the word is used in different senses, and hence equivocally, those two senses are so closely interrelated that it would be hard to disentangle them in such a way that we simply substituted a new word for one of the senses: or that we say that two words are used analogically if they are used in such a way that our normal criteria for sameness or difference of sense are not adequately sharp for us to be able to give a clear-cut answer to the question whether the word is used in the same sense or not, and where different considerations pull us in different directions over this question. Since in so many of the examples cited by Aquinas the most elementary criterion we have for difference of sense – that A can be ϕ in one use of the word, and not ϕ in the other (clearly in Aquinas' most frequently used example we may dispute Mr Desai's contention that healthy urine is *ipso facto* healthy *qua* diet or medicine) – is satisfied, in what follows I shall treat analogical predication as a species of equivocation, though this will usually affect the idiom rather than the substance of the claims I make. Secondly, Aquinas frequently asks which of the two uses of a word is primary, and although there may be cases of analogical predication where such a question has no answer of logical significance – as in the case, for example, of the use of the verb 'to see' for seeing a tree and for seeing the point of an argument – this distinction is sufficiently important in a wider range of cases and crucial for the topic I wish to explore that the notion of a primary and a secondary or derived sense requires explicit comment: a primary sense is neither (as I am using the term) necessarily the sense most frequently encountered, nor an etymologically prior sense. When we say one sense is primary and another secondary, we are saying that to explain the secondary sense one must necessarily bring into one's account the notion signified by the word in the primary sense. So that one simply could not explain the notion of a healthy climate without bringing in the notion of what it was for a man to be healthy: a healthy climate is precisely one which promotes health in an animal. No more and no less is to be read into our distinction of a primary and a secondary sense – for instance, one must be on one's guard against letting this distinction slide into no more than a claim that A is ϕ in a more eminent or fuller manner than B: if we can make sense of this second account of a primary sense, it is clearly going to be tempting to confuse two different accounts of what it is for a sense to be primary, particularly in a discussion of the relation between words signifying perfections in its application to God and to creatures. In fact, in the typical remark 'only A is really ϕ' one may find a point at which these two different notions of primacy meet: that here one is saying that although we may talk of other things than A as ϕ, A fully realizes a central notion of being ϕ, and anything else which is called ϕ is so called because it approximates to being ϕ in the sense in which A alone is ϕ. Here the notion of A being ϕ in a 'more eminent way' than anything else is spelled out so as to give purchase to the logical notion of primacy which is our main concern.

Against the background of these preliminary remarks, we wish to examine the possibility of the apparently extraordinary and paradoxical claim made both by Aquinas[5] and Barth[6] that the words used to signify divine perfections are used in their primary sense in their application to God, and that their use when predicated of creatures is a derivative sense. It is important to recognize that for both Aquinas and Barth this thesis is made on *theological* grounds – both appealing to the scriptural witness to divine revelation in support of their claim, even if there is a difference in emphasis. In Barth, the theological basis of the claim is not only made at the outset but is given concrete weight by the whole discussion of divine perfections that follows, whereas at the back of Aquinas' mind there may well also be ideas whose ultimate source is Plato's contention that it is, for example, of the form of the good and the form of the good, alone, that goodness may really be predicated. It is well worth recognizing how strong this theological appeal is before moving on to the question which is my primary concern here: the logical possibility of the truth of the claim. Besides passages referred to by Aquinas and Barth[7] there are even more striking passages which make their thesis an almost inevitable approach to the question now before us: Jesus' saying 'Why do you call me good? No one is good but God alone' (Mark 10: 18), Matt. 23: 8ff, and the discussion of the relation of the wisdom of this world and 'the foolishness of God' of 1 Corinthians 1 and 2, all emphasize in different ways that the thesis we are discussing is not arbitrary metaphysical speculation, but is a way of talking that has its roots in God's self-revelation itself.

But the thesis, as Barth himself fully recognizes – and I suspect this is what led Aquinas to maintain the contrary thesis as far as the 'mode of signification' was concerned – can appear paradoxical in the extreme. For we are maintaining that there is a series of words which, even as part of the vocabulary of those who have never heard of the God who reveals Himself in Christ, are primarily only truly predicable of God, and that when predicated of creatures are being used in a derived sense.

The paradoxical nature of the thesis we are discussing, and perhaps also the philosophical suspicion with which people treat statements such as 'only A is really ϕ' or 'nothing is really ϕ' is given clear expression by Wittgenstein in his *Remarks on Colour*:[8]

> Lichtenberg says that very few people have ever seen pure white. So do most people use the word wrongly then? And how

> did *he* learn the right use? – He constructed an ideal use from the ordinary one. And that doesn't mean a better one, but one refined along certain lines and in which something has been carried to extremes.
>
> And of course such a construction may for its part tell us something about the way we actually use the word.
>
> If I say a piece of paper is pure white, and if snow were placed next to it and it then looked grey, I would still be right in calling it white and not light grey in its normal surroundings. It might be that I use a more refined concept of white, in a laboratory, say (where e.g. I also use a more refined concept of exact time measurement).

Now this passage, I think, summarizes a feeling that is evoked by most statements that at least apparently are at odds with ordinary use, and is worth examining carefully because the defence that can be made of Lichtenberg can reveal that appeals to the way that we ordinarily speak can oversimplify our language: and if that is so in the case of an as apparently straightforward concept as 'white', then we may see how treacherous such appeals can be in the case of more complex concepts. (Would Wittgenstein have taken someone to task for saying that very few people can recognize true beauty in music? Particularly if he had hit below Wittgenstein's philosophical belt by referring to the length of time it took for Schubert's piano music to be properly appreciated.) At an earlier stage in his thinking, in the *Philosophical Remarks*,[9] Wittgenstein had allowed that a good sense could be given to the claim that no one sees an exact circle, in a discussion which was far more fully worked out than our present text.[10]

It can look as though, in the passage from the *Remarks on Colour* Wittgenstein is defending the way people ordinarily use the word 'white' against an attack implicit in Lichtenberg's remark – and certainly that is how Wittgenstein himself presents the matter. But this is in fact far from being the case: what Wittgenstein is defending here is a grossly simplified picture of the way the word 'white' is used in everyday language, and in fact is travestying the idioms to be found already *in the vernacular*: idioms in the vernacular which can themselves be seen as giving a good sense to what Lichtenberg says without Lichtenberg having to 'construct' a special use for the word 'white' or a special concept *pure white*: we could in fact, although what he says is purely in the material mode, see Lichtenberg as drawing attention to how much more complex is our use of colour words by comparison with our immediate intuitions. What makes this passage strange is that in other parts of the *Remarks on Colour*, and even more in the sustained earlier discussion of colour in the *Philosophical Remarks* (chapter XXI), Wittgenstein showed himself fully aware of what he would call the grammatical facts that could find expression in such remarks as that of Lichtenberg under debate. We may allude to some of these facts – which are all facts about the ways we all use colour words:

(*a*) We are only prepared to qualify certain of our colour words with the epithet 'pure' – roughly, we only have a totally clear use for 'pure ϕ' when ϕ is one of white, black, or a primary colour. We do not know what to do with the phrase 'pure brown' and although we can imagine a use for 'pure orange', this use is far more a way of describing a surface than a colour: 'the page was pure orange' means 'every part of the page was orange' not that this was the colour of the page *tout court*. The discussions of what lies behind this fact to be found in the *Philosophical Remarks* are far more subtle than anything I can say in the brief space at my disposal.

(*b*) There is absolutely no inconsistency in the way that we ordinarily talk between saying both that 'A is white' and that 'B is whiter than A': this would be our natural way of describing the case of the sheet of paper and the snow Wittgenstein alludes to. There is, in fact, an extraordinary neglect, on the part of philosophers of language, of the fact that a large number of our concept words are used not only simply, but have comparatives and superlatives.

(*c*) Such remarks as 'I thought my husband's shirts were white until I used Persil' are part and parcel of our *very* everyday use of the word 'white'.

(*d*) Wittgenstein does nothing with the fact that Lichtenberg qualifies the word 'white' with the epithet 'pure': it is highly questionable whether 'pure white' is in Wittgenstein's idiom in the first instance a name of a surface colour. Pure white does not have different shades, all our words for surface colours (including the use of the word 'white' as such) are used in such a way that we admit the possibility of different shades of white. In the *Philosophical Remarks* Wittgenstein alluded to this fact by means of the metaphor that the names of the primary colours are like points, but the mixed colours like lines:

that is, when we say 'orange lies between red and yellow' we are saying that orange is properly applicable to any shade lying between these two primary colours – not that it lies between some shade of red and some shade of yellow.

In fact in the *Remarks on Colour*, there seems to be a genuine tension in Wittgenstein's thinking: one element finds expression in the criticism of Lichtenberg and also in III.102: 'When we're asked "What do 'red', 'blue', 'black', 'white' mean?" we can, of course, immediately point to things which have these colours – but that's all we can do: our ability to explain their meaning goes no further.' Although from its context it is clear that he does not think this is an exhaustive account of the meaning of these words, it does relate to a much simpler notion of colour words, and how we learn their use, than the actual one. Here we find an instance of the overwhelming temptation we feel to think that explaining the meaning of a word used predicatively is simply a matter of bringing someone to recognize to which objects the predicate can be truly applied. This temptation goes with an idea of a concept like that which underlies Frege's work: that everything is in order with a concept word if and only if it is clearly determined to which objects the concept is truly applicable and to which not. And yet, even in the case of words as apparently simple as the colour words, such an account could not begin to account for the points we have sketched above, nor indeed to an enormous amount that Wittgenstein himself says elsewhere about colour words. In this connection we must remember how tentative and exploratory a work the book on colour is. In fact its brilliance lies not in giving us 'an adequate grammar of the colour words' but in its sensitivity to points which show how much more complex a task this is than we might naïvely assume. Yet even here we feel, in remarks like the one we have just quoted, how strong the pull of the naïve conception is on us – that it can manifest itself in the middle of an immensely more subtle discussion than is compatible with it.

We may, for instance, consider a remark such as II.133:

> I may have impressed a certain grey–green upon my memory, so that I can always correctly reidentify it without a sample. Pure red (blue, etc.) however, I can, so to speak, always reconstruct. It is simply a red that tends neither to one side nor to the other, and I recognise it without a sample, as e.g. I do a right-angle, by contrast with an arbitrary acute or obtuse angle.

This passage seems to have a good sense: but it only has a good sense if 'red' here does not mean a particular shade of red, but is rather pointing to the way we use the names of the primary colours as points of reference by means of which we, for example, describe the shades of other colours: the use of the word 'red' in 'a reddish-brown' – and in terms of which we say that one red is even redder than another. Here, we may say, Wittgenstein is talking in a way which approaches Lichtenberg's way of talking. If Wittgenstein were here using 'pure red' as the name of a shade of red, how could he be certain that it actually did not 'tend to one side', however slightly, or that he always reconstructed the same shade? If there is a real objection to Lichtenberg, it is not the one Wittgenstein makes, but rather that his remark seems to imply that 'pure white' is simply a very rare shade of white – much as if someone were to think that 'the Euclidean circle' was just a kind of circular object which was a rare case among our ordinary circular objects, rather than that the phrase 'Euclidean circle' indicated a technique for testing ordinary objects for how close they came to being fully circular.

Obviously if we are not to spend too much of this essay on what is only a preliminary example, we must now give a rough sketch of the position our consideration of words for the primary colours and white and black leads to. These words have two different uses; in one of them they are simply used for citing the colours of objects or comparing the colours of objects, and in the other, they provide the points of reference of a coordinate system within which we can make the ordinary colour distinctions that we do make. Here, even if the first use may be the more familiar and frequent, it is the second use which is primary, since it will be by means of colour words used in that sense that we may explain and clarify the words used in the other sense. This picture, however roughly sketched, is certainly more accurate than the one provided by the notion that the basic use of colour words is simply one of classifying objects according as they are or are not white.

The relevance of this lengthy detour into a discussion of colour words is that it illustrates how, even in as simple a case as this, our ordinary predicative expressions may well not be explained simply by showing how we classify objects according as the predicate is or is not applicable to them, and that even here we can give sense to the notion of the primary sense of these words being one which is not necessarily used *directly* in the description of any object whatsoever.

When we turn from this example to the divine perfections, the position becomes even more complicated, and complicated in such a way as to make the idea that the primary sense of the words involved here is given us by the classification of everyday objects according as the object does or does not fall under the concept referred to completely untenable. For whereas in the case of a word like 'white' we could do nothing with the idea of a man who understood the sense of the word and yet was radically mistaken about a large number of the objects to which he thought the word could be truly applied, we are perfectly prepared to say that a man has radical misconceptions about which objects are or are not beautiful – that the music he likes is all kitsch, and that he simply does not hear what there is to hear in, say, Schubert or Bach: and also we are prepared in the course of our lives radically to reassess our own views of what is beautiful. (Most of us would be embarrassed by the memory of the poetry we found so beautiful when we were younger.) And yet to make true sense of what is going on here, we have to say that the *word* 'beautiful' is used in the same sense throughout: if we criticize someone for finding Swinburne's poetry beautiful, this has no sense at all if all we are criticizing him for is using the word 'beautiful' with a different sense from our own. And similarly for the other words at stake in the doctrine of divine perfections. There may be deep disagreement as to whether a man is truly wise, or whether what he says is no more than superficial cleverness masking a real shallowness of understanding: and once again such a dispute is *not* a dispute about words. It is with these kinds of considerations in mind that we may find what Aquinas has to say about the mode of signification of the words signifying divine perfections off key, however natural they sound:

> Our knowledge of God is derived from the perfections which flow from Him to creatures, which perfections are in God in a more eminent way than in creatures. Now our intellect apprehends them as they are in creatures, and as it apprehends them it signifies them by names. Therefore, as to names applied to God, there are two things to be considered, namely the perfections which they signify, such as goodness, life, and the like, and their mode of signification. As regards what is signified by these names, they belong properly to God and more properly than they belong to creatures, and are applied primarily to Him. But as regards their mode of signification, they do not properly and strictly apply to God; for their mode of signification applies to creatures. (*ST* I.q.13ª.3)

Here, in giving an account of the 'mode of signification' of the words under discussion, Aquinas is assuming that their primary sense is given to us from their true application to creatures: and that that sense has to be refined by the removal of the imperfections necessarily present in the exemplars if we are to extrapolate to the sense of the word in which it is primarily only applicable to God. But it is part of our everyday use of such words that we are prepared to fault even what had hitherto appeared an exemplar – and a true account of the sense of such words, when used in talking about creatures, which cannot accommodate that fact is *ipso facto* wrong. Here, as with the case of the colour words we have dwelt on at length, we call men 'wise' according as we believe them to approximate to an ideal of wisdom – even if we cannot define what such an ideal would be – but unlike the case of the colour words, we are prepared radically to reassess our notions of what does and does not so approximate. It is a reasonable conjecture that there is no man who would be acknowledged by everyone to be wise – and not because there were some facts known only to some people and not to others. And yet this does not indicate that the word 'wise' is used with no fixed sense, in chaotically different ways. If this is so, Aquinas is wrong in characterizing our learning the meaning of the word 'wise' by saying 'our intellect apprehends [wisdom] as it is in creatures, and as it apprehends it, it signifies it by a name'. However difficult we may find it to give a completely plausible account of how we do learn a word like 'wise', this account does not even begin to do justice to the simplest facts about our use of this word. We may make beginnings of an account of our use of the word 'wisdom' by saying, 'A wise man behaves in ways appropriate to the situation' – but that shifts our problem to the word 'appropriate', though it does indicate why examples of wisdom are so eminently challengeable. For what one man counts as a relevant feature of the situation, may be totally ignored by another, and vice versa – and a man may, in retrospect, see that by ignoring certain features of the situation, he has ignored all that really matters.

To advance further, it seems now appropriate to look at the way that a term used theologically may be transformed by our encounter with divine revelation. But the transformation consists not in an alteration of the sense of the word but in leading us radically to reassess what it is to which the word is really applicable. Let us consider the following passage from Wrede in *The Messianic Secret*,[11] where he is advocating the view that Jesus as presented in the Gospels is not yet the Messiah:

In his sermon at Pentecost (Acts 2: 36) Peter says that God has *made* Jesus whom the Jews crucified *both Lord and Christ*. In this it is implied that this had been done through his being raised from the dead. This saying, quite by itself, would prove that there was in primitive Christianity a view in accordance with which Jesus was not the messiah in his earthly life. I shall avoid the expression 'was not *fully* the messiah'. In his earthly life, to be sure, Jesus lacks only one thing in order to be the messiah: namely, the sovereign dignity and power. But this one thing is the *whole* thing. It is precisely what makes the concept of messiah what it is, as Christianity received it from Judaism. (*The Messianic Secret*, p. 216)

We are not here concerned with the historical accuracy of Wrede's claims – whether for instance the Jewish concept of the Messiah was as clearly defined as he assumes, but with the easy assurance of his remark that Jesus in His earthly life lacked the sovereign dignity and power appropriate to the Messiah. This is particularly fascinating in someone who joined in, and contributed a great deal to, the fashionable way of describing Mark as portraying the disciples as stupid in their lack of understanding. Now there are many different instances of misunderstanding on the part of the disciples, discussed with that curious mixture of extreme intellectual alertness and yet lack of historical imagination that is for me the hallmark of Wrede's writings. But the central one is surely the series of passages beginning with the episode on the way to Caesarea Philippi[12] in which, if I read Mark aright, Jesus has a showdown with the disciples. (That is to say if one reads this passage blocking out from one's mind the Matthaean additions that inevitably become associated with the Marcan account in one's reading, the passage reads not as the first Messianic declaration on the part of the disciples, but as Jesus beginning to declare to them what His mission is, and what their discipleship to Him ought therefore to be: if they are following Him because they believe Him to be the Christ, they must be shown that they have not yet begun to understand what being the Christ really amounts to. And this account ends in the violent altercation between Peter and our Lord, in which our Lord is even prepared to say of Peter (and I think the continuity of the passage makes this condemnation include a reference to Peter for his 'rebuking' Jesus): 'For whoever is ashamed of me and of my words in this adulterous and sinful generation, of him will the Son of man also be ashamed, when he comes in the glory of his Father with the holy angels.') From this point on in Mark's

Gospel, the point at issue here is the substance of the disciples' lack of understanding and 'stupidity': they cannot comprehend that the man that they acknowledge and follow as the Messiah should be going up to Jerusalem, not to establish Himself with a mighty demonstration of power, but to undergo the death of a common criminal. In their 'stupidity', then, they are totally at one with Wrede: what, for them, Jesus is lacking, is the sovereign dignity and power which are *the* characteristic marks of the Messiah, or at least, if not lacking, resolutely refusing to exercise, while still demanding that they 'take up their crosses' and follow Him *as the Messiah*.

But there is a clearly discernible strand in the Gospels, particularly in Mark and John, which suggests that the issue here is not one of the disciples'coming to terms with a Messiah who, in His earthly ministry, lacks sovereign dignity and power, as Wrede would have it, but that recognizing Jesus as the Messiah, involves a radical reassessment of what really constitutes sovereign dignity and power, and with this, the associated notions of glory and kingship, a reassment which involves such a revaluation of so many of our ideas that it is highly intelligible that the disciples should show no progress in understanding during the course of His ministry: and what is at stake here, to iterate the theme of this essay, is not a modification of the sense of the words, but a recognition of what those words in their everyday sense most properly apply to.

Now obviously if we take up the theme of Christ's kingship within the scope of this essay, we can do no more than indicate lines of thought. But what we must do is indicate the ways in which Jesus of Nazaraeth in His ministry, even in His crucifixion – perhaps above all in His crucifixion – exercised true kingship, besides which what we ordinarily call kingship appears a perversion, and a crude analogy for what a king should be: that 'sovereignty', 'power', 'dignity' and the rest are only applicable in an attenuated and derived sense to them, and also the ways in which He talks of the 'Kingdom of God', in His 'parables of the Kingdom' He talks to those who have ears to hear of what 'kingly rule' is most properly predicated: and what we say here refers not only to the risen Christ, or the Son of Man coming again with His holy angels, but to Jesus in the form of a servant living in poverty and the obscurity of an itinerant preacher: even to Him, in His dereliction, crying 'My God, my God, why hast thou forsaken me'.[13] The resurrection or the Second Coming are not simply a reversal of all that has led up to them, but a making manifest of what was already present in His life on earth. Even if the revaluation of our values is such that it is only for us, as for the disciples, in the light of the resurrection that we can see in the culmination of His ministry at Golgotha the glory of true kingship, it is there that it is to be seen, and to be seen without any alleviation of the suffering, dereliction and humiliation to which He was subjected. And *pace* Wrede, it is to this point that the whole witness of the early Church directs our attention. We are all too ready to read such passages as Phil. 2: 5ff as though at verse 9 there is a transition from a state of humiliation to a state of glory, without seeing that the state of glory is an affirmation and declaration enabling us to see the royal dignity of the way of the cross. It is not only John who points out the terrible coming together of a hideous death and a supreme exaltation ('"and I, when I be lifted up from the earth, will draw all men to myself." He said this to show by what death he was to die.')[14] Paul talks of the princes of this world crucifying the Lord of Glory, thereby revealing their own bankruptcy, and not of them crucifying Him who is to be the Lord of Glory. And Mark takes up the altercation between Jesus and James and John ('"Grant us to sit, one at your right hand and one at your left, in your glory." But Jesus said to them, "You do not know what you are asking...to sit at my right hand or at my left is not mine to grant, but it is for those for whom it has been prepared."')[15] and echoes its phrasing at the depths of Jesus' humiliation: 'And with him they crucified two robbers, one on his right and one on his left',[16] and these almost random examples show the characteristic way of thinking of almost every New Testament author, even if we rightly see John as the author who has made the point thematic for the whole structure of his Gospel.

But how are we to understand this coming together of what appears supreme disgrace and impotence with sovereign dignity and power? Before attempting to answer, we should not forget how little we still understand – how we still only see as in a glass darkly, and commit the ultimate folly of assuming that the ways of God are already transparent to us: but under that proviso, which cannot be underlined too strongly, we must at least point to what leads us to join with the New Testament witness in this affirmation.

The synoptic account of the ministry of our Lord begins with the temptation to establish Himself as a king of this world: 'And the devil took him up, and showed him all the kingdoms of the world in a moment of time, and said to him, "To you I will give all this authority and their glory: for it has been delivered to me, and I give it to whom I will. If you, then, will worship me, it shall all be yours."'[17] But this temptation is renounced by Jesus as a demonic possibility: the kings of this world are here seen as, at least to that extent, servants of Satan. We do not need to debate the historical niceties of how far an inward struggle on Jesus' part, when contemplating His mission, has been rendered by the simplification of the language of an actual dialogue between Satan and Jesus: the reality of Satan's temptation of Jesus and Jesus' repudiation of it do not depend upon whether we are given an image of that struggle or a literal description. And the account ends with Jesus accepting the title 'the King of the Jews' and being crucified under that superscription. The contrast between the two concepts of kingship involved here recurs again and again in the interval between these two moments, with Jesus in Mark 4 giving parables to explain 'the Kingdom of God' which seem obscure in the extreme, and at first to have only the most tenuous connection with the description of the way a king rules. We, of course, misunderstand utterly the first temptation if we do not see it as including – as almost certainly referring primarily – to the temptation to become what the world would regard as a good king; in Matthew 22 Jesus explicitly repudiates the idea that the Messiah is to be 'a son of David': if His kingdom is not of this world it is not even so in its most attractive and humanly admirable form – a king after the pattern of David.

Two *loci* immediately stand out as central to our theme: the Johannine account of the confrontation of Jesus and Pilate, with Jesus accepting the title of king but glossing it as not that of a kingdom of this world, and defining His kingship: 'For this I was born, and for this I have come into the world, to bear witness to the truth. Every one who is of the truth hears my voice',[18] and Jesus' saying in Luke, chapter 22, 'The kings of the Gentiles exercise lordship over them; and those in authority (*exousiontes*) over them are called benefactors. But not so with you...But I am among you as one who serves.'[19] We shall perhaps best understand the apparently strange account of what it is to be a king in the Johannine narrative by looking first at the Lucan text.

I submit that we miss the point of the Lucan text if we think that the kings that are called benefactors are only so called out of servile flattery: these kings among the Gentiles include those who do appear to their subjects as their benefactors. We may perhaps understand this saying best if we look at two of the most profound fictional studies of the politics of kingship: Shakespeare's portrayal of Caesar in *Antony and Cleopatra*, and Eisenstein's extraordinary study of the ambiguity of earthly kingship in 'Ivan the Terrible'. Shakespeare leaves Caesar's motivation far more ambiguous than does Eisenstein: Eisenstein is concerned throughout with the conception of a man who dedicates himself totally to the service of the cause of building the Russian state, to free the Russians from exploitation by neighbouring countries and by the traditional nobility, who see in their station no more than an opportunity to further their own ends at the expense of the ordinary Russian people. This conception is undoubtedly an idealization of the historical Ivan, but this idealization serves only to make more pointed the study of the good king who can rightly be called by his subjects a benefactor. But both Caesar and Ivan, for whatever motives, are shown as benefiting the common people over whom they rule. By the end of *Antony and Cleopatra*, the *pax Romana* has been shown to have been achieved, and Ivan is shown as having defeated those who are set to obstruct his realization of his 'great cause' (and by the end of the uncompleted third part of the film, as having consummated this work in setting Russia free from her foreign enemies).

What Eisenstein is exploring is the thesis that the good king, the man who really benefits his people, must be prepared to sacrifice all moral scruples for the cause of that service, must be prepared to be brutally ruthless with all opponents, to raise the sword in the defence of his people, and bring it down if necessary again and again and again. But to do so he must also, if he is not simply a monster, do violence to himself, crush all compassion within himself, silence all self-doubts as to the righteousness of his course, treat no bond of kinship or friendship as one in which he can afford to place implicit trust, and equally, as not one which affords protection to those who are his friends or kin if they stand in the way of his political will. He must become truly *Grozny* in every sense of that word, tyrannical both towards himself and others, for the sake of his nation. What gives to Eisenstein's study both its power and its subtlety is also what is probably historically most inaccurate about the film: the extent to which Ivan is shown as becoming a tyrant for the sake of a strong Russia, within which its people can thrive, as both taking upon himself the terrible burden of solitude and also the even more terrible burden of destroying the most basic moral constraints within himself, if he is not to fail in his mission: the man whose only laws are the laws of *Realpolitik*, and who therefore deliberately but painfully destroys his own humanity just as he destroys those whom he sees as opposing his will. It is such a man, Eisenstein argues, who can be the real benefactor of his people. Eisenstein is choosing the medium of high tragedy – if it were not for the psychological subtlety and depth of his study, one would say melodrama – but there may be far less exaggeration in his central contention than we are willing to face. So, too, Shakespeare is stressing, it is not Hotspur but Henry V, not old Hamlet but Claudius, not Antony but Caesar, who create the state in which their subjects may live in peace. And although here the contrast is more between the king of the code of chivalry and the politician in the Elizabethan sense of that word – Antony may be loved by those who serve him, and Caesar repugnant in the extent to which the world he is at home in is one of cold remorseless calculation: everyone else, from Pompey to Antony, within the play, is crippled at crucial moments by moral constraints, but Caesar makes his treaty with Pompey only to deliberate the opportune moment to destroy him, is prepared to use his sister as a device to ensnare Antony into a position from which Caesar can justify his raising war against Antony, despatches Lepidus on the basis of forged evidence, with only the merest semblance of observing the forms of justice. And yet it is this man, the confines of whose constraints upon his action are self-interest and considerations of political expediency, who is establishing the *pax Romana*, who is the benefactor of the Roman people, in ways in which those who are constrained by ideals of any other kind whatsoever than the achievement of their own ends, either thereby contribute to, or at the very least do nothing to eliminate, the turmoil which is the atmosphere of the beginning of the play: the peace of the end of the play is Caesar's triumph and his triumph alone. Ivan and Caesar are the kings among the Gentiles who are rightly called by their people benefactors, but whose kingship has been expressly renounced by Jesus as of the devil.

These men changed the world, and even if their achievements were not everlasting achievements, even if the kingdoms they established were bound in the course of history ultimately to collapse, perhaps even contained in the mode of their foundation the seeds of their ultimate collapse, the benefit to the people over whom they exercised their power is, whatever qualifications we may make, indisputable. Whereas when we confront Jesus, we certainly see a man who did, out of compassion, heal those who were physically or spiritually sick, to ascribe to Him a kingship, a rule over people who in serving Him prospered, is something that we can only do if we are prepared to accept that His effect on the course of the history of the world was to all appearances slight – Pilate's judgement that this man should be set free because He had done nothing that posed a threat to Caesar, is in the terms of this world, accurate. Certainly the Church spread and became one of the realities of this world, greater in extent, and in worldly power greater than even either Octavius or Ivan. But the more we see that happen, the more the Church appears to have become just one more kingdom of this world, with Jesus as little more than its constitutional monarch. The peace of Constantine may have established by a bloodless *coup* what we now call Christendom, but the political reality of Jesus' rule in His Church becomes, in the process, more and more questionable. We are forced by Church history to raise the question 'Where is the "peace on earth" which the angels declared to have been established with the coming of this man?' – even if, in saying this, we do not deny that there have been many, many glorious moments in the history of the Church, and men who have acted as servants of the Lord whose service to mankind is real and tangible.

But the history of the Church that proclaims itself to be Christ's body is, whatever else it may be, a history of the persecution of heretics, of so-called religious wars, of anti-semitism, of a Church which, to retain its power and 'defend the truth of the Gospel', has been prepared to fight against the progress of human knowledge, which has obstructed religious liberty far more often than it has championed tolerance. It is also a history in which, though the word 'pharisaism' acquired its pejorative sense through Jesus' polemic against the Pharisees, precisely that word is one of the most useful in describing the behaviour and attitudes of so many of its members. In the face of the extent to which all this is so, we must pause before saying that what was achieved by Christ's earthly ministry was other than something that ended at Golgotha in a failure to save either the world or His people Israel. What are we saying if we say that, in renouncing Satan's temptation, He established a real power and kingdom?

It is important to recognize the continuity of the questions we are now raising with much that is discernible about the continued history of the apostasy of the people of the Old Covenant: for instance 1 Sam. 8 is so close in substance to the questions we are now dealing with to deserve quoting in full.

> When Samuel became old, he made his sons judges over Israel. The name of his first-born son was Joel, and the name of his second, Abijah; they were judges in Beer-sheba. Yet his sons did not walk in his ways, but turned aside after gain; they took bribes and perverted justice.

Then all the elders of Israel gathered together and came to Samuel at Ramah, and said to him, 'Behold, you are old and your sons do not walk in your ways; now appoint for us a king to govern us like all the nations.' But the thing displeased Samuel when they said, 'Give us a king to govern us.' And Samuel prayed to the Lord. And the Lord said to Samuel, 'Hearken to the voice of the people in all that they say to you; for they have not rejected you, but they have rejected me from being king over them. According to all the deeds which they have done to me, from the day I brought them up out of Egypt even to this day, forsaking me and serving other gods, so they are also doing to you. Now then, hearken to their voice; only you shall solemnly warn them, and show them the ways of the king who shall reign over them.'

So Samuel told all the words of the Lord to the people who were asking a king from him. He said, 'These will be the ways of the king who will reign over you: he will take your sons and appoint them to his chariots and to be his horsemen, and to run before his chariots; and he will appoint for himself commanders of thousands and commanders of fifties, and some to plough his ground and to reap his harvest, and to make his implements of war and the equipment of his chariots. He will take your daughters to be perfumers and cooks and bakers. He will take the best of your fields and vineyards and olive orchards and give them to his servants. He will take the tenth of your grain and of your vineyards and give it to his officers and to his servants. He will take your menservants and maidservants, and the best of your cattle and your asses, and put them to his work. He will take the tenth of your flocks, and you shall be his slaves. And in that day you will cry out because of your king, whom you have chosen for yourselves; but the Lord will not answer you in that day.'

But the people refused to listen to the voice of Samuel; and they said, 'No! but we will have a king over us, that we also may be like all the nations, and that our king may govern us and go out before us and fight our battles.' And when Samuel had heard all the words of the people, he repeated them in the ears of the Lord. And the Lord said to Samuel, 'Hearken to their voice, and make them a king'.

Here, Samuel is not describing a bad king, but what it is to be ruled by a king in this world. The Jews have been called by God to the high and terrible destiny of having God and God alone as their king. But as the opening verses of this chapter show, the decision to have a king in a more concrete and tangible sense, a king of this world, for all the drawbacks spelled out by Samuel, can look no more than the decision of common sense. This is nevertheless described by God as part of the continuing apostasy of this people, who, if they are described as stiff-necked and rebellious, are not so in comparison with other people, but only because they will not live according to the high destiny God has ordained for them. The issue, God or Saul, is not only an issue of who shall be their king, but in what sense of the word 'king' they shall have a king to rule over them. If the constraints and conditions of this sinful and fallen world are taken as absolute, then the good king becomes the man who uses violence and *Realpolitik* to make the best accommodation with those conditions and constraints, and so inevitably becomes one of the long line of ambiguous figures sketched by Samuel: from Saul to David, to Caiaphas and Pilate, to Octavius and Ivan. But in so doing, he does not transform his world, he affirms its constraints and conditions as absolute, he must worship Satan, the prince of this world.

It is at this point, however difficult we may find it to do more than stammer here, that we begin to discern why it is that the immediate feeling we have when we read any of the four accounts of the passion of our Lord is that the only free and sovereign man is the man under arrest as a prisoner, the only true glory present here is the glory of a man scourged and then put to one of the most grotesquely hideous deaths that the world has devised, the only trust in God is that of the man who cries 'My God, My God, why has Thou forsaken me?': and possibly beyond this, that it is not Caiaphas and Pilate, in their concern to preserve the delicate political balance between Rome and Jerusalem, who are really fighting on behalf of the Jews, but this man who does not shrink from the ultimate impotence of the Cross, who places Himself in God's hands possibly, at that point, not even Himself understanding how His death can make sense, except that it is the will of His Father. That it is the man without *hypēretai* whom He will call upon to enforce His power that is truly king.

For it is the whole of our Lord's ministry, and especially the Passion, that causes us to question where really is power and where really is impotence: is the apparently indisputable power of Pilate perhaps impotence, and the apparently indisputable acceptance of impotence by Jesus the only real power than can challenge the absoluteness of the constraints and conditions of this world which we treat as absolute and which hold us in their bondage? We may even ask, is it just hyperbole when Peter says of Jesus that it was *not possible* that He should be held by death? And this not despite the humility of His life, but because that humility constituted an irresistible challenge to all that we worship, all we treat as the absolutely given, including death itself, however paradoxical, even ridiculous in its smallness, that challenge could superficially appear. For 'God chose what is foolish in the world to shame the wise, God chose what is weak in the world to shame the strong, God chose what is low and despised in the world, even things that are not, to bring to nothing things that are'.[20]

We may have grave doubts about the historical veracity, even if only in detail of the Johannine account of the Passion and the events surrounding it – not only because of the complex question of the precise literary genre of his Gospel, but also because the account is full of episodes such as the meeting at which Caiaphas advocates the death of Jesus, or the private interviews between Pilate and Jesus, where it is hard to see how the disciples could know what actually happened. But this does not prevent the Johannine account from being a highly intelligent and deeply perceptive hypothetical reconstruction of the nature of what occurred, where the author's whole theological reflection leads him to the point where he may attempt to flesh out what was actually known by the Church into an account which does justice to his theological interpretation of Jesus' ministry. And it is this account which tries to bring out from behind the trappings of power the real inability of Caiaphas and Pilate to do otherwise than what they actually do – their impotence – because they are unable to act in accordance with anything other than within the constraints of the way of this world. Caiaphas is concerned to defend Israel: and even if he does great injustice to Jesus because of that concern, it is because he can only see a balance on one side of which is a man who threatens to create a religious revival in Israel that will, as Caiaphas sees it, inevitably have to be crushed by Rome, and on the other, the relative independence and safety which Rome does at present grant to the Jewish nation as a whole. It is his inability to look beyond that balance that dictates his action: his concern for men is seen by him as entailing that he must be prepared to allow one man to be sacrificed for that concern. Pilate's impotence is even more self-evident. After his initial concern to defend a man whom he sees to be innocent, and his superstitious fear evoked by the possibility that he may be presented here with someone who is divinely protected, he does everything in his power to secure Jesus' release, within a situation where the custom to release one man at the time of the Passover apparently gives him the full freedom to say 'Since I see this man as innocent, it is He whom I release unto you'. And yet the political dynamics of the situation are such that the Jewish leaders are actually able to use them to force him to do what he does not will to do: leaving him neither having done what he claimed it was in his power to do, nor with a clear conscience of having done what he ought to do. The apparent local representative of the whole power of the Roman empire can be manipulated into having a man crucified against his will and his conscience. The final refusal to alter the superscription on the Cross is his last futile attempt to salvage his self-respect. Here he expresses his disgust with himself that he cannot be more than the plaything of the Jews and therefore can only perform a symbolic act in a futile attempt to reconcile his conscience to what he has done, and also impotently defies the Jews at a point when they have already secured what they wanted and his last defiance of them only confirms the extent to which he has already been absolutely unable to act against them over what really mattered. The constraints and conditions of this world, which is the world in which considerations of *Realpolitik* must be allowed their weight, voids his power of any reality whatsoever. But this last futile gesture assumes the form of refusing to budge from having – and we cannot speculate what is in his mind here – the man he crucifies publicly proclaimed the King of the Jews, thereby declaring a possibly totally unconscious and ironic recognition that here is the King of the Jews and that Caesar, Caiaphas and Pilate have shown themselves powerless by comparison with this man.

But Jesus' whole ministry is a challenge to, a disregard for, those constraints and conditions of this world which the kings of this world regard as defining the absolute limits of their power. Where they say 'That is not possible' He acts, and where they say 'That alone is possible', He is constrained by the will of His Father to see the only real impossibility He will acknowledge. This of course does not mean that He acts like a superman – almost the opposite. Certainly He is portrayed as performing miracles: here confronted by human misery, He says a firm but angry No to the alleged inevitability of that misery. Moved by compassion, He says No to the incurability of leprosy, No to the irredeemability of the mentally sick and demoniacally possessed, even No to death itself, confronted by Jairus' daughter, and with an abruptness that is a minor echo of the violence of the cleansing of the temple, turns out the professional mourners who are there to worship the majesty of death. Further, He says No to the irredeemability of those who have fallen into gross sin, going among them declaring their sins to be forgiven with the same sovereign authority with which He addresses the demons, and by feasting with them, creating the possibility of a restoration of their true humanity and dignity. Even the words 'Render to Caesar the things that are Caesar's, and to God the things that are God's'[21] are a simultaneous challenge to the absoluteness both of religion and of Caesar and his world. The temple cannot claim an absoluteness which sets itself outside this world, but must acknowledge its debt to Caesar for the possibility of its continued flourishing, but at the same time limits are set to the absoluteness of Caesar. It is only in so far as he does not transgress the things which are God's that he has any power at all that one should respect.

But at Gethsemane, one feels that to continue talking like this is to trespass on holy ground, for here we must affirm a continuity of this ministry with a man who did not go to His death with serene disdain, but who underwent the full terror and horror of shrinking from what lay ahead of Him, who entered into a state of experiencing the absence of God, contemplating the defection of His disciples, and perhaps even unable to see in what way His Father's will pointed to anything other than failure. But here, confronted by all these possibilities, He did not shrink from them, but in a state of agony said to His Father, 'nevertheless not my will, but thine, be done'.[22] In so doing, He affirmed His sovereignty over failure, solitude, despair, and even death itself, not by evading them, but by willingly undergoing them if it be His Father's will. In so doing, He established His solidarity with all despairing, sinning, lonely men, with all human failure, by refusing to acknowledge the absolute nature of the need to evade their condition if possible, but to relativize it to the will of Him who sent Him. When He has arrived at His trial, while others are whirled about like leaves by the machinations of Realpolitik, He addresses them simply as men, is silent when they wish to approach Him only in their official roles, and refuses to do otherwise than bear witness to the truth, and by bearing witness to the truth, draw all those who are of the truth, whom He sets free from the lie of the absoluteness of this world, into His kingdom.

It is in this strange overcoming of death, darkness, things which are not – by not evading them, but undergoing them in their full depths, that He establishes His Kingdom. And when we say neither Caesar, Pilate, Caiaphas, nor Ivan, nor their masters, death and violence, are Lords, but Jesus alone is Lord, we, however dimly we perceive what we are saying, affirm a finality to His kingship, which makes it appropriate for us to reserve the word 'King' for Him and Him who sent Him, alone, and if we continue to use the word 'king' of the kings among the Gentiles, we see that we are now constrained to say that it is this latter sense of kingship which is the derivative one – that this kingship is only the regency for the conditions and constraints of this world that they treated as absolute, but which He treated with sovereign disdain by comparison with the will of His Father. Because he did so, He created not so much the possibility of men who live their lives here on earth without sin, but the possibility of a hope that since He has overcome the world, even the most weak and sinful of men will be raised to serve in His kingdom, when what happened at Golgotha at the end of time becomes manifest:

> For in him all the fullness of God was pleased to dwell, and through him to reconcile to himself all things, whether on earth or in heaven, making peace by the blood of his cross. And you, who once were estranged and hostile in mind, doing evil deeds, he has now reconciled in his body of flesh by his death, in order to present you holy and blameless and irreproachable before him.[23]

However far our actions may show our unbelief in the Lordship of Christ, that we too constantly act as if we had no king but Caesar, we as Christians, are such only if we are prepared to say, not in spite of Golgotha, but because of Golgotha, that Jesus alone is Lord, and that if we continue to call the kings of this world 'kings', it is *they* who are only so in a derivative sense, as perverted approximations to men of power and glory; and as we do so, we may begin to know in anticipation not the peace of the *pax Romana*, of this world, but the peace that, 'not as the world gives', He gives unto us and with that, understand what really constitutes 'peace' also in its primary and not derived senses.

Let us, in conclusion, look again at where we began: there, I argued that, contrary to many of our immediate intuitions, the primary sense of a large number of the words that we use predicatively is not to be found in their use in making predications about everyday empirical objects, but rather in their use to allude to an ideal or standard of comparison to which those objects in some way approximated. I suggested that this was in particular true of almost all the words at stake in the doctrine of divine attributes, and further that there it was true that it was by no means a necessary condition of our having understood the sense of the word that we should be able to spell out what in fact such an ideal would be like. (Here there may be idle disputes about what counts as understanding the sense of a word: I mean no more than that a man may know perfectly well how to use the word 'wise' with sense, while still being unable to describe what would constitute true wisdom.) Thus far, despite the complete difference of idiom, in these reflections in the philosophy of language, we are, it seems to me, on territory that was explored again and again by Plato in the early dialogues. There, he is concerned to show that we do not know what, for example, courage really is, and the dialogues, as is well known, continually conclude in a state of *aporia*. For this, many people have regarded Plato as involved in perverse paradox, but I hope I have given some substance to the claim that something of immense importance has been seen by Plato. For instance, in *The Blue Book*,[24] Wittgenstein takes Socrates to task for not even assembling examples as a preliminary stage in his investigation, and although, for the case cited by Wittgenstein – the discussion of knowledge in the *Theaetetus* – the charge may have some weight, Socrates' stance of treating examples as irrelevant to *his* quest is comprehensible against the background we are discussing: for what it is vital to recognize here is that the context of those dialogues is a situation where a concept is at stake for which what are and are not instances of that concept are eminently controversial. So that, for example, in the *Euthyphro*, the dialogue has its origin in a concrete case where there is deep disagreement between Socrates and Euthyphro over the question whether what Euthyphro is going to do is or is not pious. It is against that background of controversy that Socrates strives to find an account of piety by means of which the dispute can be brought within the scope of reason. Clearly, to accuse Plato of not resolving his problem by enumerating examples in such a situation, so as to learn from them what piety is, would be symptomatic of a complete misunderstanding: to think that examples would be of direct use in resolving the dilemma would be to fail to appreciate how much of the dilemma originates in the fact that here we are concerned with concepts where we do not have a notion of an example that would be in principle uncontroversial. Hence when examples are cited in these dialogues, they are not to be treated as given cases, but as cases which appear in the very nature of the case merely ways of focusing the debate – do these cases in fact fall under the concept or not?

Where few people would now contend that Plato was not misled, was when, as his thought developed, he came to think that since the primary use of the words he was concerned about was not given by their everyday predicative use in describing empirical objects, there must be an abstract object of which it was truly predicable – something that was ϕ and nothing but ϕ. It is this – the so-called theory of forms – which is the intelligible but ultimately incoherent way that Plato was to articulate his insight: in his later dialogues, Plato was himself to see many of the grave difficulties involved in positing an ideal object that was ϕ and nothing but ϕ, but did not take the further step of seeing that his quest for a point of comparison by means of which we could see whether everyday objects did or did not approximate to being ϕ was not a quest for an object that was perfectly ϕ, but for an account of the primary sense of a word where in that primary sense it was not in the first instance predicated directly of anything at all, not even an ideal form. But given the final shape of the theory of forms, it is comprehensible that many of the early theologians – even someone as late as Anselm in his early writings – should have made the equation between God and the Form of the Good. Such an identification has something right about it as well as a great deal wrong. What is wrong is what is simply entailed by the ultimate incoherence of the fully-fledged theory of forms. Nevertheless, if we are open to what Plato and his disciples among the theologians were trying to say, we can learn from them. Although I have suggested that Plato's mistake was the natural one of thinking that the primary sense of the words he was concerned with was one in which the word was used predicatively, something that did perfectly instantiate the ideal alluded to by such a word could, with an intelligible shift of perspective, have the word in its primary sense truly predicated of it. This much we may concede to the Platonic tradition in Christian theology: and also we may acknowledge that they had learnt from Plato something the full depth of which has been appreciated by few theologians outside that tradition, apart from Barth: namely the extent to which natural man may have either no idea, or a perverse misconception of what the ideal alluded to by the word may be like. The radical agnosticism that is the pervasive atmosphere of a great deal of neoplatonic theology has its roots in a genuine insight. The difference between Barth and that tradition is that he drew a completely different moral from that insight – perhaps because he himself was drawn to see what they had seen in a totally different way: whereas they pointed in the direction of theology being developed by means of a *via negativa*, he saw it as the task of the theologian to learn from God's self-revelation itself what constituted true love, true power, and so on. What Barth achieved by taking this step is something of enormous significance for theology. I am not underestimating the importance of Barth's other contributions to theology when I say that I see this step as perhaps the most profound single contribution he made to theology, and one which provides us with a way of understanding a number of his more particular discussions in the *Church Dogmatics*. Time and again in the *Dogmatics*, Barth transforms our apprehension of an entire complex of theological questions by simply challenging the assumption that we know what being ϕ really is in independence of divine revelation, to learn there what truly constitutes being ϕ, being prepared to take this to extremes that may appear paradoxical and yet which can almost invariably be given a good and profound sense. It is only for someone who does not understand what Barth has seen that it can appear a perverse eccentricity when he claims that apart from Jesus Christ we do not know what man really is. It is a central leitmotif of the *Dogmatics* and perhaps one of the deepest lessons we may learn from it, how much more radically we must be prepared to look to divine revelation – and above all to Jesus Christ – to learn about the very words we use in theology. (Even if we regard Barth's remark 'Only God has hands – not paws like ours' as only a battle cry, the point of that slogan is close to the centre of Barth's theological concern.) I am sure I am not alone in the feeling that most traditional accounts of the doctrine of divine attributes are largely sterile and simply boring, whereas when we read the second half of *Church Dogmatics* II/I the doctrine of God's perfections becomes profoundly exciting and challenging – even at times electrifying in the way that it forces one to rethink one's conception of God: and this largely because of Barth's simple but resolute refusal to look elsewhere than to God's self-revelation to learn what He is like.

It is within that context that I should like the later parts of my essay to be read: that even in the case of a word like 'king' – not a word usually under debate in discussions of analogical predication in talking about God – where we might naïvely take it as given that we know what constitutes kingship, we should, on the contrary, be prepared to have our presuppositions challenged at the deepest possible level. It is then that we realize that what had appeared an abstract exercise in the philosophy of language has implications of the deepest moment for our faith and lives as Christians. But what we may also learn from those preliminary reflections in the philosophy of language is that when we use a word to talk about God, we are not necessarily appealing to a doctrine of analogical predication so as to give us a new and purified sense of that word. We may, in fact, be using the word in a sense that is already given us in the vernacular, although not given in such a way that we know independently of God's self-revelation what such a word in this sense, which I have argued is its primary sense, truly describes. Although at the outset I described Barth and Aquinas as at one in a thesis the logical possibility of which I wished to explore, it is Barth who took the further radical step of turning the traditional doctrine of analogical predication on its head: that it is from the use of words in talking about God that we may throw light on their everyday use and not vice versa. Barth has argued with great subtlety in his doctrine of the Image of God in man for the theological possibility of our language containing words that in their full sense may only be used to describe God – and obviously an exploration of what he has to say there would take us outside the confines of this essay: we have simply been concerned with the questions raised for the philosophy of language by such a claim and its logical as well as its theological possibility: the possibility that in Barth's words, what we have when we talk appropriately about God and our Lord is 'a homecoming of concepts'.

Notes

1 Thomas Aquinas, *Summa Theologica*, 1265–1273 (ET New York, 1947).
2 Karl Barth, *Kirchliche Dogmatik*, II/I (Zurich, 1940; ET *Church Dogmatics*, Edinburgh, 1957).
3 Barth, *CD* II/I, pp. 237ff.
4 Cajetan, *De Nominum Analogia et de Conceptu Entis* (1498); ET *On the Analogy of Names and the Concept of Being*, trans. E. A. Bushinski and H. J. Koren (Pittsburgh, 1953).
5 Aquinas, *ST* I.q.13^{a}.6.
6 Barth, *CD* II/I, pp. 224ff.
7 Eph. 3: 14f; Isa. 40: 15; Matt. 7: 11; etc.
8 L. Wittgenstein, *Remarks on Colour*, ed. G. E. M. Anscombe (Oxford, 1977), I, §§ 3ff.
9 L. Wittgenstein, *Philosophical Remarks*, ed. R. Rhees (Oxford, 1964; ET Oxford, 1975).
10 Wittgenstein, *PR*, §§ 212ff.
11 W. Wrede, *Das Messiasgeheimnis in den Evangelien* (Göttingen, 1901; ET J. Greig, *The Messianic Secret*, London, 1971).
12 Mark 8: 27ff.
13 Mark 15: 34.
14 John 12: 32f.
15 Mark 10: 37–40.

16 Mark 15: 27.
17 Luke 4: 5ff.
18 John 18: 37.
19 Luke 22: 25ff.
20 1 Cor. 1: 27f.
21 Mark 12: 17.
22 Luke 22: 42.
23 Col. 1: 19–22.
24 L. Wittgenstein, *The Blue and Brown Books* (Oxford, 1960), p. 20.

12

'True' and 'false' in Christology

BRIAN HEBBLETHWAITE

The notes to this essay will be found on page 238

It may seem a far cry from contemporary philosophical analysis of the meaning of the word 'true' to the solemn use of the concept of truth in the Fourth Gospel. There the writer places on the lips of Jesus words which express his own profound conviction that the ultimate truth of God and man is revealed, indeed embodied, in the figure of Jesus himself. Before Pilate, Jesus says, 'For this I was born, and for this I have come into the world, to bear witness to the truth'. Earlier he had said to his disciples: 'If you continue in my word, you are truly my disciples, and you will know the truth, and the truth will make you free.' Similarly in the farewell discourses, he says of the Comforter, 'When the Spirit of truth comes, he will guide you into all the truth...He will glorify me, for he will take what is mine and declare it to you.' And of course, most concretely of all: 'I am the way, and the truth, and the life.'[1] But in reflecting on these pronouncements, the philosophical theologian is bound to ask himself what is the relation between the ordinary uses of the word 'true' and these profound religious uses.

The conception of personal truth which we find in the Fourth Gospel is very different from the 'personal truth' advocated by Wilfred Cantwell Smith.[2] The Jesus of the Fourth Gospel is not just speaking of a quality of personal living, by comparison with which the truth of doctrines fades into insignificance. On the contrary, embedded in the religious pronouncements of the Fourth Gospel about truth lie deep convictions about how things ultimately are with God, man and the world and about how man and the world were meant to be. These convictions can and must be expressed in propositional form, as 'proposals for belief'.[3] Consequently, analysis of the meaning of the word 'true', as used in these far-reaching religious contexts, is a necessary task for philosophical theology.

It is most unlikely that the analysis of truth in religious contexts advocated by D. Z. Phillips will be found to do justice to the pronouncements of the Fourth Gospel.[4] For Phillips, 'truth' and 'reality' are not general terms whose meaning can be fixed, irrespective of context. The sense of 'truth' and 'reality' in religion can be determined only within the religious 'language–game'. There is no analogy between everyday truth or scientific truth and truth in religion. Internal criteria alone can show what it means to speak of religious truth. I do not think that this analysis does justice to what ordinary believers mean when they affirm the truth of their beliefs. As a number of philosophers have pointed out,[5] we have here a dispute that could in principle be settled by phenomenological or sociological research. Equally, a careful reading of the Fourth Gospel will support the view that, even in the solemn passages quoted above, the word 'true' is being used in its basic, common, sense of that which expresses or shows how things really are and were meant to be.

Before considering the specific question of 'true' and 'false' in Christology, I want to explore this more general question of the nature of truth. Theories of meaning and truth are much debated in contemporary secular philosophy, as indeed are the underlying metaphysical conceptions of reality that explicitly or implicitly accompany them. No doubt it is impolitic for theology too exclusively to endorse particular – and highly controversial – philosophical theories. But the case I wish to state and examine at this stage is the threefold thesis that meaning is to be understood in terms of a combination of truth-conditions and the intentions of rational minds, that truth is to be understood in terms of that which expresses or shows how things really are and were meant to be, and that reality is to be understood in terms first of the being and nature of God and then of a universe with a given nature and destiny which we discover rather than invent or construct.

The concepts of meaning, truth and reality are closely bound up together. We specify the meaning of an assertion or belief, at least in part, by indicating what it would be for that assertion or belief to be true. We specify, that is, its truth-conditions. But assertions and beliefs are states or acts of knowing minds, and neither meaning nor truth can be defined apart from reference to the mind. A statement, a gesture, an event only means something to someone. Equally, truth is the disclosure of reality to the mind and the expression of how things are by rational minds for rational minds.

This does not mean that how things are depends on *our* minds. For the theist, God is who He is and the world is what it is irrespective of our knowing minds. On the other hand, the world's reality does depend on the mind and will of God. In this sense, the world and man are mind-dependent. They depend on God for their being, their nature and their destiny. This is the element of truth in the metaphysical theory known as idealism. But of course philosophical idealism has tended rather to assert the dependence of the world on *our* minds. This is the dominant characteristic of those post-Kantian strands in western philosophy, which, losing confidence in the objectivity of God and His creation, have tended greatly to exaggerate the contribution of the human mind to the constitution of how things are. Phenomenalism and other forms of idealism are united in opposing the view that things are what they are independently of specifically human ways of knowing and of human powers of verification. This is equally true of the most popular form of anti-realism today, the philosophical position or cluster of positions known as constructivism, whereby the objects of our thought and discourse are held to be constituted by our socially constructed projections, categorial frameworks and webs of meaning.

Against these theories metaphysical realism insists that the world is what it is irrespective of *our* knowing minds. We discover rather than constitute reality. Christian theism asserts the given nature of the realities which we come to apprehend. God gives Himself to be known by us in revelation and He gives the world its nature and rational structure which we discover through interaction with it both in everyday life and in science. Further, just because the world is in process, we need to discern not only how things are but where they are going. Not only the present reality of the world, but also its future, according to Christian theism, is governed by the divine intention. We have also, therefore, to discover what it was meant to be.

One of the merits of theism is that it makes it possible to retain the connection between reality, truth and knowability, without either according implausible powers to our human minds or collapsing into scepticism. Plato held categorically that ultimate reality was entirely knowable by us, and in his exaggerated confidence in the scope of philosophy, believed the supreme realities to be accessible to any properly trained mind.[6] Heidegger, more realistically for a non-theistic philosopher, held that the being of things was hidden and concealed and only came to expression fitfully and enigmatically in poetry and in a philosophy that rejected most of its own past.[7] Karl Jaspers was even more pessimistic about our ability to know transcendent being. For him, metaphysics, religion and poetry all provide no more than 'ciphers' of an essentially unknowable and inexpressible transcendence.[8] By contrast with the excessive optimism of Plato and the excessive pessimism of Heidegger and Jaspers, Christian theism has retained the conviction of the inseparability of reality, truth and knowability, without supposing ourselves to be capable of knowing all there is to be known. It is enabled to do this by its postulation of God's knowledge as alone commensurate with how things really are. But God's knowledge of what He has made and God's creative power ensure the objectivity and stability of what there is for us, with our limited powers of cognition, to come at least partially to know.

Michael Dummett has pointed out the close connection between anti-realist metaphysics and verificationist theories of meaning and truth, whereby only what is in principle verifiable *by us* can have any claim to truth-content.[9] A theory which grounds objective truth and knowability in the mind and will of God frees the notions of meaning and truth from that anthropocentric verificationism which characterizes those post-Kantian phenomenalist or constructivist philosophies mentioned above.

There are interesting possibilities of *argument* for theism here. For if we can defend the notion of objective reality being what it is independently of human minds and there for us to discover as we aim at truth only on the supposition of its knowability by transcendent mind, then perhaps there is a rational argument from truth to God. At first sight this looks a viciously circular argument. Are we not appealing to objective truth as a ground for belief in God and at the same time to God as a guarantor of objective truth? But I do not think that the argument is circular. For I notice that in everyday life and in science alike, we find an enormous resistance to idealist, phenomenalist and constructivist ways of thinking. Working scientists, for the most part, think of themselves as probing the secrets of a universe that exists over against them, with a structure and a rationality which are not imposed by the human mind, but rather discovered through interaction by trial and error between the scientist and his subject-matter, a structure and a rationality that may well exceed our human powers of comprehension. If it is the case that our experience of the world prompts this realist view of objective truth, then, perhaps, a springboard for theistic argument is achieved.

As in other spheres, Nietzsche was more perceptive about what is at issue here than many modern philosophers and indeed some modern theologians. His rejection of the notions of absolute and objective truth was part and parcel of his rejection of Christian theism. As in the ethical sphere, Nietzsche's explicit avowal of the consequences of atheism – in this case, complete relativism and the theory of truth as fiction – is perhaps an indication of the fact that objective truth and theism belong together.[10]

Turning to the theory of truth that most readily reflects the metaphysical and theological realism which I have been defending, I want now to consider the merits and demerits of the correspondence theory of truth, as a general theory capable of covering all the diverse uses of 'true' in everyday talk, in inter-personal discourse, in historical research, in science and in religion. In its most general form, the correspondence theory of truth is surely unassailable and indispensable. It affirms that a statement, belief or theory is true just when it expresses or shows how things are in reality. It does not necessarily involve the view, which the early Wittgenstein held, that statements somehow picture states of affairs, still less the view that there is a one-to-one correlation between words and things or between sentences and states of affairs. All that is needed is Aristotle's basic definition: 'To say of what is that it is not, or of what is not that it is, is false, while to say of what is that it is, and of what is not that it is not, is true.'[11] In other words, truth is correctly predicated of statements, opinions, beliefs, claims, theories etc., when reality is in fact as they hold it to be. The basic claim of the correspondence theory, then, is that truth is a relation between the knowing mind and how things really are.

The problem with the correspondence theory lies in the difficulty and complexity – at least for creatures such as ourselves – of articulating and expressing in our own human thought and language how things are. This difficulty can be brought out if we begin with simple everyday cases such as saying truly of my hat that it is on the peg and moving rapidly on to more complex subjects such as inter-personal relations, historical judgements, scientific knowledge and religious awareness. In the simple everyday cases it is clear that all we need are conventions of reference, so that we succeed in picking out my hat as the object of discourse, and conventions of description or predication, so that we succeed in saying that it is on the peg. It seems prima facie reasonable to presume that we shall continue to need conventions of successful reference and appropriate predication when we move on to the more complex areas of discourse. The trouble is that that they are much more difficult to achieve. It has become increasingly apparent to philosophers and sociologists of knowledge that many of the things we say about the world are only partly or roughly true, and, moreover, are bound up with whole conceptual frameworks and ways of looking at the world which are highly conditioned historically, culturally, and socially. This has led to widespread scepticism about our ability to say how things are in themselves irrespective of our human modes of apprehension. These difficulties, however, need not deflect us from a correspondence theory of truth as broadly defined in its most general form above. For we can still suppose that humanly conditioned theories aim at truth in the fully objective sense of correspondence with reality. Awareness of the partial, approximate, theory-laden and often distorted nature of our affirmations need not deter us from the aim of discovering and bringing to expression how things are.

This analysis applies no less in the sphere of religion than it does in other spheres of human interest. Our aim, in religious discourse, is to bring to expression how things ultimately are with man, the universe and God. Of course the subject-matter of religion is such that we shall not be able to rest content even with the partial articulation of how things ultimately *are*. Since we are now talking about, among other things, the will of God for man and the world, we shall no doubt find ourselves endeavouring to express how things were meant to be as well. We have already had occasion to avert to this extension of the theory of truth at earlier stages in this essay and we shall naturally be developing it when we return to the question of 'true' and 'false' in Christology. Suffice it to say here that the correspondence theory of truth is not overthrown when we extend its scope from characterizing the relation between the knowing mind and things as they are to characterizing the relation between the knowing mind and things as they were meant to be. Objectivity is secured both for actual and intended truth by reference to the creative will of God.

It will be apparent that, for all spheres of discourse, the broad correspondence theory of truth defended here is quite capable of embracing recent philosophical theories of meaning and truth which stress the 'holistic' or 'network' character of human modes of representing how things are. Only when allied to constructivist, non-realist, *metaphysical* theories of the kind referred to above, are these theories inimical to the conception of truth sketched here.

In summary, we may suggest that in all spheres of thought and discourse, human minds inherit and refine ways of representing to themselves and to each other, however partially and approximately, how things are. In discovering how things are, they become aware of a world in process, with a given structure, about which they learn more and more, always aiming at truth in the sense of that which expresses or shows how things are. Led beyond this objective truth to its source in the mind and will of God, they may hope to learn something of the divine intention for the world and man, and so progress to the question of how things were meant to be. The concept of truth is then deployed within a larger horizon, as we endeavour to articulate not only present truth, but future truth and ideal truth too, in the light of God's intention.

This larger horizon will naturally come into focus as we turn now to the question of 'true' and 'false' in Christology, and especially when we come back to the pronouncements of the Fourth Gospel with which this essay began. But Christology, as a branch of Christian theology – that is, as a reflective second-order discipline – is not itself a matter of religious pronouncements. It is rather the attempt to analyse and articulate the doctrine implicit in the Church's witness to Jesus Christ, including the pronouncements of the Fourth Gospel. It is therefore just as much concerned with present truth as it is with future or ideal truth. It is concerned both to state, as carefully and fully as human language permits, who Christ is and what he reveals about the being and nature of God, and also to state, as carefully and fully as human language permits, what he reveals and embodies of God's intention for man and for the world. The remainder of this essay is devoted to these two aspects of Christology and their claim to truth.

It is an implication of the main theme of this essay that, when the Christian theologian claims that the doctrines of the Trinity and the Incarnation are true – that they state truly how things are with God and Jesus Christ – he is using the word 'true' in the same basic, common, sense as that in which it is used in any other sphere of discourse. These doctrines, he holds, correspond with reality. What is special about these doctrines is not the sense in which they are held to be true, but rather their peculiar subject-matter and the difficulty, for human beings, of cognitive access to it. Of course, the theologian does not hold that these doctrines tell us the whole truth about God and Jesus Christ. He is perfectly well aware that the realities into cognitive relation with which they put us are much greater and more mysterious than we can comprehend. But this transcendence of the reality of God over all our modes of apprehension, including the doctrines of the Church, does not mean that the doctrines in question are false. We do not have to have complete comprehension of every aspect of the being and nature of God in order to make *some* true affirmations about Him. In fact, human beings do not have complete comprehension of every aspect of any reality with which they have to do, but this does not prevent them from making some true statements about many things. Each reality, even a stone, transcends our ways of apprehending it, as both scientists and mystics have observed. But that does not prevent many true remarks being made about the stone.

Nor does the partial and approximate nature of our grasp of truth mean that the distinction between true and false statements is eroded, either in simple cases such as talk of stones or in complex cases such as talk of God. An intermediate example, talk of other people, may be used to illustrate this point. When I say that X is an honourable man, the complexity of my subject-matter, a human being and his character, no doubt transcends my relatively simple remark. (I deliberately choose an example of evaluation. Such remarks are clearly true or false. There are recognized criteria of what is to count as consistent honourable conduct.) But my remark may very well be true and be known to be true, none the less. A malicious rumour to the effect that X is a dishonourable man would, in that case, be false. The conventions of successful reference (I am talking about X, not Y) and of appropriate predication ('honourable' is rightly predicated of X, not 'dishonourable') are not rendered impotent by the difficulty of knowing the full truth about a man. Similarly, in the much more complex case of talk of God, if I say that, in one of the modes of His triune being, God became man in Jesus of Nazareth, I may be speaking truly, notwithstanding the much greater difficulty of making successful reference to the subject of my affirmation (the triune God, not Wotan) and of appropriately predicating something of Him (that, in one of the modes of His being, He became man, not that He was busy completing Valhalla).

In this difficult and complex sphere, it may not always be so easy to identify incompatible claims as it is in the examples I have given, let alone to say which has the greater claim to truth. This is true both of disputes within a particular religious tradition and still more of disputes between religions as they come to expression through comparative study or through inter-faith dialogue. In neither case should we assume that prima facie differences represent irreconcilably conflicting truth-claims. It is a prime task in comparative theology to search out what common ground there may be behind the apparently different religions. Consideration of the many-sided nature of divine reality and of the different cultural and historical backgrounds to the conceptual frameworks in terms of which different traditions endeavour to articulate their experience of God may well enable us to resolve some prima facie incompatibilities and recognize a single reality lying behind the different modes of apprehension. P. T. Geach, in a well-known article,[12] has argued forcefully against any easy assimilations here, but he shows insufficient sensitivity to the possibility that, beneath the differences, there remains some more or less vague apprehension of the same reality. It may well be admitted that the price of agreement in these matters is often greater vagueness. Moreover some incompatibilities may well remain. Participants in inter-faith dialogue may reluctantly be driven to insist that some at least of the proposals put forward for acceptance by their partners in dialogue actually contradict their own beliefs. Here questions of truth and falsehood cannot be avoided.[13]

Much the same situation obtains within a single tradition. Recent christological controversy within Christian theology illustrates this. Admittedly there is less disagreement here about the referents of Christian discourse. We are all talking about the God of the Christians and about Jesus of Nazareth. What is in dispute is what is said of these subjects. The controversial area is that of appropriate predication. But, as in the case of the dialogue between religions, it is important to search out what common ground there may be behind the christological disputes. Apparently different proposals for belief in this area too may turn out, on closer inspection, to be conveying in different ways the same underlying doctrine. For example, proponents of incarnational and non-incarnational Christology respectively may be brought to agree on the central significance for Christianity of Paul's affirmation that 'God was in Christ reconciling the world to himself'.[14] But the price of such agreement is likely, once again, to be a greater measure of vagueness. By contrast, when pressed on what he understands this Pauline affirmation to mean, the incarnational christologian will insist that Christ must be thought of as coming to us from the side of God, the ultimate subject of his words and deeds being God Himself in one of the modes of His triune being, while the non-incarnational christologian will suggest that it is enough to speak of God's unique acts by His Spirit in and through the man, Jesus of Nazareth. So it may well turn out that the disagreements are deep ones after all. The rival Christologies cannot both be true, even though both parties have *some* awareness of the religious realities whose more specific interpretation is in dispute.

I detect in the arguments of recent proponents of non-incarnational

Christology both an implicit trading on the greater vagueness of the agreed statements held in common such as the Pauline affirmation quoted above and at the same time an explicit defence of a less vague but definitely non-incarnational interpretation of such statements.

These disputes raise interesting questions about the use of 'true' and 'false' in Christology. Vague statements can certainly be true or false, in any sphere of discourse ('There's something in the cupboard'). And if we were right to emphasize the partial and approximate nature of all human awareness, we shall expect relative degrees of vagueness in all statements about any subject-matter. No doubt religious statements are more prone to vagueness than many others. They employ many extended and figurative modes of expression – analogy, metaphor, symbol, parable, myth – modes of expression which are certainly not equivalent, and all of which are open to scrutiny and analysis. The distinction between 'true' and 'false' is perfectly applicable to all these modes of discourse as well as to the attempts at more specific doctrinal interpretation of what they convey. But a vaguely grasped truth may, when explored more precisely, come to be falsely interpreted. As in all spheres, in religion too, the scope for error becomes greater the more specific the articulation. This is not a reason for resting content with vague generalities about which we can all agree. For it may be the case that the religious power of Christianity depends on relatively precise beliefs about Jesus Christ being true.

So far I have only adverted to certain basic doctrines about the Person of Christ. No doubt it is much more important for Christian theology to articulate the moral truths about God's nature and providence, embodied and enacted in Christ and his Cross. But my point is that to see the Cross of Christ as God's Cross in our world implies an incarnational Christology. The moral truths and the doctrinal truths are inseparable.

This means that the question of future truth and ideal truth – the question, that is, of what the world and man were meant to be – are also questions of christological doctrine. Christology is not only concerned with Christ as the human face of God, but also with Christ as the pattern of what man was meant to be. The will of God for the world and for man comes to expression in the incarnate one.

These reflections lead us to recognize the all-important fact for a proper analysis of the use of the term 'true' in Christology that truth is not only expressed and shown in statements and beliefs, but is also embodied and enacted in a human life. The life of the incarnate one itself discloses the reality of God and embodies His creative will for man. Christ himself corresponds with these realities. Now language is certainly the basic medium of the conveyance of truth. But we have noted something of the difficulty, for limited human powers of expression, of bringing divine realities to expression in words. Hence, we may suppose, the revelatory power of the Word of God made flesh. We are not left alone to struggle with the gap between our words and the divine reality. God comes to meet us where we are in the incarnate Word. This is presumably what the author of the Fourth Gospel means us to understand by the words, 'I am the truth', placed on the lips of Jesus, namely, that Jesus himself embodies and expresses both the truth about God and the truth about man as he was meant to be. This is the truth to which Jesus and the Spirit bear witness. It is this truth that will make men free.

The notion of truth which is not just expressed in words but embodied in human life is not peculiar to religion. A 'true friend' is a friend who embodies in life and in action the ideal reality of friendship. He corresponds with that ideal. We discover the truth about friendship from our dealings with him. In the context of Christian incarnational religion this usage becomes central. As Austin Farrer put the matter, with characteristic lucidity, 'Men may construct a myth expressive of divine truths as they conceive them, and the stuff of that myth will be words. God has constructed a myth expressive of the living truths he intends to convey, and the stuff of the myth is facts'. God's parable, on Farrer's view, is a real human life and death.[15]

When it is claimed in the Fourth Gospel that the truth will make men free, this is not to be understood in a gnostic sense, as if certain esoteric truths brought to our awareness had an automatic liberating effect. The truths in question are moral and spiritual truths of compelling practical significance. But again it is not a peculiar religious sense of 'truth' that has these practical implications. It is rather the realities disclosed in the words and works of Christ and in the Person of Christ himself that lay upon us these constraints to action.

It must be pointed out that even in these profoundly religious contexts of incarnate, moral and practical truth the same basic sense of 'truth' is still maintained – namely, that which expresses or shows how things are and were meant to be. Nor does any of this absolve us from attention to the second-order question of the truth of christological doctrine. The Christian Church may claim that Jesus is the truth. We have seen what that claim means. But the question remains, whether that claim is true.

Notes

1 John 14: 6. The other references are 18: 37, 8: 31f, and 16: 13f.
2 W. Cantwell Smith, *Questions of Religious Truth* (London, 1967).
3 See W. A. Christian, *Meaning and Truth in Religion* (Princeton, N.J., 1964).
4 D. Z. Phillips, *Faith and Philosophical Enquiry* (London, 1970).
5 E.g. A. Jeffner, *The Study of Religious Language* (London, 1972) and R. G. Swinburne, *The Coherence of Theism* (Oxford, 1977).
6 Plato, *The Republic*, books V–VII.
7 M. Heidegger, *Discourse on Thinking* (ET, New York, 1966).
8 K. Jaspers, *Philosophy of Existence* (ET, Oxford, 1971).
9 M. Dummett, *Truth and other Enigmas* (London, 1978), p. 24.
10 Nietzsche, *The Twilight of the Idols*. We may remind ourselves that Nietzsche once said that it was a definition of truth that anything said by a priest was false.
11 Aristotle, *Metaphysics* 1011b, 26ff.
12 P. T. Geach, 'On worshipping the right God', in *God and the Soul* (London, 1969).
13 See W. A. Christian, *Oppositions of Religious Doctrines* (London, 1972).
14 2 Corinthians 5: 19.
15 A. M. Farrer, 'Can Myth be Fact?', in *Interpretation and Belief* (London, 1976).

Donald MacKinnon's published writings 1937–1980

Compiled by PAUL WIGNALL

1937

Review of W. G. de Burgh, 'Towards a Religious Philosophy', *Laudate*, XV (1937), 224.

1938

'Recall to what?', review of *The Recall to Religion*, London, Eyre and Spottiswoode, 1937, in *Christendom*, VIII (1938), 48–56.

'And the Son of Man that thou visitest him', *Christendom*, VIII (1938), 186–92 and 260 72.

'Church, Community and State', report of proceedings of the 1937 Life and Work Conference in Oxford, *Oxford Magazine*, LVI (24 February 1938), 448–51.

'Jeeves on sartorial obligation' (signed Empiricus), *Oxford Magazine*, LVI (16 June 1938), 767.

Review of M. B. Reckitt, 'Religion in Social Action' (Christian Challenge Series), *Christendom*, VIII (1938), 149–51.

Review of L. J. Collins, 'The New Testament Problem' (Christian Challenge Series), *Christendom*, VIII (1938), 308–10.

Review of A. A. Bowman, 'Studies in the Philosophy of Religion' (2 volumes), *Oxford Magazine*, LVII (17 November 1938), 194.

1939

'Are there *A Priori* Concepts?' (with J. L. Austin and W. G. Maclagen), in *Hume and Present Day Problems* (being the proceedings of the symposium of the joint session of the Mind Association, the Scots Philosophical Club and the Aristotelian Society, held in Edinburgh, July 1939, to mark the bicentenary of David Hume's *Treatise of Human Nature*), *PAS*, Supp. vol. XVIII, 49–54.

'The Task of the Christendom Group in Time of War', *Christendom*, IX (1939), 139–43 and 201–6.

'No Way Back', review of P. Drucker, *The End of Economic Man*, in *Christendom*, IX (1939), 292–8.

'Vexilla Regis: Some Reflections for Passiontide, 1939', *Theology*, XXXVIII (1939), 254–9.

'Christian Social Thought: A Survey', *Theology*, XXXVIII (1939), 378–82.

Letter on 'Ecclesiastical Transcendentalism', *Theology*, XXXIX (1939), 452–5.

Review of L. A. Reid, 'Preface to Faith', *Laudate*, XVII (1939), 190.

Review of W. G. de Burgh, 'Knowledge of the Individual', *Laudate*, XVII (1939), 249.

Review of W. G. de Burgh, 'Through Morality to Religion', *Oxford Magazine*, LVII (26 January 1939), 322–3.
Review of E. Gilson, 'The Unity of Philosophic Experience', *Oxford Magazine*, LVII (9 March 1939), 514–15.
Review of C. Dawson, 'Beyond Politics', *Oxford Magazine*, LVII (25 May 1939), 660–2.

1940

God, the Living and the True (*Signpost*, no. 1), London: Dacre, 1940.
The Church of God (*Signpost*, no. 7), London: Dacre, 1940.
'What is a metaphysical statement?', *PAS*, XLI (1940–41), 1–26.
'Flesh and Blood hath not revealed it unto thee', *Theology*, XXXIX (1940), 426–31.
Review of E. Barker and R. H. Preston, 'Christians in Society', *Christendom*, X (1940), 206–7.
Review of C. Rankin, 'The Pope Speaks', *Christendom*, X (1940), 205–6.
Review of A. H. Rees, 'The Worship of God', *Christendom*, X (1940), 270.
Review of J. Dewey, 'Logic: The Theory of Enquiry', *Oxford Magazine*, LVIII (13 June 1940), 388–9.

1941

'Revelation and Social Justice' in *Malvern 1941, The Life of the Church and the Order of Society*, London: Longmans, Green and Co., pp. 81–116.
'Christianity and Justice', *Theology*, XLII (1941), 348–54.
'The function of philosophy in education', *Blackfriars*, XXII (1941), p. 413. Reprinted in *Cambridge Review*, LXIII, no. 1534 (1 November 1941), 52–3.
'The Malvern Conference', *The Student Movement* (1941).
Review of A. G. Hebert, 'The Throne of David', *Christendom*, XI (1941), 261–3.
Review of Sir Edwyn Hoskyns, 'The Fourth Gospel', *Oxford Magazine*, LIX (1 May 1941), 268–9.
Review of C. S. Lewis, 'The Problem of Pain', *Oxford Magazine*, LIX (8 May 1941), 286.
Review of N. Kemp-Smith, 'The Philosophy of David Hume', *Cambridge Review*, LXIII, no. 1536 (15 November 1941), 92–3.

1942

'Survey of Devotional Books', *Theology*, XLV (1942), 107–10.
'Where do we go from here?', *Blackfriars*, XXIII (1942), 353–8.

1943

'Some Questions for Anglicans', *Christendom*, XIII (1943), 108–11.
'Problem for Pilgrims', review of J. Baillie, *Invitation to Pilgrimage*, *Christendom*, XIII (1943), 25–6.

1944

'Some Reflections on Democracy', *Christendom*, XIII (1944), 175–7.
Review of J. Maritain, 'Redeeming the Time', *Christendom*, XIII (1944), 248–51.
Review of A. H. Smith, 'A Treatise on Knowledge', *Oxford Magazine*, LXII (20 January 1944), 119–20.

1945

'Verifiability', *PAS*, Supp. vol. XIX, 101–18. Reprinted in *Borderlands of Theology* (London, 1968), pp. 232–48.
'Some Reflections on the Summer School, 1945' (based on the concluding address at the 1945 Church Union Summer School for Sociology), *Christendom*, XIV (1945), 107–11.
Review-article of M. B. Reckitt, ed., 'Prospect for Christendom', *The Student Movement* (1945).
Review of R. Kroner, 'How do we know God?', *JTS*, XLVI (1945), 108–10.

1946

'The Tomb was Empty', *Christian Newsletter*, no. 258 (1946), 7–12.

1947

'Kant's Agnosticism', *Blackfriars*, XXVIII (1947), 256–63.
Letter on 'Bomber Offensive', *Christian Newsletter*, no. 283 (1947), 1–5.
Review of R. G. Collingwood, 'The Idea of History', *JTS*, XLVIII (1947), 249–53.
Review of F. Thompson, 'There is a Spirit in Europe' (signed Empiricus), *Adelphi*, 1947.

1948

'Things and Persons', *PAS*, Supp. vol. XXII (1948), 179–89. Reprinted in *Borderlands of Theology* (London, 1968), pp. 131–41.
Untitled essay on the Sacraments in *Report of the Sixth Anglo-Catholic Congress: The Church*, London: Dacre, 1948, 130–7.
'The Christian Understanding of Truth', *SJT*, I (1948), 19–29.
'Moral Problems of Atomic Warfare', *Humanitas*, II, 3 (1948).
Broadcast Talk: 'Where the Report Fails' (BBC Third Programme). Reprinted as 'An Approach to the Moral and Spiritual Problems of the Nuclear Age' in *Borderlands of Theology* (London, 1968), pp. 175–83.
Review of J. M. Middleton Murry, 'The Free Society', *Christian Newsletter*, no. 310 (1948), 9–16.
Review of D. M. Baillie, 'God was in Christ', *SJT*, I (1948), 207–9.

1949

Preface to the English edition of G. Marcel, *Being and Having*, London: A. & C. Black (Dacre Press), 1949. New edition: London and Glasgow: Collins, Fontana Library, 1965.

Preface to J. Coventry, *Morals and Independence*, London: Burns Oates, 1949.
Review of P. Tillich, 'The Shaking of the Foundations', *The Student Movement* (1949).
Review of W. W. Bryden, 'The Christian Knowledge of God', *SJT*, II (1949), 208–10.

1950

Review of J. G. Lockhart, 'Cosmo Gordon Lang', *New Statesman* (19 May 1950).
Review of I. Henderson, 'Can Two Walk Together?', *SJT*, III (1950), 94–6.

1951

Critical notice of G. Ryle, 'The Concept of Mind', *Philosophical Quarterly*, I (1951), 248–53.
Review of J. Baillie, 'The Belief in Progress', *SJT*, IV (1951), 415–20.
Review of H. Butterfield, 'Christianity and History', *SJT*, IV (1951), 415–20.
Review of R. Niebuhr, 'Faith and History', *SJT*, IV (1951), 415–20.

1952

'Christian Optimism: Scott Holland and Contemporary Needs', *Theology*, LV (1952), 407–12 and 448–53. Reprinted in *Borderlands of Theology* (London, 1968), pp. 105–20.
Article on the Lund Conference on Faith and Order, August 1952, *New Statesman* (12 September 1952).
Untitled contribution on the preliminary papers for the Evanston Assembly of the World Council of Churches, *Ecumenical Review*, IV (1952), 293–5.
Review of T. Preiss, 'La Vie en Christ', *SJT*, V (1952), 306–7.

1953

Edited, with concluding essays on 'Christian and Marxist Dialectic' and 'Prayer, Worship and Life' (pp. 229–56), *Christian Faith and Communist Faith*, London: Macmillan, 1953.

1954

On the Notion of a Philosophy of History (L. T. Hobhouse Memorial Trust Lecture, 1953), Oxford: University Press, 1954. Reprinted in *Borderlands of Theology* (London, 1968), pp. 152–68.
'Metaphysical and Religious Language', *PAS*, n.s. LIV (1953–54), 115–30. Reprinted in *Borderlands of Theology* (London, 1968), pp. 207–21.
Broadcast Talk: 'Reflections on the Hydrogen Bomb' (BBC Third Programme). Reprinted in *Borderlands of Theology* (London, 1968), pp. 184–92.
Review-article on E. W. F. Tomlin, 'R. G. Collingwood', *New Statesman* (24 September 1954). Reprinted in *Borderlands of Theology* (London, 1968), pp. 169–74 as 'R. G. Collingwood as a Philosopher'.
Review of C. A. Coulson, 'Christianity in an Age of Science', *CQR*, CLV (1954), 392–3.
Review of J. Wisdom, 'Philosophy and Psycho-Analysis' and 'Other Minds', *Aberdeen University Review* (1954).

1955

'Sacrament and Common Meal' in D. E. Nineham, ed., *Studies in the Gospels: Essays in Memory of R. H. Lightfoot*, Oxford: University Press, 1955, pp. 201–7.

'Creation' (with A. Flew), *CQR*, CLVI (1956), 18–32. Reprinted in A. Flew and A. MacIntyre, ed., *New Essays in Philosophical Theology*, London: S.C.M. Press, 1955, pp. 170–86.

'Death' in A. Flew and A. MacIntyre, ed., *New Essays in Philosophical Theology*, London: S.C.M. Press, 1955, pp. 261–6.

Review of H. W. Cassirer, 'Kant's First Critique', *CQR*, CLVI (1955), 427–30.

Review of C. A. Peirce, 'Conscience in the New Testament', *CQR*, CLVI (1955), 430–2.

Review of Sir Thomas Murray Taylor, 'The Discipline of Virtue', *Aberdeen University Review* (1955).

1956

'Philosophy and Christology', in T. H. L. Parker, ed., *Essays in Christology in Honour of Karl Barth*, London: Lutterworth Press, 1956, pp. 269–97. Reprinted in *Borderlands of Theology* (London, 1968), pp. 55–81.

'Ethical Intuition', in H. D. Lewis, ed., *Critical British Philosophy*, 3rd series, London: Allen and Unwin, 1956, pp. 311–33.

'Some Notes on Kierkegaard', *Cambridge Review*, LXXVII, no. 1888 (9 June 1956), 676–8. Reprinted in *Borderlands of Theology* (London, 1968), pp. 121–8.

Review-article on R. B. Braithwaite, 'An Empiricist's View of the Nature of Religious Belief', *Cambridge Review*, LXXVII, no. 1878 (25 February 1956), 375–8. Reprinted in I. T. Ramsey, ed., *Christian Ethics and Contemporary Philosophy*, London: S.C.M. Press, 1966, pp. 77–84.

Review of D. Baumgardt, 'Bentham and the Ethics of Today', *Philosophical Quarterly*, VI (1956), 183–4.

1957

A Study in Ethical Theory, London: A. & C. Black, 1957.

1958

Appreciation of Professor Alexander Stewart Ferguson, *Aberdeen University Review*, 1958. Reprinted in University College, Oxford, *Chronicle* (1958). Also obituaries in *The Times* and *The Scotsman*.

Review of C. A. Mace, ed., 'British Philosophy in the Mid-Century', *CQR*, CLIX (1958), 112–14.

Review of E. L. Mascall, 'Words and Images', *CQR*, CLIX (1958), 114–17.

Review of J. Pieper, 'Justice', *CQR*, CLIX (1958), 117–19.

Review of R. Bultmann, 'History and Eschatology', *JTS*, n.s. IX (1958), 205–8.

1959

'A. E. Taylor' in *Dictionary of National Biography 1941–1950*, L. G. Wickham Legg and E. T. Williams, ed., Oxford: University Press, 1959, pp. 864*a*–5*b*.

Oration to Arts Graduates at Aberdeen University on 9 July 1959, *Aberdeen University Review* (1959).

Review of C. A. Parkin, 'The Moral Basis of Burke's Political Thought', *Philosophical Quarterly*, IX (1959), 183–4.

Review of M. B. Foster, 'Mystery and Philosophy', *Philosophical Quarterly*, IX (1959), 283–5.

1961

The Borderlands of Theology (Inaugural Lecture as Norris-Hulse Professor of Divinity, University of Cambridge), Cambridge: University Press, 1961. Reprinted in *Borderlands of Theology* (London, 1968), pp. 41–54.

'A Finishing School?' (on Cambridge University admissions policy), *Cambridge Review*, LXXXIII, no. 2009 (14 October 1961), 7–9.

1962

'Revised Reviews: XIII – Barth's Epistle to the Romans', *Theology*, LXV (1962), 3–7.

'Intercommunion: A Comment', *Theology*, LXV (1962), 51–6. Reprinted in *The Stripping of the Altars* (London and Glasgow, 1969), pp. 62–71.

'Teilhard de Chardin: a Comment on his context and significance', *The Modern Churchman*, n.s. V (1962), 195–9.

Broadcast Talk: 'Our Contemporary Christ', printed in *The Listener* (6 June 1962), 990. Reprinted in *Borderlands of Theology* (London, 1968), pp. 82–9.

'A Note on Paragraphs 34 and 35 of the Bridges Report' (on Cambridge University policy), *Cambridge Review*, LXXXIII, no. 2027 (12 May 1962), 437–8.

1963

'Moral Objections' in D. M. MacKinnon, H. A. Williams, A. R. Vidler and J. S. Bezzant, *Objections to Christian Belief*, London: Constable, 1963, pp. 11–34. Reissued, Harmondsworth: Pelican, 1965, pp. 9–29.

'Ethical Problems of Nuclear Warfare' in D. M. MacKinnon, H. E. Root, H. W. Montefiore and J. Burnaby, *God, Sex and War*, London and Glasgow: Collins, Fontana edition, 1963, pp. 11–29. Reprinted in *Borderlands of Theology* (London, 1968), pp. 193–203.

'Justice', *Theology*, LXVI (1963), 97–104. Reprinted in A. R. Vidler, ed., *Traditional Virtues Reassessed*, London: S.P.C.K., 1964, pp. 65–75. Reprinted in *Borderlands of Theology* (London, 1968), pp. 142–51.

'God and the Theologians 2: Grammar and Theologic', *Encounter* (21 October 1963), 60–1.

Broadcast talk: 'Order and Evil in the Gospel', printed in *The Listener* (4 April 1963), 587–8. Reprinted in *Borderlands of Theology* (London, 1968), pp. 90–6.

Review of R. Niebuhr, 'Radical Monotheism and Western Culture', *JTS*, n.s. XIV (1963), 256–9.

Review of C. Lewy, ed., 'The Commonplace Book of G. E. Moore, 1919–1953', *JTS*, n.s. XIV (1963), 555–6.

Review of T. F. Torrance, 'Karl Barth: An Introduction to his Early Theology', *JTS*, n.s. XIV (1963), 556–9.
Review of J. Collins, 'God in Modern Philosophy', *Philosophical Quarterly*, XIII (1963), 91–3.

1964

Introduction to new edition of J. M. Creed, 'The Divinity of Jesus Christ', London and Glasgow: Collins, Fontana edition, 1964.

1965

'Aristotle's Conception of Substance' in R. Bambrough, ed., *New Essays in Plato and Aristotle*, London: Routledge and Kegan Paul, 1965, pp. 97–119.
'Teilhard's Vision', *Frontier*, VIII (1965), 169–71.

1966

The Resurrection: A Dialogue arising from Broadcasts, with G. W. H. Lampe (W. Purcell, ed.), London: Mowbray, 1966.
'Subjective and Objective Conceptions of the Atonement', in F. G. Healey, ed., *Prospect for Theology*, Essays presented to H. H. Farmer, London: Nisbet, 1966, pp. 167–82.
'Natural Law' in H. Butterfield and M. Wight, ed., *Diplomatic Investigations*, Harvard: University Press, 1966, pp. 74–88.
'Diakonia in Modern Conditions' ('Some Reflections on Secular Diakonia'), in *Service in Christ*, Essays presented to Karl Barth on his 80th birthday, J. I. McCord and T. H. L. Parker, ed., London: Epworth, 1966, pp. 190–8.
'Can a Divinity Professor be Honest?', *Cambridge Review*, LXXXIX, no. 2134 (12 November 1966), 94–6.
Broadcast Talk: 'P. F. Strawson's *The Bounds of Sense*', printed in *Borderlands of Theology* (London, 1968), pp. 249–56.

1967

Articles on 'Jeremy Bentham', 'Joseph Butler', 'Faith', 'Happiness', 'Intuition', 'John Locke', 'John Stuart Mill', 'Plato and Aristotle', 'Platonism and Aristotelianism', 'Pleasure', 'Socrates', 'Sophists', 'Utilitarianism', in J. Macquarrie, ed., *A Dictionary of Christian Ethics*, London: S.C.M. Press, 1967.
'Atonement and Tragedy' in *Le Mythe de la Peine*, Report of the Rome Colloquium on philosophy of religion, 1967, Paris: Aubier, 1967, pp. 373–8. Reprinted in *Borderlands of Theology* (London, 1968), pp. 97–104.
'Theology and Tragedy', *Religious Studies*, II (1967), 163–9. Reprinted in *The Stripping of the Altars* (London and Glasgow, 1969), pp. 41–51.
'John Wisdom's *Paradox and Discovery*', *CQR*, CLXVIII (1967), 67–74. Reprinted in *Borderlands of Theology* (London, 1968), pp. 222–31.
Broadcast Talk: 'Authority and Freedom in the Church'. Reprinted in *The Stripping of the Altars* (London and Glasgow, 1969), pp. 52–61.
Broadcast Talk: 'The Controversial Bishop Bell'. Reprinted in *The Stripping of the Altars* (London and Glasgow, 1969), pp. 83–94.

Tribute to J. S. Bezzant, *The Modern Churchman*, n.s. x (1967), 306–7.
Review of J. Macquarrie, 'Studies in Christian Existentialism', *JTS*, n.s. XVIII (1967), 294–5.

1968

Borderlands of Theology and Other Essays, G. W. Roberts and D. E. Smucker, ed., with an Introductory Essay by D. M. MacKinnon, London: Lutterworth Press, 1968.
'Autorité et conscience' in *L'Herméneutique de la Liberté Religieuse*, Report of Rome Colloquium on philosophy of religion, 1968, Paris: Aubier, 1968, pp. 425–30.
'What sort of radicalism?', *Frontier*, XI (1968), 116–17.

1969

The Stripping of the Altars, London and Glasgow: Collins, Fontana edition, 1969.
'Kenosis and Establishment', the Gore Memorial Lecture, 5 November 1968, printed in *The Stripping of the Altars* (London and Glasgow, 1969), pp. 13–40.
'The Problem of the "System of Projection" Appropriate to Christian Theological Statements', in *L'Analyse du Langage Théologique: Le Nom de Dieu*, Report of Rome Colloquium on philosophy of religion, 1969, Paris: Aubier, 1969, pp. 81–100. Reprinted in *Kerygma und Mythos*, VI, 7 (1976), 49–60. Reprinted in *Explorations in Theology* (London, 1979), pp. 70–89. (See also the debate with P. van Buren and others in *Débats sur le Langage Théologique*, Paris: Aubier, 1969, pp. 31–51.)
'Moral Freedom' in D. M. MacKinnon, ed., *Making Moral Decisions*, London: S.P.C.K., 1969, pp. 1–23.
'Masters in Israel III: Hans Urs von Balthasar', *The Clergy Review*, LIV (1969), 859–69. Reprinted with Postscript in H. U. von Balthasar, *Engagement with God*, London: S.P.C.K., 1975, pp. 1–16.
'The Future of Man', *Theology*, LXXII (1969), 145–53. Reprinted in *Explorations in Theology* (London, 1979), pp. 1–10.
'Freedom Defended', *Church Quarterly*, I (1969), 314–19.
'Ian Duthie: a personal tribute', *Aberdeen University Review* (1969).
Broadcast Talk: 'Is Ecumenism a Power Game?' printed in *The Stripping of the Altars* (London and Glasgow, 1969), pp. 72–82.
Review of T. F. Torrance, 'Theology as Science', *Tablet* (November 1969).

1970

Introductory Essay to J. H. Newman, *University Sermons* (D. M. MacKinnon and J. D. Holmes, ed.), London: S.P.C.K., 1970, pp. 9–23.
'Finality in Metaphysics, Ethics and Theology' in *L'Infallibilité: Son Aspect Philosophique et Théologique*, Report of Rome Colloquium on philosophy of religion, 1970, Paris: Aubier, 1970, pp. 357–74. Reprinted in *Explorations in Theology* (London, 1979), pp. 99–115.
'The Case for Disestablishment', review-article on the Chadwick Report, 'Church and State', *Tablet* (19/26 December 1970), 1229–30.

Review of H. Kung, 'Infallibility', *Glasgow Herald* (June 1970).
Review of A. MacIntyre, 'Marxism and Christianity', *JTS*, n.s. XXI (1970), 274–7.

1971

'Absolute and Relative in History...', in *La Théologie de l'Histoire: Herméneutique et Eschatologie*, Report of Rome Colloquium on philosophy of religion, 1971, Paris: Aubier, 1971, pp. 121–35. Reprinted in *Kerygma und Mythos*, VI, 7, 1976, 107–15. Reprinted in *Explorations in Theology* (London, 1979), pp. 55–69.
'Lenin and Theology', *Theology*, LXXIV (1971), 100–11. Reprinted with Postscript in *Explorations in Theology* (London, 1979), pp. 11–29.

1972

'The Euthyphro Dilemma. Part I', *PAS*, Supp. vol. XLVI (1972), pp. 211–21.
'Evidence: Preliminary Reflections' in *Le Témoignage*, Report of Rome Colloquium on philosophy of religion, 1972, Paris: Aubier, 1972, pp. 111–23. Reprinted in *Kerygma und Mythos*, VI, 7 (1976), 145–52. Reprinted in *Explorations in Theology* (London, 1979), pp. 116–28.
'"Substance" in Christology: a cross-bench view' in S. W. Sykes and J. P. Clayton, ed., *Christ, Faith and History. Cambridge Studies in Christology*. Cambridge: University Press, 1972, pp. 279–300.
'Theology as a Discipline of a Modern University' in T. E. Shanin, ed., *The Rules of the Game (Cross-Disciplinary Essays on Models in Scholarly Thought)*, London: Tavistock, 1972, pp. 162–74.

1973

'Idéologie et Croyance' in *Démythisation et Idéologie*, Report of Rome Colloquium on philosophy of religion, 1973, Paris: Aubier, 1973, pp. 207–18.

1974

The Problem of Metaphysics (Gifford Lectures, 1965–1966), Cambridge: University Press, 1974.
'Parable and Sacrament' in *Le Sacré: Études et Recherches*, Report of Rome Colloquium on philosophy of religion, 1974, Paris: Aubier, 1974, pp. 151–67. Reprinted in *Explorations in Theology* (London, 1979), pp. 161–81.
'Coleridge and Kant' in J. Beer, ed., *Coleridge's Variety*, London: Macmillan, 1974, pp. 183–203.

1975

'Kant's Philosophy of Religion', *Philosophy*, L (1975), 131–44.
'Some Notes on the Irreversibility of Time' in *Temporalité et Aliénation*, Report of Rome Colloquium on philosophy of religion, 1975, Paris: Aubier, 1975, pp. 39–47. Reprinted in *Kerygma und Mythos*, VI, 7 (1976). Reprinted in *Epworth Review*, III (1976), 92–102. Reprinted in *Explorations in Theology* (London, 1979), pp. 90–8.
Review of R. Bambrough, ed., 'Wisdom: 12 essays', *Aberdeen University Review* (1975).

1976

'Idealism and Realism: An Old Controversy Renewed', the Aristotelian Society Presidential Address, 11 October 1976, *PAS*, n.s. LXXVII (1976), 1–14. Reprinted in *Explorations in Theology* (London, 1979), pp. 138–50.
'The Relation of the Doctrines of the Incarnation and the Trinity' in R. W. A. McKinney, ed., *Creation, Christ and Culture*, Studies in honour of T. F. Torrance, Edinburgh: T. & T. Clark, 1976, pp. 92–107.
'La communication efficace et les tentations de Jésus' in *Herméneutique de la Secularisation*, Report of Rome Colloquium on philosophy of religion, 1976, Paris: Aubier, 1976, pp. 373–82.
'The Inexpressibility of God', *Theology*, LXXIX (1976), 200–6.
Tribute to J. MacMurray, *Tablet* (June 1976).

1977

'The Conflict between Realism and Idealism: Remarks on the significance for the philosophy of religion of a classical controversy recently renewed' in *La Philosophie de la Religion: L'Herméneutique de la Philosophie de la Religion*, Report of Rome Colloquium on philosophy of religion, 1977, Paris: Aubier, 1977, pp. 235–45. Reprinted in *Explorations in Theology* (London, 1979), pp. 151–65.
'Weimar's Theologian', review of W. & M. Pauck, 'Paul Tillich: his life and thought, vol. I', *The Guardian* (15 February 1977).

1978

'Law, change and revolution: some reflections on the concept of raison d'état' in Report of Rome Colloquium on philosophy of religion, 1978. Reprinted in *Explorations in Theology* (London, 1979), pp. 30–54.
'Return to Scotland', *The Scottish Review: Arts and Environment*, no. 11, 16–20.
Review of S. Pétrement, 'Simone Weil: a life', *SJT*, XXXI (1978), 471–6.

1979

Explorations in Theology: 5: Donald MacKinnon, London: S.C.M. Press, 1979.
Preface to C. Ernst, 'Multiple Echo', London: Darton, Longman and Todd, 1979.
'Ethics and Tragedy' in *Explorations in Theology* (London, 1979), pp. 182–95.
'Tillich, Frege, Kittel: Some Reflections on a Dark Theme' in *Explorations in Theology* (London, 1979), pp. 129–37.
Review of G. C. Stead, 'Divine Substance', *SJT*, XXXII (1979), 271–3.

1980

'Power-politics and religious faith', the Martin Wight Memorial Lecture, 8 March 1979, *British Journal of International Studies*, VI (1980), 1–15.
Review of B. Stendhal, 'Kierkegaard', *Scandinavica* (May 1980).
Review of J. Sobrino, 'Christology at the Cross-roads', *SJT*, XXXIII (1980).
'Reflections on Mortality', *The Scottish Journal of Religious Studies*, I, 1 (spring 1980), 40–4.
'Some Reflexions on Time and Space', in memory of Enrico Castelli, *Archivio di Filosofia* (1980), 369–75.

Index